Maritime Dynamics in the Indo-Pacific

Maritime Dynamics in the Indo-Pacific

Editors
Vijay Sakhuja
Kapil Narula

National Maritime Foundation

Vij Books India Pvt Ltd
New Delhi

Published by

Vij Books India Pvt Ltd
(Publishers, Distributors & Importers)
2/19, Ansari Road
Delhi – 110 002
Phones: 91-11-43596460, 91-11-47340674
Fax: 91-11-47340674
e-mail: vijbooks@rediffmail.com
we b: www.vijbooks.com

Copyright © 2016, *National Maritime Foundation*

First Published : 2016

ISBN: 978-93-85563-47-8 (Hardback)

ISBN: 978-93-85563-48-5 (ebook)

FOREWORD

In a world experiencing epochal changes, there are few maritime regions which are transforming more dramatically than the Indo-Pacific region. In the midst of such an environment which is fueled by the growing economic clout of China, the security dilemmas for the littoral nation states are quite discernable. China's growing power projection capabilities have further strained the delicate and the fragile relationships with its neighbours due to its existing boundary disputes, excessive maritime claims and non-conformity to the existing norms.

This has led to new challenges and the maritime security architecture is in a flux due to the strategic power play and realignments leading to an increased potential for conflict. Further, the US rebalance strategy and the emerging relationship between Australia, India and Japan is shaping the regional balance of power. Therefore the region presents a unique challenge for geopolitics, oil and trade flows as these shape the strategic and economic imperatives.

India's maritime interests in the region are largely predicated on economic, security and strategic considerations. Further, the deepening bonds of inter-dependency which result from India's 'Act East' policy, makes India a major stakeholder in the region.

It is in this context that a Seminar on '*Maritime Dynamics in the Eastern Indian Ocean Region and the Western Pacific Ocean*' was organized at Vishakhapatnam in July 2015, jointly by the Eastern Naval Command and the National Maritime Foundation. This book emerges from the papers presented at the Seminar which was an intellectually stimulating event. The participants included academics, students from colleges, eminent citizens of Visakhapatnam, naval fraternity and the media. This event also contributed to the NMF's goal of promoting maritime awareness and encouraging informed public debate.

The chapters in the book, authored by academics and practitioners are rigorous and capture the emerging regional maritime dynamics. This book addresses various strategic aspects such as geopolitics, economics, diplomatic and environmental dynamics in the east of India and deciphers the posturing and alignment of various countries in the Indo-Pacific region with their possible implications for India.

The complex cross-linkages in the above dimensions are analysed to draw out India's salient strategic imperatives and options and it is in this context that the book assumes importance. I hope that this book adds to the existing discourse on maritime power and serves as a repository of the process behind the changing dynamics in the Indo-Pacific region.

Admiral DK Joshi
PVSM, AVSM, YSM, NM, VSM (Retd.)
Chairman
National Maritime Foundation

29 Feb 2016
New Delhi

वाइस एडमिरल सतीश सोनी, पी वी एस एम, ए वी एस एम, एन एम ए डी सी
फ्लैग अफ़सर कमान्डिंग-इन-चीफ
Vice Admiral Satish Soni, PVSM, AVSM, NM, ADC
Flag Officer Commanding-in-Chief
Tele : 0891-2577399

मुख्यालय
पूर्वी नौसेना कमान
विशाखापट्टणम - 530 014
Headquarters
Eastern Naval Command
Visakhapatnam - 530 014

ADDRESS

The maritime theatre in the Indo-Pacific is gaining increasing strategic importance and with it the role of the Eastern Naval Command (ENC) is also evolving. Starting from a very modest beginning in 1939, the Navy has grown with the city of Visakhapatnam. Today, the ENC is the largest Command and the only one with nuclear assets. Basing of the Shivalik and Kamorta class ships, P8I and AJT aircraft, Chakra and Arihant nuclear submarines have given a new impetus to operations on the Eastern seaboard. The ENC is also preparing to base the Vikrant with her MiG 29 complement in the near future.

The Eastern Naval Command also has ambitious plans for development of infrastructure on the Eastern seaboard. These include an air station at Bobilli, a second VLF Station at Vikarabad in Telangana, and a naval base at Erawadi near Tuticorin. Commissioning of new detachments in Behala, West Bengal, Bhubaneshwar, Vijaywada, Paradip, Kakinada and Ennore are also on the anvil.

Visakhapatnam will host India's second ever International Fleet Review (IFR) in early February 2016. Till now, 37 countries have confirmed attendance by way of ships, Chiefs of Navies or delegations. The Presidential Review will witness participation by 90 ships. Other events would include an Operational Demonstration, International City Parade, Band Concerts, Maritime Conference, Presidential Banquet and setting up of an IFR Village to showcase Indian culture and technological capabilities. The President, Prime Minister, Governor, Chief Minister of Andhra Pradesh, Raksha Mantri and other dignitaries are expected to grace the occasion.

The Bay of Bengal is witnessing an exponential growth of new ports with plans for more in the offing. Dhamra, Gangavaram, Krishnapatnam,

Katupalli, Karaikal and Ennore have been in existence for some time, and new ports along the approaches to Calcutta and along the Andhra coast are planned. Finalisation of the maritime boundaries between India, Bangladesh, Thailand and Myanmar, commissioning of Kyaukpyu and Sittwe in Myanmar, and the proposed port of Sonadia in Bangladesh are likely to contribute to increased economic activity in the region. Consequently, various regional navies are also set to become more active. Bangladesh and Thailand are shopping for submarines. Myanmar has an ambitious ship construction programme and Singapore Navy punches much above its weight.

As can be expected of a rising economic power, the Chinese are making their presence felt in the Western Pacific and Indian Ocean. A near continuous deployment of a naval Task Force in the Gulf of Aden since 2009, inclusion of a submarine and depot ship for anti-piracy operations, deployment of scientific research vessels and seabed mining assets in the Southern Indian Ocean, declaration of an ADIZ in East China Sea and massive construction programmes in the contested South China Sea reefs and islands are indicative of abandoning the traditional continental mindset, and shifting focus from offshore waters to open seas protection, as emphasised in the latest Chinese Defence White Paper. The Belt and Road initiatives aim to link 60 countries ostensibly for economic benefits, but the proposal could well have military overtones. The Chinese are also building their humanitarian credentials. Extensive deployment of a hospital ship to African and ASEAN ports in 2010 and 2013, evacuation of foreigners and Chinese nationals from war-torn Yemen, responding to the water crisis in Maldives and to the massive earthquake in Nepal are some of their initiatives in this regard.

Countries of the region are reacting, slowly but surely. Philippines has taken their maritime dispute with China to an International Tribunal for arbitration. Japan, Australia and Malaysia are now more vocal in the international fora. South Korea has avoided taking sides due to its own geo-strategic and historical compulsions but has been helping Philippines of late. The Vietnamese do not hide their concerns and are developing robust naval capabilities. All ASEAN navies appear to be in sync with some more expressive than others. While smaller countries like Brunei would like to play it down and solve issues bilaterally, there are others like Indonesia who, while remaining silent, are slowly developing infrastructure on maritime frontiers such as the Natuna Archipelago.

A substantial rise in naval cooperation is also being witnessed. Philippines has just concluded a first ever bilateral exercise with the Japanese. The Philippines and Australians are keen to conclude Defence Contracts with the Japanese defence industry. China was invited for the 2014 edition of the Rim of The Pacific Exercise at Hawaii for the first time. There is a growing convergence between Russia and China. The bilateral exercises which began in 2012 in East China Sea have gradually expanded in scope and we saw the two navies exercising for the first time in the Mediterranean in 2015. Closer home, the Eastern Naval Command is all set to carry out bilateral exercises with Russia, Australia, United States, Japan and Sri Lanka.

The US has announced a Pivot to the East which is not viewed favourably by China. US military aircraft flew through the Chinese Air Defence Identification Zone (ADIZ) in the East China Sea last year, and more recently over the Fiery Cross Reef to publicise Chinese construction activity and to register a protest. The US Secretary of Defence Mr Ashton Carter made a brief but symbolic stopover at the Eastern Naval Command during his visit to India in early June.

We are, therefore, living in interesting times and there is much to share and discuss with regard to maritime dynamics in the Indo Pacific. We look forward to hearing the views of our distinguished panellists as to how they perceive developments in the region. Where do India and the Indian Navy stand? What must be the takeaways for us? How must we respond to the Chinese proposal of participation in the Maritime Silk Road initiative? What should be our reaction to developments in the South China Sea? Should ASEAN countries develop an intra-ASEAN consensus against construction in South China Sea to preserve the sensitive ecosystem? What of recent reports of the possibility of the Chinese declaring an ADIZ over South China Sea; and what should be our options in case this happens? How do other nations and their navies perceive our actions, especially the frequent joint exercises with so many navies including some trilateral ones? How will our decision to host the IFR 2016 at Vizag be viewed by countries in the region? Are we doing enough to promote harmony and stability in our neighbourhood?

Seminars such as these must debate controversial issues and throw up options for the younger generation. I look forward to the discussions and deliberations and wish the Seminar all success.

Date: 09 Jul 15

CONTENTS

Foreword   v

Address   vii

Introduction   xiii

1.   Maritime Dynamics In The Indo-Pacific: Setting The Scene   1

     Arun Prakash

2.   US Rebalance to Asia   11

     K Raja Menon

3.   Southeast Asian Countries and their Alignment   21

     Anup Singh

4.   Strategic Power Play in East Asia   36

     Yogendra Kumar

5.   South China Sea Dispute and its Impact on Regional Stability   55

     Kamlesh K Agnihotri

6.   Relevance of UNCLOS and other Legal Instruments
     in Resolving Maritime Disputes In The South China Sea   73

     Raghavendra Mishra

7.   Regional Environmental Challenges   97

     Kapil Narula

8. China in the Indian Ocean: Foreign Policy and Maritime Power 120

   Gurpreet S Khurana

9. India and Multilateral Security Architecture 137

   Anurag G Thapliyal

10. India's Act East Policy: Adding Substance to Strategic
    Partnerships 151

    Shankari Sundararaman

11. Seminar Takeaways 168

    Antara Ghosal and Kapil Narula

Contributors 173

Index

INTRODUCTION

The 'rise' of Asia is a major factor shaping the global order, which is caused largely due to the economic progress of its maritime-configured rim-land, comprising established and emerging powers such as the US, China, Japan, Korea, India and the Southeast Asian countries. The shift of power to Asia in the 21st century has transformed the geopolitical and security landscape. The rapid economic growth of the region has resulted in strong interdependence within and beyond Asia; yet the region faces many challenges. Being a predominantly maritime configured region, the emerging regional order is closely linked to affairs of the sea.

The maritime dynamics in the region are highly pronounced, and these bear on the regional security, particularly on India's national interests. The key dynamics are India's engagement with major powers, modernization of regional navies, maritime-territorial disputes, challenges to established international norms, and the persistence of non-traditional security threats. While the multilateral security mechanisms are considered essential, their effectiveness would be premised on regional geopolitics and the security interfaces that the regional powers succeed in forging amongst themselves and with other countries in the region.

This book is an attempt to examine the emerging geopolitical developments and the related trends in the region, including the drivers and regional responses, thereof. This volume is based on the papers presented at the Seminar on 'Maritime Dynamics in the Eastern Indian Ocean Region and the Western Pacific Ocean' jointly organized by the National Maritime Foundation and the Eastern Naval Command (ENC) of the Indian Navy and attempts to answer certain key questions.

The first session of the seminar discussed the Regional Geopolitical and Geostrategic Dynamics in the region and provided a broad canvas to address the maritime dynamics and the responses thereof. The geopolitical rivalry in the region manifests in various forms such as China's increasing politico-military assertiveness to further its maritime-territorial claims, US 'rebalance' to Asia, and Japan's efforts to shake off its constitutional constraints. The other dimension is represented by the economic rise of countries like China, Japan Korea and other Southeast Asian countries. This is leading to a concurrent increase in the national power of the established and emerging powers, with possible ramifications for international order and inter-state relations. These dynamics are also closely linked to a complex interplay of cooperation and competition which affect the regional balance of power.

The key questions which were addressed were:

- How is balance of power evolving in the region?

- How is the U.S. responding to the changing regional dynamics?

- How are regional maritime strategies evolving?

The next session addressed the Maritime Disputes and Challenges. Considering the predominantly maritime configuration of the region, the security environment is largely shaped by events and developments in the maritime and littoral spaces. More prominent, however, are the regional insecurities based on maritime disputes. Some of the many potential flashpoints in the region are located in the disputed maritime areas and islands in the South and East China Seas, Taiwan, and the nuclear-weaponised Korean Peninsula. The concerns are aggravated by the rapid augmentation of maritime military capabilities by the regional countries, with a particular emphasis on sea-denial and anti-access. These pose major challenges for regional stability. The key issues in this session were:

- Assessment of maritime disputes which have the potential to escalate into an armed conflict in the region.

- Likely conflict scenarios, triggers, signposts and escalation dynamics for an increased threat of military confrontation in the region.

- Importance of UNCLOS and other legal instruments in resolving the maritime disputes.

Another facet of regional geopolitics is the growing economic integration. The region has been in the forefront of economic multilateralism and widespread economic growth, which has led to strong interdependencies amongst countries. This has also led to an increased strategic and economic competition for resources and markets in the region. At another level, environmental challenges driven by global warming are also having an increasing impact on the region. The threat of sea level rise, frequent natural disasters, over-exploitation of marine resources and its effect on coastal sustainability is emerging as a growing cause of concern. Regional Economics and Environmental Dynamics were addressed in Session 3 and the key questions which were addressed in this session were:

- How is regional economics and trade influencing maritime security?

- What are the emerging environmental challenges in the region?

Diplomacy and Strategic Posturing was the theme of Session 4. Regional countries have diverse national objectives which are often contradictory and certain countries perceive it as a zero-sum game. These countries are leveraging their political, diplomatic, economic, and military power, to further their foreign policy objectives. This has also led to increased engagements at the diplomatic level and strategic posturing. The key questions to be addressed in this session were:

- How are major powers in East Asia leveraging maritime capabilities to further their foreign policy objectives?

- What are the potential areas of China- India strategic discord in the Indian Ocean?

Evolving Maritime Security Architecture and India was the theme of the last session. The unfolding maritime dynamics in the region has led to institutionalisation of multilateral security structures such as the ASEAN Regional Forum (ARF), ASEAN Defence Ministers' Meeting Plus (ADMM+), East Asian Summit (EAS), Expanded ASEAN Maritime Forum (EAMF), etc. This has contributed to regional stability as it encourages furthering of cooperative mechanisms. India has significant economic and strategic stakes and its role in maintaining security in the region is clearly acknowledged. India's engagement in the Asia-Pacific security multilateralism is a part of its 'Look East' policy, which has now evolved as 'Act East' Policy. In context of the foregoing, Session 5 focussed on the following questions:

- What role can India play in shaping the structural and normative parameters in the existing multilateral security architecture in the region?

- What are the perceptions of regional countries towards India's role in the region?

- What are India's strategic options for enhancing its role and influence in the region?

The book attempts to provide answers to the above questions and brings together leading experts in the area to provide an assessment of the emerging dynamics in the Indo-Pacific, with a focus on Eastern Indian Ocean and Western Pacific Ocean region. We hope that the book serves as a milestone in recording the maritime dynamics in this region.

– **Vijay Sakhuja**

– **Kapil Narula**

1 MARITIME DYNAMICS IN THE INDO-PACIFIC: SETTING THE SCENE*

Arun Prakash

Introduction

While 'Samudra Manthan' the title of Raja Mohan's book may be just an allegorical reference to the Sino-Indian maritime rivalry in the Indo-Pacific, but there are many other who foresee growing competition in the Indo-Pacific region. U.S. analyst Robert Kaplan goes a step further and visualizes the Indo-Pacific as the setting where, 'the rivalry between the U.S. and China interlocks with the regional rivalry between China and India'.

Many other developments in the recent past have seen the world becoming distinctly more fraught with perils of every kind. The ongoing proxy war in the Ukraine has created a chill in East-West relations, reminiscent of the Cold War era. There are civil wars and simmering conflicts in the Middle East, Africa, South Asia and South China Sea which have the potential to spark widespread conflagrations. The sudden and stunning success of non-state entities like the Islamic States and Boko Haram, which marry fanatical ideology and military prowess with social media, adds a new dimension to the threat scenario.

The economic arena had looked fairly placid till the recent Greek crisis. However, as the RBI Governor reminds us, there are many possible scenarios, in which, geopolitical events could trigger a severe crisis. In the fickle world of finance, the BRICS grouping, i.e. Brazil, Russia, India, China and South Africa seems to have disappointed and the focus has,

---

* Adapted from the 'Keynote Address' delivered in the Inaugural Session of the Seminar.

now, shifted to MINT: Mexico, Indonesia, Nigeria and Turkey. Energy has always been a powerful economic weapon and the development of fracking techniques in the U.S. has caused major upsets in Russia and the Middle East; with deep geo-political ramifications.

In the mid-18th century Asia had more than half of the world population and represented more than half its product. Just a hundred and fifty years later, European mercantilism and the industrial revolution had reduced Asia's share of products to 1/5th of the world's total. The steady shift of power and of productive base from the Anglo-Saxon world to the East has led to predictions that the 21st century will witness the restoration of Asia to its position of economic prominence.

A century ago, American strategist, Admiral Mahan had described the Indian and Pacific Oceans as future *'hinges of the world's geo-political destiny'*, because he felt that control of this region could empower a maritime nation to influence political developments deep into Eurasia. Today, when it appears that the Indo-Pacific may become a theatre for rivalry and power-play, it is important that India's eastern maritime domain is explored as an area of strategic interest.

After decades of focus on the western seaboard, both the nation and the navy have rightly turned their attention eastwards. As U.S. Defence Secretary Ashton Carter's recent visit demonstrated, the strategic significance of the Eastern Naval Command (ENC) has been duly recognized and the port of Vishakhapatnam as well as its neighbourhood are well on the way to becoming our eastern maritime bastion.

India's Area of Interest and its Relationship with the Indian Ocean

The core interests of colonial powers that dominated the Indian Ocean for 400 years lay, back home, in Europe. The strategic importance of this region was, therefore, downplayed and it was regarded merely as a cross-road for shipping traffic. Even in the heyday of the Raj, when the Indian Ocean was considered a 'British Lake', there was little interest in its consolidation. The British saw the Indian Ocean as a collection of sub-regions like Southern Africa, East Africa, Middle East and the Far East.

The US, which succeeded Britain as the predominant Indian Ocean power, remained focused on security of Middle East oil, and the containment of communism through a system of treaties and alliances. The America's fixation with the Atlantic and the Pacific has tended to relegate the Indian Ocean to the periphery of its consciousness. The U.S. has further aggravated the situation by trifurcating the Indian Ocean between three geographic Combatant Commands; PACOM, CENTCOM and AFRICOM. Independent India, too, contributed to the region's isolation by making an abortive attempt at creating an Indian Ocean Zone of Peace which would bar the entry of extra-regional navies.

Today; a thousand years after the zenith of Chola sea-power and three hundred years after Kanhoji Angre sailed the Arabian Sea in triumph, there are clear signs of India's renaissance at sea. As a major economic, military and maritime power, India can change the character of the Indian Ocean littoral through strategic and economic relationships. At the same time, there are many pointers that India also needs to look beyond the Indian Ocean.

Apart from its evolving 'Look East' and 'Act East' initiatives, nearly 55% of India's trade with the greater Asia Pacific transits through the South China Sea (SCS). India has also invested heavily in hydrocarbon ventures in the Russian Far East as well as in Vietnamese waters. India, thus, has a stake in the freedom of navigation and stability of sea lanes, right from Oman in the west to the Okhotsk Sea in the east. The rapid warming of Indo-Japanese and Indo-Australian ties is a recent development which could have far-reaching implications for the region.

The US 'pivot to the east' has also seen a subtle shift in strategic perspectives. The use of the term 'Indo-Pacific' instead of 'Asia-Pacific' by the State and Defence Departments seems to be an acknowledgment of the concurrent rise of China and India. Simultaneously, the need for a 'dynamic coupling' of the Indian and Pacific Oceans, in order to reflect changing geo-political realities began to be articulated at the highest political levels in the US and Asia.

Interestingly, the 2015 US Maritime Strategy has coined yet another geo-political term; the 'Indo-Asia-Pacific'. This term is said to span the region from the West Coast of the US to the East coast of Africa and contains eight of the world's ten most populous countries. Indian academics need to reflect on which of these terms has more validity and relevance. Or should we play safe and stick to the phrase, 'Eastern Indian Ocean and the Western Pacific,' used in title of this seminar?

Leaving aside, semantics; given the navy's role as an instrument of state policy, a naval officer is liable to find himself as the first responder, not just in disaster-relief incidents but also in, political or diplomatic situations; as happened in the 2004 tsunami or in Lebanon, Libya and Yemen. Since Rules of Engagement don't cover all eventualities, it is important that views and especially, 'snap-appreciations' by commanders at sea are based on practical considerations and not on woolly notions.

International Relations Theory

19th century British PM Lord Palmerston had said of his foreign policy: "*We have no eternal allies, and we have no perpetual enemies. Our interests are eternal and perpetual, and those interests it is our duty to follow.*" Palmerston's maxim is a good start point for a quick guide to State behaviour.

The concept of political-realism in international-relations conveys a warning that states acts in pursuit of their self-interest, with the primary goal of ensuring their own security and survival. To this end they gather military, economic, and political power as well as territory. The prevailing international system is defined as anarchic since there is no universal authority, including the UN, which can resolve disputes or maintain international order. There is a theory which says that the international system requires a hegemon, or a dominant single state, in order to maintain stability. It cites historical precedents of the past 500 years, to show that global hegemonic dominance is a cyclical phenomenon lasting between 100 to 150 years, after which the title of 'most powerful nation in the world' changes hands. Such a change is considered to be due now. States can guard against hegemony and enhance national security by ensuring - through coalition formation - that a balance of power exists; i.e. no single state is strong enough to dominate others. Finally; a state's behaviour can be predicted if you can classify it either a *status quo* or a revisionist power. A *status quo* power is one that is satisfied with the existing international system and seeks to work within it without change. A revisionist state, on the other hand, is primarily concerned with its own power and prestige and seeks to remodel the existing order for its own benefit. Against this backdrop, the realities of the Indo-Asia-Pacific region i.e. its potential 'hotspots' and sources of tension are outlined in the next few sub-sections.

Sources of Tension in the Indo-Asia-Pacific

In a unique but dangerous juxtaposition, three out of the region's four declared nuclear weapon states, China, India and Pakistan, live in uncomfortable proximity. While North Korea's nuclear devices and ballistic missiles have kept the neighbourhood on tenterhooks, Iran's long-term intentions are still not quite clear.

In South Asia, the 68-year old Indo-Pakistan tensions, far from abating, flare-up periodically to keep the border 'hot and live'. The Sino-Indian disputes, going back to China's take-over of Tibet and the subsequent border war of 1962, seem to be getting more complex and convoluted. Despite an exchange of visits between Chairman Xi Jinpeng and PM Modi in quick succession, there has been little progress on thorny issues like territorial claims, delineation of the Line of Actual Control (LAC) and information on trans-border rivers.

In East Asia, many countries like Japan, China and the Koreas, carry burdens of the past, and perceptions of historic wrongs that tend to prevent reconciliation. North Korea has, technically, remained in a state of war for the past 62 years with the USA and South Korea. While tensions across the Taiwan Strait have eased in recent times, mainland China has neither slackened its military build-up, nor renounced the use of force against Taiwan.

Most of the historic differences in the region are linked to maritime disputes. They impinge upon the freedom of shipping, and international trade and energy traffic. Of late, freedom of air-navigation, too, has become an issue. UNCLOS, unfortunately, has many lacunae which do not properly address overlapping sovereignty claims in the South China Sea. This has led to diplomatic and military standoffs in an area which sees dense international shipping traffic.

The East China Sea dispute over the Senkaku islands, has led to heightened tensions between Japan and China. Apart from the two disputants an added complication is the possible involvement of the US on account of the US-Japan Security Treaty.

Finally, a symptom of the region's acute 'security dilemma' is the naval arms race, which has been in progress across the Indo-Pacific for some time. An interesting manifestation of this phenomenon is the way in which many SE Asian nations have rushed to acquire submarines to counter China's maritime assertiveness. The past decade has seen Singapore, Malaysia and Vietnam, join the submarine club whose original members were Australia and Indonesia. New aspirants in the race are Bangladesh, Thailand, Philippines and Myanmar. India and Pakistan are, of course, much older participants in this race.

India is often accused of being over-possessive of the Indian Ocean; even to the extent of attempting to impose its version of the 'Monroe Doctrine' in the region. This criticism is, largely, misplaced, and India has provided enough evidence of its intention to be a benign 'security provider' for the region.

On the other hand, the far-reaching influence of a rapidly growing China on the global power balance has become a matter of intense discussion. China's new Military Strategy expresses the pious hope that 'in the foreseeable future, a world war is unlikely and the international situation is expected to remain peaceful.' However, it also speaks of 'operational and tactical offence' embedded in 'strategic defence'. The PLA Navy will shift focus from 'offshore waters defence' to 'open sea protection', 'strategic deterrence', 'counter-attack' and 'maritime manoeuver.' Therefore there is a need to penetrate the dialectic and gauge China's intended policy objectives.

China's Policy Objectives

In 2010, Beijing declared its 'non-negotiable' claim to sovereignty over almost the entire South China Sea, along with islands, reefs and rocks; many within the territorial waters of other countries. It has also been, vigorously, re-asserting its claim to Arunachal Pradesh, which it calls 'South Tibet.' In 2013, China unilaterally proclaimed an Air Defense Identification Zone (ADIZ), to cover some South Korean as well as Japanese territory. Currently, it is engaged in feverish activity to create artificial islands in disputed areas of the South China Sea, after which it may establish another ADIZ that will cover the entire sea.

There are only two ways in which a country can hope to achieve ambitions of such breath-taking audacity: either by brute intimidation or by war. The first does not seem to be working, as a defiant Philippines has shown, by approaching the International Court of Justice. So, there is a talk in the Chinese media, of 'inevitable war'.

A muted belligerence does run through the new Military Strategy document as it refers to 'anti-China' forces instigating Tibet and East Turkistan 'independence movements'. There is also mention of 'maritime rights and interests' and warnings to external countries against 'meddling in South China Sea affairs'. Repeated exhortations to the PLA to uphold the Party's 'absolute leadership over the military' only highlight the underlying insecurity of the Politbureau and a possibility that conflict could break out through sheer militarism, overconfidence or miscalculation on part of the PLA leadership.

A Different View of China

China's economic and military rise has been so spectacular that many have failed to notice that it is also busy reshaping the geopolitical fundamentals of global power. Given the scanty understanding of China, the world may be emulating the blind men who touched different parts of an elephant and came to different and erroneous conclusions.

Therefore, let us put aside, the concept of sea power propagated by Mahan and his acolyte KM Panikkar to focus the attention on an alternate oracle of strategic wisdom - Sir Halford Mackinder – for a different perspective on China. Mackinder, who is known as the 'father of geo-politics', wrote a paper in 1904, in which he pronounced that the era of sea power, that had lasted for 400 years, was over and the age of land power had arrived.

On his new map which combined parts of the three continents into a unitary land mass or 'World Island' he declared that the 'Heartland' of Eurasia, corresponding to the then Russian Empire, would be the pivot that held the key to world-domination. Mackinder argued that the future of global power lay not, as most then imagined, in controlling the global sea lanes, but in controlling the vast land mass of 'Euro-Asia. Whoever ruled the 'heartland', he said, would command the 'world-island' and whoever ruled the world-island would command the world.

Today, the focus has shifted from Russia to China, whose grand-strategy seems to have adopted two canons of Mackinder's thesis. On one hand, it is creating a trans-continental infrastructure for the economic integration of the world-island from within. This plan includes a vast and expensive internal network of high-speed railways as well as oil and natural gas pipelines, within China. This network will be linked to a trans-continental Eurasian grid. At the same time it is also building a sophisticated military to guard its maritime flanks and preclude attempts at containment.

To bypass the Straits of Malacca, China constructed a pipeline in 2013 that carries both Middle Eastern oil and Myanmarese natural gas from the Bay of Bengal to south-western China. In addition, China is building two spur lines, southwards, toward the world island's maritime margins; one to Gwadar in Pakistan and another to Singapore via Laos.

There is substantive evidence to show that China's grand strategy has been carefully crafted to take care of every detail. The creation of the Asian Infrastructure Investment Bank (AIIB) and the Silk Road Fund will serve to capitalize the gigantic expenditure of these regional growth plans.

In the last paragraph of his 1904 paper, Mackinder had offered an ominous proposition. He wrote: '*Were the Chinese, for instance, to overthrow the Russian Empire and conquer its territory, they might constitute the "yellow peril" to world freedom just because they would add the advantages of an oceanic frontage to the resources of a great continent.*'

If Mackinder's apprehensions come true, China, by befriending, instead of conquering Russia, will not only become a land and sea power but also gain control of the global economy by coupling its own industries to the vast natural resources of the Eurasian heartland. The Indo-Asia-Pacific will then have to make an agonizing re-appraisal, not just of the maritime dynamics but, of the far more serious geopolitical ramifications of China's rise.

Hedging Strategies

Hegemonic competition is a zero-sum game and the prospect that China may, one day, achieve its ambition of becoming America's peer in economic and military power is unnerving for everyone in the region. Indo-Pacific stake-holders, small or big, want to ensure that international norms and laws are respected, commerce and navigation remain unimpeded, and that strength or coercion does not decide the outcome of disputes.

The anarchic nature of the international system has not changed since the mighty Athenians exercised the right of unbridled power 2400 years ago, telling the islanders of tiny Melos: *'right is only in question between equals in power...the strong do what they can and the weak suffer what they must.'*

The choices are stark. A strategy of 'Containment' is clearly infeasible; given China's deep economic and trade linkages with the US as well as with other Asian countries. Power-balancing and alliance formation could lead to tensions and even confrontation. The approach to China must, therefore, encompass a basket of strategies that combine active engagement with a subliminal deterrence. Even as nations continue to build trade and economic relations with China, they must retain sufficient leverage to ensure that it remains within the bounds of normative behaviour. Another component of this policy would require a credible military counterpoise – not in the form of a formal coalition but possibly as a 'force in being'.

Conclusion

At this juncture, India cannot stand up to China on its own. However, as a democracy, a nuclear weapon state and an emerging economic power, it is seen by others as a possible bulwark against regional hegemony. It is in this context that India must, with subtlety and sophistication, remain a pole or rallying point for countering China. To this end India's diplomats need to craft hedging strategies that will ensure peace with honour.

India is in the unusual position of being a developing nation as well as a rising power. While its delicately poised economy requires peace and stability for growth, its rise to great power status will depend on adroit management of geopolitical challenges which can only be achieved through regional cooperation.

Historically, regional diversity, combined with chauvinistic self-interest have combined to prevent the formation of pan-Asian institutions which could facilitate dialogue, or help create a cooperative response to developments affecting the whole region. While many sub-regional groupings and organs like ASEAN, APEC, ARF and ADMM have been success stories, others like SAARC, IORA, IONS and BIMSTEC have shown relatively less dynamism.

It is encouraging to see India's new leadership reaching out to the Indo-Pacific neighbourhood to create partnerships and cooperative mechanisms for mutual benefit. China, too, must remain a part of India's new economic and strategic outreach. In fact, there are suggestions that India's and China's mutual dependence on the same sea lanes could become the rationale for a cooperative maritime relationship.

As the maritime dynamics of this region unfold, India's policy-makers and diplomats must learn to play hardball with a soft touch. However, they need to be constantly reminded that navies make extremely useful instruments of state policy; especially when practicing realpolitik, in the tradition of Lord Palmerston.

2   US REBALANCE TO ASIA

K Raja Menon

The Unified Command Plan

Over the cold war years and afterwards, the US has set in place an organization for the application of power worldwide through what is called a Unified Command Plan. Under this plan the world has been subdivided into combatant commands under the pentagon and the President. Fig. 1 shows the command structure of the unified command plan. As can be seen there are some areas which are dense with populated countries and there are others like the Pacific command which has two fifth of the world's population and covers half the globe.

Fig. 1. The Unified Command Plan divided into tri-service command areas

The division of commands and the lines of demarcation affect countries and their relationship with the US. This is particularly so in the case of India where the separation line between central command and Pacific command areas runs along the Indo-Pak border, thereby placing the two countries in two separate commands. But clearly, the Indian relationship with Pakistan is so uneasy and the US intervention plays such a large factor, that Indians have never ceased to complain to PACOM that this division is inconvenient. The US has however taken no heed to these complaints and have adhered to the Unified Command Plan. Lately, the demarcation has been seen to be advantageous in that the area of responsibility for PACOM automatically upholds the idea of the Indo-Pacific as being one coherent strategic area.

The pivot to the East must be understood as being a diplomatic, an economic and a military rebalancing and the last one- the military cannot be understood without knowing what the force structures looked like before unbalancing. The Pacific Command Area is the biggest, command area covering half the globe and is a unified tri-service command including the army, navy and air force. The military forces allocated to this region include two fleets and three air forces apart from an army contingent. Under the army there are troops in Japan (1 corps), in Korea (8 corps) and in Hawaii – the 25 Division. There are two Fleets – the 3rd fleet in San Diego in the US and the 7th fleet based out of Hawaii. There are three air forces – the 5th air force in Japan, the 11th air force in the US and the 13th Air force in Hawaii. There is a B52 squadron based at Guam and 7 nuclear submarine squadrons are distributed between the US, Hawaii and Guam. Marine expeditionary forces are positioned in Japan, Hawaii and the US.

Hence, the command structure has not been affected by the rebalancing but the actual allocation of forces has been adjusted in that there is now, a total of six Carrier Battle Group (CVBGs) in the East where there was formerly five. A CVBG includes a carrier, its air component, a destroyer squadron, some SSNs and a tanker for refueling.

Why the Rebalancing?

The US acknowledges that as the production center of the world's economy, maritime Asia (from Japan, across China and South East Asia to South Asia) is the new center of gravity of the world due to its economic strength and its large military expenditure.

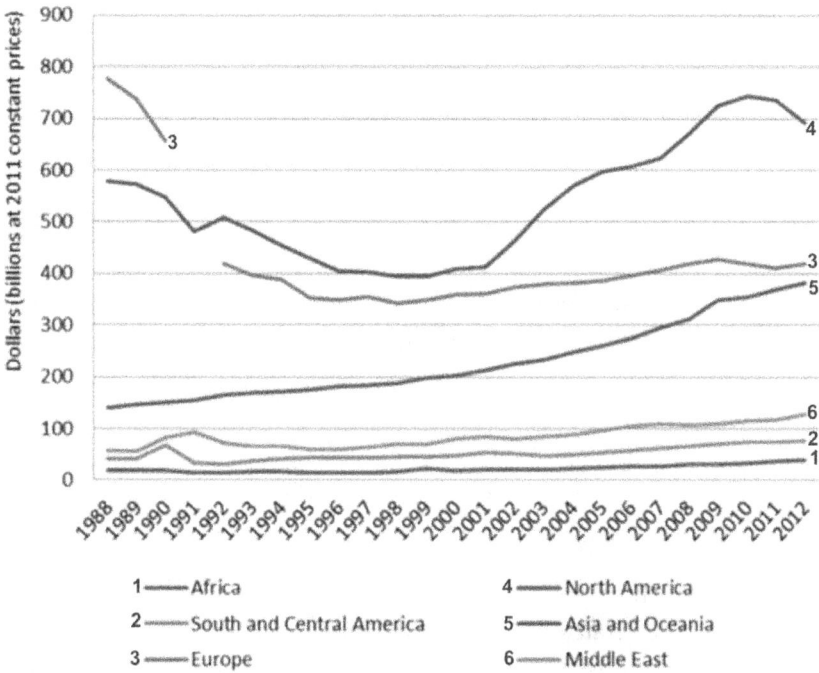

Fig. 2. Trends in regional military expenditure (1988-2012)

[Source: SIPRI Military Expenditure database]

Fig. 2 shows the trends in regional military expenditure. While the expenditure of Europe has remained steady, for Asia and Oceania, it has risen steadily and is set to overtake that of Europe. This region is also the only area where the nuclear arsenals are still growing and there is an ongoing power struggle that is reminiscent of 19th century politics with 21st century economics.

There is also a growing realization that the global system will be shaped by the East, and particularly by the increasing economic clout of China, which is close on the heels of the US economy in terms of size. This rise of China or rather the return of China to its former position of pre-eminence economically is going to place severe strain on the world system, currently dominated by the US. It is imperative from the US point of view that China be engaged and brought into the world system so that the 'rise' of China is managed peacefully, a process that has not occurred in history previously.

Why Containment is not the Option

During the cold war, the famous Kennan letter led the US to contain the USSR, which successfully isolated the country, until the USSR collapsed economically. Containment today is not an option, as the decision to integrate China's economy into the world economy was taken as early as 1978. At that time it was not forecasted in US strategic circles that the move would be a stunning success and that China would eventually invest US $ 1.4 trillion in US treasury bonds and would be able to build a trade surplus of US $ 343 billion in 2014 with Chinese exports being US $ 466 billion and imports being only US $ 123 billion. There are other indications, for instance, the Chinese students in the US numbered 274,000 in 2014. So there is clearly no possibility of containment when the two countries are so closely engaged. In fact the engagement of the US with China is probably one of the closest between any two countries, although they remain strategic competitors.

The important aspect is that the US has decided that the close engagement is a strategic asset and has no intention to disengage from the closeness and revert to encirclement or containment – although there are efforts towards creating a balance of power in which India may have an intended role. The grand strategy of the US foreign policy is to engage more with China and draw that country into the international system. The Chinese of course see the pivot as a hostile move aimed at containment and Chinese think tanks constantly tell Indians that the US talk of engagement is all deception. It is however true that if the US had calculated differently in 1978 that engaging China would eventually create a competitive giant which would threaten US hegemony, the decision may not have been taken to integrate China with the world's economy.

The US is at pains to point out that engaging China has a threefold strategy - a diplomatic, an economic and a military aspect. Underlying the statement is an acknowledged position that eventually the relationship with China will be competitive as China seeks to plough a different furrow in world affairs. Quite often the Chinese foreign policy seems to take a delight in a deliberate anti-US position for the sake of annoying the US – as for instance in the area of supporting dictatorial regimes in South America, - in the US backyard, or taking contrary stands on Weapons of Mass Destruction (WMD). So it is true that engaging China has a strategic objective, which is to 'manage' China. This is different from dealing with the USSR which only had to be deterred and could not pose an economic challenge to the US. So the game with the USSR was essentially a zero- sum game and achieved an equilibrium quite early on.

So how does one run a military competitive relationship simultaneously with a cooperative economic one? Furthermore how does the US reassure its allies that the cooperation with China stops short of their treaty obligations in the face of a China deploying its missiles in the South and East China Seas? The military competitiveness is often driven by Chinese aggression. Its determination to claim sovereignty of the nine-dashed lines, combined with the A2/AD concept clearly puts the Americans on warning that China will resist US interference close to its own coast, either in defence of Taiwan or in intervening in the South China dispute.

Under the A2/AD concept, the US has a problem to diplomatically reassure the smaller nations in the region that the US can be relied upon. What, they ask is the US strategy? The Pentagon places its reliance on the Air –Sea battle concept, but there is insufficient demonstration that this is an up and running idea, which has been tested out. In the capitals of the SE Asian countries, leaders have to make up their minds on the basis of little evidence as to whether the Air-Sea battle concept can overcome the A2/AD concept. No one believes that it will come to a shooting war, but reassurance rests on that very possibility – that in the end, there is a guarantee that the Air – Sea battle concept will stand the test of time.

Chinese Reaction to the TPP

It is impossible to separate the institution of the Trans-Pacific Partnership (TPP) with the pivot to the East although secret negotiations began as early as 2006. When one states that the center of gravity of the world is shifting to the East, necessitating a US relationship to the East, one is largely referring to economic realities. The chief economic reality has been the rise of China and its massive achievement of lifting 400 million people into the middle class. So it is a mystery as to why a US relationship, and a TPP would leave out China. Was it because the TPP had its early beginning as a Trans Pacific Strategic Economic Partnership? Because even today, the total two way trade between the US and China which is close to US $ 450 billion dwarfs all other statistics.

Not surprisingly many have made the accusation that the TPP might be a move to drop China from being a favoured source of imports, but this doesn't make sense, for it was the US firms like Walmart that enabled China to rack up the amazing trade imbalance with the US. Also, two of the big contributors to the TPP are Mexico and Canada which are in any case tied to the US through the North American Free trade Agreement (NAFTA). Underlying the getting together of the TPP was talk about new labour standards of countries from which the US would import goods and this was deemed to be a move against Chinese goods and a US strategy to rebalance trade with China to a more favourable level. The other accusation was that the TPP would have strong barriers against currency manipulation, particularly the deliberate under-valuation of national currencies so as to sell more goods. So there are analysts who believe that the purpose of the TPP is the exclusion of China. Certainly the current TPP negotiation does not include China, nor is the TPP seen to be keen to provide incentives to make China want to join. This is a bizarre situation when China is at the head of the supply chain. Not surprisingly, China is keen on building its own China centered trade relationships. This again makes little logic because China and Japan are close to making a free trade agreement between them. But the hawks in the US say that the TPP is about who gets to write the rules in Asia, and if the US doesn't seem to do so, then China will.

The Maritime Silk Route vs the American Pivot and the TPP

The Pivot has occurred more in the economic sense than in the other two -- diplomatic and strategic. Planners say that without progress on the TPP all that the US has succeeded in doing is setting off a Chinese reaction of triggering an economic grouping – namely the Maritime Silk Route (MSR). In pushing the MSR, China is attempting to create its own economic grouping in reply to an almost moribund TPP. China realizes that it cannot win the hearts and minds of the Asian countries without financial blandishments. The MSR builds on a 2000 year old idea of creating mutual prosperity through common manufacturing and trading links. The MSR is advertised by Admiral Zheng He's famous voyage to the Indian Ocean. After visiting all the main ports of SE Asia with a fleet of 40 vessels and 27,000 soldiers and sailors, reaching upto the Persian Gulf and Africa. With rising costs in China, many SE Asian countries could become manufacturing hubs financed by China. As a competitor to the TPP, the MSR would set a very low standard for entry, with no contention criteria like institutional property rights and minimum labor standards.

Furthermore China is willing to put money up front to set up port infrastructure, communications and manufacturing support. Many predict that in a few years upto 100 billion dollars worth of capital would flow from China along the MSR, replicating the ancient era when with Chinese investments would come Chinese materials, as they have done in Africa to push the idea of absorbing Chinese capital.

The continental vs the maritime strategy for China

Chinese strategists are keeping both options open i.e. building a rail connection to transport containers from Shanghai to Germany which would be a faster connection. However sea transport would remain cheaper.

China will however not depend on overseas Chinese national to push investments as they are aware that politically, overseas Chinese have little in common with the Chinese community. The implications for India are interesting and speculative. Originally the MSR was only for SE Asia but was later extended to the Indian Ocean. New Delhi has ambiguous feelings towards the MSR which is not very clearly articulated. India is however keen to absorb Chinese capital for infrastructure projects and almost US $ 34 billion have been committed during the top level visits. At the same time, New Delhi has carefully skirted around the MSR idea keeping a wary distance from it for reasons that are not clear. Chinese money for infrastructure whether it comes from the MSR or directly should make no difference. India believes that the objectives of the MSR are opaque, but this shows a lack of confidence that a Chinese port may be used as a base later on. This uncertainty weighs too heavily on Indian minds.

The Strategic Competition – A2/AD vs Air-Sea Battle

The Chinese certainly believe that the US pivot is a strategic move to 'contain' China. This chapter has argued that containment is not a relevant strategy in the era of globalization, but the Chinese are not convinced. They believe that the US wishes to limit their power to continental China and prevent it from becoming a world power. The internal Chinese debate must be going on but one is not privy to the contents of that debate. All one knows is that China is determined to break out both overseas, through the A2/AD and the MSR as well as continentally through the Silk Road with the ability to send a container from Shanghai to Rotterdam overland.

In the meanwhile the Pentagon has been pushing the Air-sea battle concept as the method by which the US retains the ability to intervene on the Asian scene in support of treaty obligations. These obligations tie the US to Japan, Korea and the Philippines. There is also the US unilateral interest in preserving the freedom of the seas from China's excessive sovereign claims in the South China Sea. The nations in-between do not have a formal position, but would prefer that the international system be run by the US rather than China. So while it may not come to a shooting war between the US and China, each nation would have to take a call on whether the US Air Sea Battle concept can overcome the A2/AD concept or not. The US pivot is therefore far more about a strategic relationship of naval and air forces to the East. The Air Sea Battle concept is therefore eventually about building counter access capabilities.

The anti-access strategy details are contained in detail elsewhere but essentially the Chinese claims that they can use a DF 21 missile with a terminal homing capability to hit a large warship like the US aircraft carrier upto a range of about 1500 km from the Chinese coast. The system consists of other nodes such as the Beidou satellites and OTH radars to locate the carrier to some degree of accuracy. The Department of Defence (DoD) literature specifically states that the ASB is a concept or strategy to 'counter' area denial capabilities. That over time many states have tried to develop anti-access strategies, but that these have had to be overcome through innovative ideas and aggressive tactics. The DoD's problem statement says that A2/AD forces US to operate from disadvantageously longer distances and prevents build up of US forces and their ability to maintain freedom of action. The DoD memorandum goes onto say that

(a) A2/AD activities will occur without any notice.

(b) As a result US forces will be within lethal range, initially.

(c) US supporting bases will be targeted simultaneously with US forces.

(d) All domains will be contested at the same time -- space, cyberspace, air and maritime.

(e) Lastly, no domain can be ceded to the adversary and superiority in any domain can be used to challenge the adversary in other domains.

In reply to these challenges the ASB is a supporting strategy to the joint operational access concept and it is therefore an analysis of how to shape the A2/AD environment. The ASB idea is to develop networked integrated forces capable of attack in depth of the interdependent domains of the enemy and destroy and defeat his integrated plan. US forces will be made available to any commander irrespective of the choice of command to destroy any of the enemy's domains. Traditional service barriers will be done away with thereby giving any commander the ability to call upon any space, air or maritime capability to attack the enemy domain.

According to US naval literature the ASB is not aimed at the power of an enemy but at his anti-access capability to facilitate further joint operations. The concept has been institutionalized and presumably been gamed extensively although there are no reports of the concept having been tried out on the ground at any time. The US literature sounds positive that the Chinese attempt at area denial is another attempt in the history of asymmetric warfare to deny entry to an offensive power and the US feels that it can handle it, like previous occasions.

Effects on Indian Strategy

The competition between the US and China will have downstream effects that will affect the Indian strategic scenario, by either facilitating or blocking the Chinese entry into the Indian Ocean. The Chinese desire to enter the Indian Ocean in a permanent way, forced by their need to protect the burgeoning SLOCs in the Indian Ocean. Their ability to enter the Indian Ocean would be largely dependent on the outcome of their competition with the US – or in other words the perceived outcome of the A2/AD concept vs the ASB. For instance, if they see that they are heavily outweighed in the Western Pacific, they are unlikely to foray into the Indian Ocean. In such a case they will push continentally westwards overland through the Silk Road.

Conclusion

Beijing has kept its options open, by making forays into the MSR as well as the Silk Road, which could have an early exit from Kashgar down to Gwadar. In the meanwhile, the foray into the Indian Ocean would be heavily dependent on the pressure the US and Japan can mount in the Western Pacific. Despite this pressure, if they come into the Indian Ocean, their force would not be significantly large.

The only problem is that the Chinese entry into the Indian Ocean is not likely to be a foray, but of a semi-permanent nature. To facilitate such a move the Chinese will need a base on the Indian Ocean littoral. Could the MSR be a clever ploy to lay the groundwork for an Indian Ocean base? Such is New Delhi's worry – that Chinese money may lay the foundation for a base in the Indian ocean littoral, if a littoral nation was to accept the billions that are being offered for joining the MSR. However even a base in the Indian Ocean littoral would not be an insurmountable obstacle to Indian ambitions.

3 SOUTHEAST ASIAN COUNTRIES AND THEIR ALIGNMENT

Anup Singh

Introduction

Southeast Asia (SE Asia) is that region in the Indo-Pacific geography, which is located South of China, North of Australia, East of India, and West of Papua New Guinea. Southern China provides the proverbial roof to the region. That has meant not just physical proximity, but also increasing influence due to the interconnectedness between China and SE Asia since the end of the cold war because of the intense economic engagement between the two.

The region has often been considered the barometer for how China's rise would ultimately affect the world. For about two decades after the cold war, it was felt that if China's economic and foreign policies were accepted by SE Asia, these will find easy acceptance in the rest of the world. That situation meant that other than those countries which had (land) boundary disputes with China, the larger world would easily accept China's rise if the SE Asian countries did. And SE Asia was engaged so effectively by China that apart from its economic relations, it also projected a peaceful and soft side of its demeanour through a new and "open" form of diplomacy. China gained acceptance through renewed trust and started spreading its influence through attractive packages for the lesser developed countries in the region. All that changed in 2009, when China pulled out its nine-dash line map, annoying those littorals in the South China Sea whose Exclusive Economic Zones (EEZ) saw conflicting overlap with the nine dashes. Yet, ASEAN saw reason to believe that normalization could be restored, and many an attempt was made to improve relations through the economic and diplomatic route. One such effort succeeded in conclusion of the landmark deal on the China-ASEAN Free Trade Agreement (CAFTA).

This gave hope to all ASEAN members, of a possible thaw and mutual trust due to the economic strings attached to this arrangement. Over the last five years, however, relations between China and SE Asian nations have become increasingly strained due to overlapping territorial and maritime jurisdictional claims, and due to unseemly clashes at sea.

In so far as alignments are concerned, good relations, pacts for mutual cooperation, and partnerships in economic or security arrangements make for harmonious relations, and a penchant on the part of the Client State to back the Patron State's call in international institutions. Such a relationship also makes clients view their patron's role in regional or global politics with a positive bias. The opposite takes place when there is increased regional conflict – may be diplomatic or military, or both – which works against the mechanism of quid pro quo, resulting in the affected client state opposing alignment in international or regional politics of the patron. This is the current story of the affected parties in the South China Sea in particular, and SE Asia in general.

It is security concerns that are mainly responsible for the turmoil that is raging in the region. All the important countries in the region – from the Philippines, Vietnam, Malaysia, to Brunei – have been affected. Indonesia, which did not protest till now, as none of the islands, reefs, or shoals within its EEZ get encroached by the nine-dashed line, too has now joined the rest of the littorals in making a bold statement that China's nine-dash line has no basis in International Law. This has happened in President Jokowi's time, and is being brought up because of the realization that even if none of Indonesia's features get covered by the line, it heavily intrudes in to its EEZ – claimed around the Natuna Islands in the North. If Indonesia had kept quiet (as in its previous dispensation), it could well have resulted in China continuing to indulge in illegal fishing, and exploratory actions in that area.

To add to the tension, these countries are now worried at the pace of Chinese military modernization amidst unprecedented growth. There is no stopping its military budget from moving on a predetermined linear graph that even in 2015 has been declared at 10% over the last, as announced on 04 Mar 2015.[1] Though lower than the previous year's 12.2% increase, the current allocation still marks the fifth consecutive year with double digit growth in defence expenditure, and that too in the "white" budget (official military spending). The actual military spending is thought to be much more.

It is a well-known fact from history that "dominant" regional powers that rely too heavily on coercion instead of consensus in their interactions with other countries of the region, actually end up pushing such countries to find counterweights by forging alliances and security pacts with outside forces. Outsiders are normally too happy to oblige as such alliances and their entry into the affected region would end up undermining the prowess, and curb the rise of a peer. Such alliances guarantee security and defence cooperation. They also ensure for the external power, an exchange bonanza in terms of support for its own agenda, and economic benefits in some cases. Such models were witnessed during the cold war when the two super powers were in competition to enroll client states from each other's 'camps'.

One issue that heavily impinged upon geopolitics in the region was President Obama's announcement of a shift of US' foreign policy focus to the East, referring to it as the *Pivot to Asia*, later dubbed as *Rebalancing* under indirect pressure from China as well as its European allies. This announcement infused tremendous confidence amongst all SE Asian countries, apart from the important ones in the Far East (like Japan and South Korea), and is already showing signs of realignment by some.

Country Alignments

Philippines

The sore point in Philippines-China relations has been the contentious Scarborough Shoal – just 100 nautical miles from Subic Bay (well inside Philippines' EEZ). The low in their relations came in the spring of 2012, when vessels from the Philippines and China engaged in a week-long standoff near this shoal. The incident was triggered by the Filipino sailors having boarded a Chinese fishing vessel inside their EEZ. The confrontation ended a few months later with China having effected physical control of the disputed waters with an overwhelming force.

Philippines was a US colony from 1898 to 1946, followed by the signing of a Mutual Defence Treaty between the two in 1951, five years after the former gained independence. Even before conclusion of that treaty, the Philippines continued to allow America to operate from two of its bases established during the war, the Clarke Air Force Base, and the Subic Bay Naval Base.

While the 1951' Mutual Defence Accord stipulates that the US or Philippines would support the other if one came under attack, it is not very sure if it will be applicable to its ongoing troubles with China in the South China Sea. Therefore, Philippines has started wooing the United States to come back in a form that would introduce an element of deterrence against China. On its part, the US has signed an Enhanced Defence Cooperation agreement with Philippines, in 2014, for a period of 10 years, which allows US ships to rotate through Philippine Naval Bases (operational turn around). In 2014, the US also granted US $ 50 million in military aid, a 100% hike from the previous year's allotment, and pledged US $ 40 million for the year 2015[2]. In so far as actual hardware is concerned, the US transferred two Vietnam-era Coast Guard cutters to Philippines, at US $ 10 million apiece. These vessels, intended by the US to be used as frigates by the Philippines Navy, are considered *peanuts* by the latter. Clearly, Philippines is ruing the fact that in 1992, it wrongly threw out the US out of its two bases, and perhaps the only way to provide security and deterrence against China is for the US Navy and Air Force to be present on its territory and to operate out of the old bases. Japan, on its part, has started helping the Philippines with sales of helicopters, patrol craft, and two C-130 planes for humanitarian assistance and disaster relief (HADR) missions.

While China seems satisfied with the break in relations with Philippines (having expanded its maritime jurisdiction), it is *Advantage America* in terms of alignments here – something unthinkable in the early nineties. Philippines – which wished to stay neutral after the cold war – has decidedly aligned itself with the United States for now.

Malaysia

Malaysia has had strong bilateral ties with China ever since establishment of their diplomatic relations in the mid-seventies. Malaysia's tilt towards China became even more conspicuous during the Mahathir years, when it tended to give the benefit of doubt to China, in many a niggling problem with Southeast Asia. That tendency grew from a penchant to maintain a certain distance from the West – despite its strong ties with the West in many areas including the Five Power Defence Arrangement (FPDA) with UK, technology infusion, industrial infrastructure, and acquisition of hardware for all three arms of the Defence Force. Mahathir Mohammad is in fact known to have differentiated between "Eastern Values" that he felt Malaysia shared with China, and the liberal democratic values espoused by the West.[3]

Actually, successive Malaysian regimes sought to benefit from China's economic rise, to perhaps build on their political stock at home. That meant pursuing a policy that tended to prioritise immediate economic benefits over potential security concerns. This became more conspicuous with the end of the cold war. One more reason that brought Malaysia close to China was the 1997 Asian financial crisis. While the West imposed unwelcome and embarrassing conditions for financial assistance, Malaysia was attracted towards its larger neighbour for solace, due to a feeling of hurt slapped by the West. Therefore, unlike other littorals in the region, Malaysia did not insist too much on its maritime claims against China when others did. But China's increasing assertiveness since its Nine-Dash Line claim and the growing international attention to Chinese encroachments in 2013 and 2014 into Malaysian waters, combined with the former's annoyance at Malaysia's handling of MH 370 tragedy in 2014, has made Malaysia reconfigure its policies towards China for the first time in decades. Its long-established non-confrontationist approach towards China has changed tack in a conspicuous manner. And evidence came at the ASEAN summit held in April 2015 when Malaysia fully supported the statement criticizing China for its land reclamation drive in the South China Sea. Till a couple of years ago, it was different. Malaysia used to bat for China in a not-so-hidden manner, whenever ASEAN's forums debated admonition for China's actions. Things seem to be changing, and Malaysia is tending to somewhat dilute its alignment with China.

Brunei

The only problem preceding the Nine-Dash Line was the Malaysia-Brunei maritime boundary overlap. The idea to resolve that was first thrown up in 1994. The issue of overlapping claims was finally resolved in August 2008, and officially agreed to, in March 2009. The two have lived happily thereafter – with their maritime boundary line demarcated, as mutually agreed upon. The residual problem with Brunei – as in the case of Malaysia – is the Nine-Dash Line cutting through its EEZ. That is just not acceptable to Brunei which still harbours pride over its glorious past when it used to control seaborne trade and coastal ports in the region in the 14th-15th centuries.[4] Of course it helps the US to seal an alliance for furthering its political, diplomatic, and military interests in the region. Not just because that means adding more partners to its kitty for the upcoming Trans-Pacific Partnership (TPP), or for its rebalancing strategy, but it makes so much sense in creating "dependencies" in a region where the aim of the US is to reduce China's stock as a contender for 'Great Power' status. Despite some Chinese companies having recently entered into oil extraction business in Brunei's oil fields, Brunei is now conspicuously aligned with the United States of America.

Indonesia

During his election campaign in mid-2014, President Joko Widodo (Jokowi), had promised to strengthen Indonesia's maritime security, expand regional diplomacy to cover the entire Indo-Pacific, and most significantly, project the Indonesian Navy as a respected regional maritime power in East Asia. Soon thereafter, he announced that he aimed to transform Indonesia into what he called as the "Global Maritime Axis". These objectives were reaffirmed by him after his victory, while invoking the slogan *Jalesveva Jayamah* (in the ocean, we triumph).

Compared to the rest of the South China Sea littorals, Indonesia had no (or negligible) claims for the first five years. China therefore found Indonesia a benign stakeholder, but also a very important actor in the region – because of its archipelagic sea lanes that provide China, and the whole of East Asia its lifeline for transit to the Indian Ocean and beyond. Therefore, China considered Indonesia a very valuable "neutral" player in the South China Sea imbroglio, which did not have any dispute like the other five littorals, and could be used as a friend in the politics of ASEAN. So, Indonesia was wooed at many a forum including the Western Pacific Naval Symposium (WPNS) biennial in China, in April 2014. In return, Susilo Bambang Yudhyono (then President) did not publicly object to the Nine-Dash Line, and Indonesia remained a moderate in many ASEAN deliberations where anti-China discussions were being pursued.

All that changed on arrival of Jokowi on the scene. Early this year, the new Indonesian President made it clear that the Nine-Dash line has no basis in International Law. Actually, such a line was also taken by Indonesia in 2009, while submitting its claims for delimitation, without broadcasting it to the world.[5] But this time, the tone and tenor were different, and a certain boldness is being projected by the current dispensation under Jokowi. Indonesia is a country that has always projected the image of being neutral, and now it is being not just neutral but also bold in calling a spade – a spade.

Vietnam

From the very beginning of its birth as a nation, Vietnam had been fiercely independent. Even during the two periods of colonization by the French, and the United States, it fought alone, without seeking external help. During the cold war, though, it was openly allied with the Soviet Union, but that had more to do with the apprehension of China repeating a 1979' type episode and also because of ideological reasons. Being a relatively poor country those days, it had to depend almost entirely on the USSR for military hardware and training. In return, Cam Ranh Bay was a Soviet base. After the cold war, it had adapted to the principle of "no alliance and no alignment". But, with China becoming increasingly assertive in the South China Sea, Vietnam is once again being seen moving closer to partnerships through defence cooperation mechanisms.

After the oil rig incident of May 2014, a shift in Vietnam's outlook towards China became very evident. It saw China as an unreliable power in the region – one that cannot be trusted, and decided that it had to take a call on its alignments. Though it had aligned itself with the Soviet Union during the cold war, today, it cannot trust the Russian Federation because of the very close links that country has suddenly forged with China. Nor does it want to be dependent as an "ally" of any other power. But it has established close defence and security relations with those in the region who are facing similar postures from China, i.e., Philippines and Japan. Even the United States is a welcome partner in strengthening Vietnam's security, though without a military alliance. In terms of alignments, Vietnam continues to nurture its political independence.

Laos

Since independence, Laos has generally been described as a "have-not" country, sandwiched between five others, with no access to the sea, and hamstrung by its subsistence-oriented economy. That, however was not the Laos that history had known as a dynamic trading economy which thrived on its integration with the entire region. This landlocked state shares a long history with China, and is remembered in the archives for its cherished era during the heyday of the 'Caravan Trade' between China and Southeast Asia.

The Vietnam War offered a great opportunity for the Chinese, as American presence indirectly revived Chinese migration. The US gave enormous assistance to Laos, to prevent the fall of Laos to the Communist *Pathet Laos* which could have had a cascading effect on the entire Southeast Asian region. But that economic assistance and the accompanying boost in trade with Thailand encouraged a large number of Chinese from Thailand to settle on the banks of the Mekong. Later, in 1956-57, it was the turn of the Chinese from Hong Kong and Saigon to take full advantage of mismanagement of the US Aid program.[6] The 60s saw a large number of Peoples Liberation Army (PLA) troops pouring in to Laos to "correct" the deficiencies of mismanagement during the American aid era. They built a vast network of roads, and other infrastructure. The 70s, however, saw the withdrawal of Chinese military workers, owing to a cooling of diplomatic relations between the two.

The end of the cold war, once again, led to a fresh and lucrative economic package by the Chinese to regain their place in the "centre" of SE Asia. With this package came a fresh wave of Chinese immigrants – as workers and traders. China has been aggressively pouring Foreign Direct Investment (FDI) for large projects in Northern Laos – from agriculture to mining, to running casinos. Before the Chinese, nobody wanted to invest in, or go to the North of the country. Now that that area has been developed, everyone from the West, or from the region itself, wants to first go there. Even Special Economic Zones (SEZs) have been established by the Chinese.

Today, once again, thousands of Chinese migrants have started pouring in to Laos, through the North-South economic corridor linking Kunming to Bangkok, thanks to the Greater Mekong sub-region program launched by the Asian Development Bank (ADB).[7] As a result, the number of Chinese migrants has soared over the past few decades and many more are bound to follow because of some of the largest infrastructure projects being on the anvil including the railways. The Chinese are quite firmly embedded and can be given the "credit" for building the Laos economy. And so, Laos is indebted as a client state, and has its alignment clearly and firmly defined with China.

Cambodia

Cambodia and China have had ancient ties, even though the two established diplomatic relations only in 1958. During the cold war, Prince Norodam Sihanouk had decided to adopt non-alignment as the primary focus of its foreign policy. The West however, never trusted him due to suspicions of a special relationship with China – at the leadership level. Then again, China supported the infamous Khmer Rouge regime – blamed for the massacre of 1.7 million people and for ruining the country. China remained a suspect even after restoration of normalcy in the wake of the Paris Peace Agreement in 1991. As a result, the Cambodia People's Party (CPP) remained suspicious of China – till 1997. China readjusted its approach thereafter, suddenly becoming one of Cambodia's most important donors, and strengthened Cambodia's security forces with abundant supplies and training. After the suspect elections of 2013 (in which the CPP won), the CPP suddenly became friendly to China, and even supported the "one-China policy". During the ASEAN ministerial meeting in Phnom Penh in 2012, Cambodia was accused of using its role as chair to prevent ASEAN from making a strong statement regarding the South China Sea dispute, in order to "please" the Chinese leadership.[8] As a result, ASEAN failed to issue a joint communique, for the first time in its 45 years of existence. Relations between Cambodia and China are now stronger than ever before and Cambodia can be said to be firmly aligned with China.

Thailand

Thailand and the United States have been long term allies. During the Cold War, Thailand was one important country that provided seven bases to host 27,000 US troops in the fight against communism in Southeast Asia.[9] The US flew its bomber sorties to Vietnam from Thai bases. But this bonding is showing strains of an uneasy relationship due to the coup by the Thai military in May 2014. This weakening relationship has meant losing the special position that Thailand was always considered as having with America. It also implies losing a privileged central position in America's Lower Mekong Initiative – meant to boost American engagement with continental Southeast Asia.

Some influential elites in the Thai society have been critical of the United States' interference – first in the campaigns against the drug smuggling/human trafficking menace in the region, and now because of

American disappointment with the coup. China, on the other hand, has seized the opportunity by capitalizing on the Thai sentiment of the hour. Shortly after the coup, China offered "continued" support to Thailand's development and hosted a senior Thai Military delegation in Beijing, sealed new deals in the telecom and infrastructure sectors, and most importantly, it won Thai approval for a new railway line from Kunming to Bangkok, through Northeastern Thailand.[10] Once completed, this project is obviously intended to tie Thailand's economy more closely to China's – ironically modelled on the principle that Thailand's seaports had moved Thailand closer to the West earlier. With new trade routes already being built through Laos and Cambodia, Thailand's trade has a new direction, having already veered away from its sea ports, towards its Northern routes that finally lead to China. Of course, Japan is trying to woo Thailand away from China, but for the moment, the Generals have been feted to satisfaction by China, and are in no mood to let go of that influence.

The worst thing that the US did – to its own detriment recently, was scaling down its own contingent and enthusiasm in the annual exercise, Cobra Gold. China is thrilled. And Thailand has clearly signaled a slight change in its alignment.

Myanmar

Myanmar and China have had extremely close links because of history, geography, culture, and even in a substantial way, economy. There are common tribes that live on both sides of their border in Myanmar's Shan and Kachin States and in China's Yunnan Province. Both have enjoyed cordial relations since Myanmar's independence. However, there was a dark period of relations during China's cultural revolution when the PLA joined (to support) the communist insurgency in Myanmar. But the situation reversed itself during the popular uprising in 1988 which led to a new Military Junta taking over in Rangoon (now Yangon). Consequent sanctions imposed by the West brought China very close to the country. It became the prime source of support and protection in international fora.

China also became the primary source of military hardware and military training, and a major (at one stage, the only) investor in Myanmar's economy, including through import of all precious raw materials from that country. But after the new Government took over in 2011, there has been a sharp decline in Chinese investments. This happened because of large scale protests by the civil society and environmental activists who were against the mega Myitsone Dam project. After the new government took office in 2011, that project (half done) was shelved. This has given a rude shock to the Chinese, and has created tensions between the two governments. Some other projects including a few in the mining sector too were shelved – only to be revived with altered scope of work. As a result of this situation, China has been hoping to see revival of such stalled projects after a new government takes over. They are therefore treading with caution – aiming to avoid the spectre of another popular uprising from the local people. Despite all this, China and Myanmar still enjoy satisfactory relations.

Since 2012, Myanmar has been getting close to the United States, apart from India. In fact, economic ties with Japan, RoK, ASEAN, and the West have been on the surge, with a Japanese funded SEZ, an Indian sponsored infrastructure project, and US investments. China's apprehension that the US is in Myanmar in order to "encircle" it or sideline it, is being carefully treated by Myanmar as it does not wish to annoy China. At the same time, it is being politically strong in not allowing China to treat it like Cambodia – as when it came to chairing ASEAN in 2014.

On its part, India is doing its best to reap the benefits of changed alignment after the transition, but when it comes to economic engagement, it is limiting its act to importing beans and pulses and exporting the proverbial *peanuts*. But India can do much better with regard to strategic sectors of industry, infrastructure and most importantly, defence.

In terms of alignment, Myanmar could still be seen supporting China in some ways in international institutions. However for the moment, the scales are almost equally balanced with other powers.

Singapore

Six years before his death, late Lee Kuan Yew had remarked: "*We are a little red dot but we are a special red dot. We are connected with the world, we play a special role. And we are not going to be in anybody's pocket.*" For a small city state with just five million population and 700 sq km of land, Singapore has made remarkable strides in its economy, political independence, and occupies an important position within ASEAN. In its foreign policy towards major powers, notably the USA and China, it has always tended to be neutral, and has refused to be drawn into any alliance. Though, it has always called upon the United States for "balancing" against regional actors and China, it refuses to qualify itself as a *dependent ally* of the US.

Its regional cultural concerns vis-à-vis China, Malaysia, and Indonesia find prominence in its foreign policy formulations. Economically, Singapore has been balancing between the major powers, and the ASEAN region. Even though it has been in competition with Hong Kong, in terms of foreign investment into China, it also sees its strategic relationship with the US as a hedge against increasing Chinese economic dominance and uses its deepening engagement with its ASEAN partners as another avenue to diversify away from China.[11]

Singapore, like some of its ASEAN partners, has been encouraged by America's *Pivot* or *Rebalance* to Asia. Having been one of the original Asian Tigers, it guards its economic miracle more than any other asset or condition. It has forged close economic ties with regional, middle and great powers, to ensure smooth, uninterrupted economic growth. To give an example, it has signed bilateral free trade agreements (FTAs) with both the US (2004), and China (2009).[12] The strong sinews of Singapore's foreign policy with regard to political and economic independence have ensured that despite having impressive trade ties with both the countries, Singapore does not fall into either's dependency trap. In fact, Singapore accords equal importance to all its trading partners – particularly Japan, Korea, and China, apart from ASEAN.

With India, Singapore's relationship has been special. India was among the first countries to establish diplomatic relations with it. The Comprehensive Economic Cooperation Agreement (CECA) signed in Jun 2005 has provided strength to both countries' economic engagement with each other. Singapore continues to remain cautious of neither getting too deeply involved with China, nor annoying China on any count, and is substantially aligned with the United States.

Actions by United States

On its part, the United States first made a lot of noise after China's declaration of the Nine-Dash Line in 2009. At any event when it was asked about its views on the imbroglio in the South China Sea, it indirectly disapproved of China's assertiveness and advocated freedom of navigation in any water body in the world. And in July 2010, then Secretary of State

Hillary Clinton gave a very clear message at the ASEAN Regional Forum (ARF), saying the US supported a collaborative diplomatic process by all claimants for dispute resolution without coercion, and opposed use or threat of use of force by any claimant. She also offered services of the United States to facilitate initiatives and confidence building measures in this regard.[13] Chinese Foreign Minister Yang Jiechi reacted with a strong 30 minute speech, accusing the US of plotting against China, poked fun at Vietnam's socialist credentials, and made a surprising statement, staring directly at Singapore's Foreign Minister, George Yeo: "China is a big country and other countries are small countries, and that's just a fact".[14] That said a lot about China that its neighbours in SE Asia had not realized till then!

In 2011, the Obama Administration announced its famous (strategic)"Pivot" to Asia, hurriedly re-labeled as "Rebalancing" soon thereafter. This strategy is aimed at strengthening bilateral security alliances, deepening relationships with emerging powers (including with China), engaging with regional multi-lateral institutions, expanding trade and investment, forging a broad-based military presence, and advancing democracy and human rights.[15] In other words, the strategy seeks to generate confidence in America's future leadership role in the region and perhaps respect for its capacity and ability to "change" things in Asia.

Many countries are happy that the US is coming to their rescue, and will manage to keep China in check. But there are also others who do not wish to be seen by China as dumping their relationship with it at the arrival of the US. None of them want to see competition or containment turn into "confrontation". But America's announced arrival has tilted alignments in the region.

Conclusion

In April 2015, for the first time since the formation of ASEAN, SE Asian leaders openly criticized China for its land reclamation in the South China Sea. The event was ASEAN Leaders Summit at Kuala Lumpur, on 26 Apr 2015.[16] The showstopper at that summit was supposed to be the regional forum's progress on economic integration, but the annoying pace of China's illegitimate creation of real estate over shoals, reefs, rocks and islets diverted the SE Asian region's attention. Moreover, China's curses on Philippines for having "counter-claimed" a reef / maritime zone where China is already building an island, and for having filed for international arbitration, have, for the first time united the ASEAN into making a common response. Compare this to the summit in 2012, when the Philippines pushed hard for a statement by ASEAN on the maritime disputes which resulted in an embarrassing failure to release a joint statement, and a lot of hard feelings on all sides.

The last six years have seen a shift of foreign policy preferences in most SE Asian countries. The primary reason has been China's changed posture in assertiveness, and its tendency in being hegemonistic over the region. There are of course some who fear retribution and therefore continue to be aligned in favour of China. And there are yet a few others who do not see anything wrong in accepting China's full involvement in their countries' development (at China's cost), and are still aligned in the old mould. On the whole however, alignments are conspicuously changing and changing for the better. This change is bound to invite some restoration of the tilt that the balance of power equation had assumed in the region. Some more instances of assertiveness, a few more cases against China in international tribunals, and (hopefully) adverse impact of shifting alignments to its economic and political wellbeing, may be the only way China will alter its attitude towards its neighbours.

NOTES AND REFERENCES

1   "China's Defence Budget" on GlobalSecurity.org, downloaded at http://www. globalsecurity.org/military/world/china/budget.htm, on 13 June 2015, at 1630 hrs.

2   "Philippines to the United States: We Want You Back" by Siddhartha Mahanta, published in Foreign Policy, June 01, 2015, downloaded at https:// foreignpolicy.com/2015/06/01/philippines-china-military-carter/ on Jun 14, 2015.

3   Felix K Chang, "A Question of Rebalancing: Malaysia's Relations with China", Foreign Policy Research Institute, downloaded at http://www.fpri.org/ contributors/felix-chang on Jun 22, 2015, at 1150 hrs.

4   "How a Tiny, Anti-Gay Monarchy Became a US Ally" By Bill, published by Arsenal for Democracy, May 10, 2014, downloaded at http:// arsenalfordemocracy.com/2014/05/10/why-brunei-how-a-tiny-anti-gay-monarchy-became-a-u-s-ally/#.VY6GRhuqjGe on 25 Jun, 2015 at 1245 hrs.

5   "China's Main Claim in South China Sea has no Legal Basis", Reuters, Mar 23, 2015, downloaded at http://www.reuters.com/article/2015/03/23/us-indonesia-china-southchinasea-idUSKBN0MJ04320150323 on 23 Jun, 2015

6   Danielle Tan, "Chinese Engagement in Laos", ISEAS Perspective 2015 #07

7   Ibid.

8   Phoak Kung, "Cambodia-China Relations: Overcoming the Trust Deficit", The Diplomat, downloaded at http://thediplomat.com/2014/10/cambodia-china-relations-overcoming-the-trust-deficit/ on 27 Jun, 2015, at 1945

9   Felix K Chang in the FPRI Blog "Geopoliticus" downloaded at http://www.fpri.org/geopoliticus/2015/02/wanting-it-both-ways-principled-and-practical-us-policy-toward-thailand on 28 Jun 2015 at 1030 hrs.

10 Ibid.

11 Robyn Kingler Vidra, "The Pragmatic 'Little Red Dot': Singapore's US Hedge Against China", P. 70

12 Ibid, P. 70

13 Comments by Secretary Clinton in Hanoi, Vietnam, Jul 23, 2010, US Dept of State, IIP Digital, downloaded at http://iipdigital.usembassy.gov/st/english/texttrans/2010/07/20100723164658su0.4912989.html#axzz3dmtfv77c on 20 Jul 2015.

14 "US Takes a Tougher Tone with China" by John Pomfret, The Washington Post, Jul 30, 2010, downloaded at http://www.washingtonpost.com/wp-dyn/content/article/2010/07/29/AR2010072906416.html on 20 Jun, 2015.

15 Clinton, Hillary "America's Pacific Century", in Foreign Policy magazine.

16 "Chinese Island-building in South China Sea", The Guardian, 27 Apr 2015, downloaded at http://www.theguardian.com/world/2015/apr/27/chinese-island-building-in-south-china-sea-may-undermine-peace-says-asean on 12 Jun 2015, at 1545 hrs.

4   STRATEGIC POWER PLAY IN EAST ASIA

Yogendra Kumar

Introduction

The strategic power play in East Asia - geographically covering, for the purposes of this chapter, the South China Sea and the Western Pacific regions - has become extremely complex and fluid in recent times due to the toxic mix of several factors, both contemporary as well as historical. Historically, post-Second World War, the force posture of the US in the Western Pacific was aimed at the Soviet Union with China still having a continental outlook with the sole exception of Taiwan. The only legacy of that period is the absence of an inclusive regional security architecture in the Western Pacific given the non-conclusion of peace treaties between the Soviet Union/Russia and Japan due to the dispute over the Kurile Islands and between US and North Korea.

The post-Cold War period has witnessed a strategic shift which has a significant maritime dimension. In the case of the South China Sea, a certain undercurrent of tension has existed post-Second World War after the withdrawal of the Imperial Japanese navy from the region which led to the revival of competing historical claims by regional countries on both the Paracels and the Spratlys islands chain spurred by the realisation of their strategic location and the prospects of hydrocarbon reserves. Unlike the Western Pacific, the South China Sea had a regional organisation in ASEAN to manage regional differences starting, initially, to cope with communist subversion and to supplement the US-created security architecture of 'Hub-and-Spokes' effected through individual security guarantees and the US overseas bases in the region.

The current geostrategic landscape, in East Asia, has dramatically altered since the end of the Cold War. From a 'neat situation' of US-USSR contestation, backed up on each side by a stack of nuclear weaponry, the current geostrategic landscape consists of a large number of 'moving parts', any or all of which may not move according to script. The strategic geography, under the changed circumstances, is acquiring a different salience. The dramatic rise of China, which is seen by the US as challenging the strategic equilibrium established by it and which is rapidly modernising its armed forces, is a critical development. There is also the growing tension between China and Japan as the latter is modernising its Maritime Self-Defence Forces and expanding their area of operations. The perennial uncertainty regarding an 'autonomous' North Korea, with its state fragility and growing nuclear capability, has become an aggravated 'wild card' in the equation.

Strategic Maritime Geography

Western Pacific Region

The global commerce having become overwhelmingly seaborne has meant an exceedingly high salience of maritime geography, especially in the Indo-Pacific region. The opening of the 'northern route' for commercial navigation through the Arctic Circle brings Russia into the picture and, now, especially so with the onset of 'Cold War.2' between Russia and the US. The circumstances, prevailing in the South China Sea region, are shaping up to be analogous to those in the East China Sea due to the spilling over of strategic rivalry between the great powers and by the focused bellicosity, presently, on the Spratlys. How is the geostrategic landscape, then, panning out in the Indo-Pacific region?

The East China Sea and the Western Pacific waters have several potential flashpoints drawing in major global powers with implications for a stable maritime order for the 21stcentury; India has many stakes in these flashpoints apart from commercial navigation. The Kurile Islands chain has become important once again with the Russian government investing in the Sea of Okhotsk with a strategic role in the emerging Arctic Ocean's geopolitics; there are also reports that Russia is fortifying the southern Kurile Islands which has security implications for Japan. There is a military delimitation line between the North and South Korea involving various islands occupied by the former. There are disputes between China and

Japan (Senkaku/Dioyu islands and the Okinawa Trough); between Japan and South Korea (Takeshima/Dokdo islands in the Sea of Japan), and, between China and South Korea (EEZ claim lines, submerged rocks and fishing zones in the Yellow Sea). The grand strategies of the key contesting powers in these waters, especially of the US and China, revolve around the so-called 'First Islands Chain' comprising Japan and their Ryukyu Islands, the "half island" of the Korean peninsula, Taiwan, the Philippines and Indonesia to, potentially, blockade China. The one exit point for China is North Korea's Rason (former Rajin-Sonbong), under a 50 year lease, for access to Vladivostok and the northern East Sea. A reference also needs to be made to a so-called 'Second Island Chain' comprising Guam and the Mariana Islands where the US is expanding its capabilities.

South China Sea

The South China Sea, comprising an area from the Malacca Straits to the Straits of Taiwan hosts several chokepoints: the Straits of Singapore and Malacca, the Karimata Strait (connecting the Java Sea and thence to the Sunda and the Lombok Straits), the Balabac Strait (connecting with southern part of the Sulu Sea and thence to the Pacific Ocean via Surigao Strait and the Philippine Sea), the Mindoro Strait through the northern Sulu Sea, the Verde Island Passage to the Pacific ocean, the Bashi Channel and the Balintang Channel and the Taiwan Strait.

The South China Sea contains over 250 small islands, atolls, reefs etc. grouped into three archipelagoes two of which, the Spratly Islands and the Paracels Islands, are hotly disputed; conflicts have been waged over them during periods of geostrategic fluidity. The Paracels were captured by China, first, from Taiwan (1950) and, later, from Vietnam (1974). The Spratlys have been contested between the Philippines, Indonesia, Brunei, Malaysia, Vietnam and China and Taiwan, last two also laying claim to the enclosed waters through 'nine dotted lines' ('eleven dotted lines' for Taiwan). Apart from various instances of military conflict over them, a trigger for the escalating tension in the Spratlys are the attempts, through reclamation and other artificial measures, to "prove" the ability of various land features to support claims for maritime zones under the UNCLOS.

There are several, additional, maritime disputes between the various littorals: Vietnam and China over the Gulf of Tonkin; maritime boundary along the Vietnamese coast between Vietnam, China and Taiwan; waters north of Natuna islands between Indonesia, China and Taiwan; waters north of Borneo between Vietnam, China, Taiwan, Malaysia and Brunei, off the coast of central Philippines and Luzon between the Philippines, China and Taiwan; and, maritime boundary in the Luzon Strait between the Philippines and Taiwan.

Drivers of Strategic Geography

The various flashpoints dotting across this complex strategic geography are overlaid by historical and current drivers causing regional tension and aggravated prospects for instability. The East China Sea region has no overarching security architecture where the situation is characterised by growing strategic contest between the US and China; the Cold War phase had witnessed this contest between the US and the Soviet navies which is, now, getting revived between the former and Russia, USSR's successor state, in the form of naval infrastructure buildup and the resumption of Russian strategic bomber flights up to Guam since 2007. US has maintained peace in this region through security guarantees to Japan, Taiwan and South Korea and through maintaining bases in Japan and South Korea although these are being reduced in size with some forces being relocated to Guam. Although there is no upgrade of weaponry, in recent times in Taiwan, the US offers it a security guarantee and an undercurrent of tension between China and Taiwan still exists despite a measure of stability in their relations in the last few decades. The 'strategic equilibrium' is sought to be maintained by the US building up its, essentially, naval 'pivot', consisting of bulk of its SLBMs and ships with Aegis systems, to Asia-Pacific to "bottle up" the Chinese navy within the 'First Islands Chain' making China's overseas installations vulnerable to destruction; this is sought to be supplemented by its 'Air Sea Battle' concept (2010) to aggressively attack Chinese onshore strategic installations. In this scheme, the Japanese Maritime Self-Defence Forces capabilities are being strengthened. Chinese response has been to develop its 'anti-access/area denial' (A2/AD) capabilities to prevent the US navy and air force to dominate the area in its proximity; its missile forces are sought to be neutralised by US deploying, along with Japan and, now, South Korea, anti-ballistic missile defences in the Pacific Ocean, Alaska and California. This uneasy 'equilibrium' is being constantly tested due to regular confrontation between China and Japan over the Senkaku/Diaoyu dispute.

There is also the, almost, daily provocative activity between the Koreas with the potential spillover involving the principal backers, namely China and the US, a prospect darkened by the possibility of state collapse in North Korea. The latest, in this series of provocations, is the purported test firing of SLBM by North Korea in May, 2015. Russian strategic bomber flights in the Pacific have introduced yet another wild card and the US asked Vietnam not to allow the Russian bombers to refuel at its bases. Even more disturbing is another aspect: the Chinese nuclear missile submarines capability, confined presently to the coastal waters of the South China Sea, the East China Sea and the Yellow Sea, raises the prospect of a "pre-emptive" first strike from Chinese SLBMs in the face of pressure from the ballistic missile installations in South Korea, Japan and US onshore establishments as well as from the overall US posture. The strategic equilibrium in the East China Sea is not only fragile due to the entrenched action-reaction syndrome between the principal actors but also due to multiple 'wild cards' which are not under anyone's control.

In the South China Sea, the historical tension between the claimant countries over the Spratlys has triggered occasional flare-ups but the transformative changes in the strategic situation have taken place only at historical inflection points such as the Chinese capture of the Paracels islands, first from Taiwan after the defeat of Chiang Kai Sheik and, then, from Vietnam after the collapse of the US-backed South Vietnamese regime. The regional flare-ups over Spratlys have occurred due to high distrust level amongst claimant countries and their efforts to create 'facts-on-the-ground' to take advantage of the provisions of the UNCLOS. The strategic equilibrium has begun to change in recent years with growing Chinese assertiveness about its Spratlys' claims backed by the continuous building up of its naval capabilities in South China Sea and, thereby, causing heightened anxiety amongst the ASEAN countries. The US 'pivot' to Asia has a South China Sea focus at least since 2011.

Foreign Policy Objectives of Major Powers

The foreign policy objectives of both the regional and extra-regional powers, in East Asia, are, clearly, to manage the rising regional tension and strategic flux while expanding seaborne trade and commerce. They also have interests in meeting non-traditional security challenges, such as disaster relief, protecting marine ecology as well as constabulary responsibilities for combating, *inter alia*, human trafficking and piracy.

Whilst these objectives can be seen to be almost universally shared by the powers in the region, there are considerable number of challenges in pursuing them, in the current strategic flux. The biggest problem inheres in the existing strategic equilibrium being challenged by the rise of China in both economic and military terms. China remains suspicious of the US aims to 'contain' it through bolstering the existing strategic equilibrium in its favour and is pursuing its own grand strategic objective to "break out" through attempts to neutralise the US military superiority as well as through connectivity projects skirting around the naval chokepoints; these, it considers necessary, to protect its extensive overseas interests and to nurture relations with friendly countries to balance US and allied influence in its areas of interest. The US has its own, independent, relationship with China to pressurise as well as to incentivise the latter for the purpose of leveraging, also, its security relationships in the region drawing upon its partners' anxieties *vis-a-vis* China. The US objective is to maintain the regional equilibrium, respectively in the East China Sea and the South China Sea, as it exists today and, at the same time, involve China in humanitarian and disaster relief programmes and for constabulary functions such as anti-piracy operations. This also involves cooperation in preserving the marine ecology.

In recent times, the US's alliance relationships have been reaffirmed, in strong terms, at the highest level in respect of Japan, South Korea and the Philippines; and, it is strengthening security-based friendships in the region, especially with Vietnam and Singapore. Although welcomed by East Asian countries, the US is strengthening its own capabilities to counter China in the region through bolstering the current favourable strategic equilibrium by leveraging the military capabilities of the regional countries. As it strengthens regional military capabilities, it also seeks to manage them such that there is no unintended escalation in the military situation to undermine its overall objectives vis-a-vis China. Tempering 'competitive' hyper-nationalism in the region, especially in Japan, is part of the US approach.

The foreign policy objectives of the major powers in the East Asian region are clearly territorial defence – an objective complicated by the existence of large number of maritime and territorial disputes. By their very nature, the strategic and diplomatic posturing is spurred by hyper-nationalism amongst the claimant countries; whilst in some cases, this high emotional content may be spontaneous, in the case of China and Vietnam – and, to an extent, Japan – it is stoked by the respective leaderships which tends, not infrequently, to get out of hand. China has nurtured it proactively *vis-a-vis* Japan, the most recent manifestation being over the Senkaku/Diaoyu Island. As China is strengthening its economic as well as – military power, its inability to moderate its domestic hyper-nationalism has made it appear intimidating against the smaller neighbours in the region, even, amongst friendlier countries such as Malaysia and Indonesia. The Chinese leadership, apparently, feels confident, even though there are reservations amongst its own strategic community, that it can sustain its regional relationships on the strength of its economic power and programmes despite the rising distrust which, even, have the potential to reorder regional political economy; its economic strength diminishes its earlier anxieties about not being seen as being 'isolated' diplomatically. The US's return to the Pacific, including the South China Sea, has been welcomed by the ASEAN countries which is seen by the latter as strengthening their hand, in the midst of mutual recriminations about non-observance of the ASEAN-China Declaration on conduct in South China Sea (2002), in the negotiations with China for a binding Code of Conduct. The Chinese activities in creating military infrastructure in the Spratlys, are, now, being challenged by the US as the US Secretary of Defence has declared that it will assert its navigational rights irrespective of the interpretation of UNCLOS rights by China. Whilst this does act as a constraint, because of the US being much more powerful than China, it, also, has the potential for escalation in a vicious action-reaction cycle. In this charged atmosphere, the military postures of the regional countries are becoming more pro-active and battle-ready.

Maritime Doctrines of Major Powers

The latest, March, 2015, US non-classified strategy document, 'A Cooperative Strategy for 21st Century Seapower' (CS-21R), provides a conceptual construct entailing a "global network of navies" with "plug-in-and-play" capabilities – mentioning countries such as Bangladesh, Brunei, India, Malaysia, Micronesia, Pakistan, Singapore and Vietnam; this is in addition to its alliance partners in South-East and East Asia. China is seen as a challenge and an opportunity to be managed "through our continued forward presence and constructive interaction with the Chinese maritime forces". In a foreword to the US non-classified, 'National Military Strategy', (released in June, 2015) Chairman, Joint Chiefs of Staff Committee, states, "The probability of US involvement in interstate war with a major power is low but growing"; the reference has been interpreted to be directed at Russia.

'China's Military Strategy', the official White Paper released on May 26, 2015, admits, in a nuanced difference, to the possibility of a local war but has its major theme, according to Dennis Blasko is "long-standing task for China to safeguard its maritime rights and interests" as it refers to US's 'rebalancing' strategy, Japan "overhauling its military and security policies", some "offshore neighbours" taking provocative actions against "China's reefs and islands" and "external powers... meddling in South China Sea affairs" (Blasko, 2015)1. A new strategic task is "to safeguard the security of China's overseas interests." The PLA Navy "very gradually shift its focus from 'offshore waters defence' to the combination of 'offshore waters defence' with 'open seas protection.'" By comparing with the original Chinese text of the White Paper, Ryan Martinson states that it envisages "strategic management... of the seas and oceans and protecting maritime rights and interests." (Martinson, 2015)2

Japan's Prime Minister Abe has set up a National Security Council and has revised defence guidelines emphasising military capabilities, lifting the previous ban on arms exports and a cabinet reinterpretation of the Japanese Constitution to exercise collective self-defence for assisting friendly states under attack. It also revised, as announced at a joint press conference by the US and Japanese foreign and defence ministers in New York on April 28, 2015, the US-Japan Defence Guidelines to allow greater interoperability between the US and Japanese forces including use of force if a clear danger to Japan's existence arises due to an attack on a country with which it has close ties. These also include US and Japanese cooperation in intercepting ballistic missiles, targeted at allies, including US. Protection of critical sea lanes is envisaged as one of its major activities.

India's own 'India's Maritime Military Strategy' (2007) puts the South China Sea and the West Pacific region amongst its "secondary areas" of responsibility envisaging both military as well as benign roles in an environment of strategic flux.

Defence Policies of Major Stakeholders

Driven considerably by extra-regional interests, the volatility has increased in the entire East Asian region and the risk of a minor incident getting out of control has risen greatly in an atmosphere of incandescent nationalism. So has the distrust level amongst the stakeholder countries. As a result, military preparations, especially naval, have increased amongst all countries putting in jeopardy the possibility of cooperation on substantive aspects of good order at sea. Following is a brief account of the policies of various countries' drawn upon, largely, from the IISS' (International Institute for Strategic Studies) 'Strategic Survey 2014' and 'Military Balance 2015'.

Russia

In the current context of growing tensions between Russia and the Western world, Russia is also 'pivoting' to the East by developing relations, primarily, with China but also with other countries in the region across a wide variety of spheres including a strong focus on establishing links in energy trade. It is looking to substantially expand its Pacific Fleet with adding new surface combat vessels and attack as well as nuclear ballistic missile submarines. The Russian Navy Chief, Admiral Viktor Chirkov, has been quoted as saying that the upgrade of the Navy's SSBN Base in Kamchatka will be ready by October, 2015, to house its latest 'Borei' class submarines which at the height of the Cold War, housed nearly a dozen SSBNs (LaGrone, 2015)3. It is also projecting its power in the Indo-Pacific and in the South China Sea through regular naval patrols. Several countries are trying to source Russian military hardware. Vietnam's offer, at Cam Ran Bay, of the facility to refuel Russian strategic bombers on the deterrence patrol in the western Pacific has drawn a negative reaction from the US.

China

China's broader approach has been assertive and, is backed by a rapidly growing military strength. As reported in the International Crisis Group (ICG), the Central Leading Small Group on the Protection of Maritime Interests, created in 2012 and reportedly led, at least initially, by President Xi, is seen as taking critical decisions where regional expertise is not adequately considered; the result has been - as stated in the report written on the basis of personal interviews of officials in Beijing - the adoption of a more hardline, nationalistic approach and to view all developments through the prism of US-China relations[4]. China's budgetary allocations and their rate of growth is the highest amongst the Asian countries. There are frequent confrontations with Japan over the Senkaku/Diaoyu islands and its declaration, moreover, of Air Defence Identification Zone (ADIZ) covers these islands even though it is not fully able to enforce it. With Vietnam, although there is an agreement between the two prime ministers, in late 2013, to resolve maritime disputes peacefully, there is incremental assertiveness in the form of fisheries zone enforcement announcement (December, 2013) and in bringing oil exploration rigs in areas claimed by Vietnam as its EEZ (May, 2014). Apart from this assertiveness of the Spratlys, where it is building the airstrip (Fiery Cross Reef), its naval exercises in South China Sea are also signals about its intention of projecting its power: senior US naval officers have expressed an apprehension that the Fiery Cross Reef facility, with its acquired capability for hosting all types of aircraft, can lead to China-proclaimed ADIZ in South China Sea. It is also building second airfield in Subi Reef and expanding the Woody Island (Paracels) runway. The power projection objective has been evident in exercises by the Chinese Navy held close to the Philippines coast, involving its aircraft carrier and the Chinese nuclear submarine in the South China Sea and in the crossing of a surface action group with an amphibious transport battleship into the Indian Ocean. Its vessels are, now, seen in the EEZs claimed by Malaysia and Indonesia which could be interpreted as the Chinese intention of pressing its claim over the waters covered by its 'nine dash line'. This assertiveness is manifest in activities *vis-a-vis* the US Navy as well as its frequent encounters at sea exemplify. Its relations have become particularly tense with the Philippines following its confrontations over the Scarborough Shoal (occupied by China in 2012) and over the Second Thomas Shoal, 194 kms from Palawan and within its EEZ.

China hopes to temper the resulting regional anxieties through its economic diplomacy. Its trade relations with all the Asian countries remain robust. Its latest initiatives are 'One Belt One Road' (OBOR) and the 'Maritime Silk Road' (MSR). These initiatives aim to develop infrastructure and economic zones surrounding them; the OBOR aims to link the adjoining regions to the mainland Chinese economy whilst MSR initiative aims to develop their infrastructure in the South China Sea littoral and beyond. Whilst pledging commitment to resolving disputes peacefully, the negotiations between China and ASEAN over a binding Code of Conduct are, yet, to move decisively forward. For addressing non-traditional challenges, including disaster response and search and rescue, it participates actively in regional programmes as well as bilaterally with US. Most recently, it participated in the WPNS (Western Pacific Naval Symposium) exercises. It is also an active participant in the ASEAN-related organisations dealing with maritime issues, including ARF, ADMM Plus and EAS (East Asia Summit).

In 2012, it conducted trials for J-15 combat aircraft for its first aircraft carrier, 'Liaoning'. Its own sea exercises signal PLAN's aim of developing a carrier battle group. Additionally, development and construction of Type-052D destroyer and Type-55 cruiser programme are reportedly underway.

United States

The US alliance system in East Asia has remained intact since the end of the Second World War. Its troops deployed in Japan and South Korea signify its security guarantees to both countries which also extend to Taiwan. By way of restraining Japanese nationalism, as manifest in Prime Minister Abe's policies, it has cautioned that disputes need to be resolved peacefully while stating, that its security guarantees extend up to the Senkaku islands. There is some Japanese anxiety as to whether the US would live up to its commitment for Japan's territorial defence should a conflict break out with China. The US concerns, about Prime Minister Abe's variant of Japanese nationalism, include respecting imperial Japanese figures, condemned as war criminals at the US-led Tokyo War Crimes Trials at the end of the Second World War, and have been publicly stated due to the resulting adverse reactions in East and South-East Asian regions. Japanese anxieties about the depth of US military commitment also exist, especially following President Xi Jinping's visit the US for extended meetings with President Obama in June, 2013, as portending a possible emergence of 'great power relationship' or – in other words – a US-China global condominium. At the same time, US has prodded Japan to revise its national security doctrine for the more expanded role for its Self-Defence Forces; on April 28, 2015,the revised US-Japan Defence Guidelines were unveiled envisaging extended cooperation between the US and the Japanese forces. With Republic of Korea (ROK), US commitment has been reiterated but its insistence that the former should assume responsibility for wartime operational control of the joint forces of ROK and US have triggered similar concerns about US commitment as is the case with Japan. US is also expanding its infrastructure in Guam for 'forward posture' *vis-a-vis*

China. Its rebalancing in the South China Sea has meant deployment of a Littoral Combat Ship (LCS), in Singapore, a number which is expected to be increased to four by 2018, rotating 1,100 (2,500 in 2018) marines at Darwin, Australia and pre-positioning of equipment and acquiring similar logistical support at the Philippines bases under a ten-year Enhanced Defence Cooperation Agreement. Although, there have been assurance of security guarantees, under the US-Philippines Mutual Defence Treaty (1951),there have been doubts in the Philippines leadership, also, about the US interpretation covering their claims concerning the Spratlys as evident in the lack of US action against the Chinese dispossessing the Philippines from the two islands claimed to be within its EEZ. US has also developed a limited defence partnership with Vietnam allowing it to acquire patrol vessels from the US. Apart from its ability to quickly mobilise its naval forces, its public concerns over the Chinese reclamation activities in the Spratlys have taken the form of forcibly asserting its navigation and flight rights to test the limits of Chinese claims; the most recent being one of its P-8A Poseidon Surveillance Aircraft flights, in May, 2015, assertively ignoring Chinese instructions to terminate the flight over Fiery Cross Reef. This is being accompanied by public debate, attributed to US military sources, about its Navy testing Chinese claims of 12 nautical miles coastal waters zone around these islands. The US has declared that it takes no sides on the dispute itself and has asked the concerned parties to conclude negotiations for a binding Code of Conduct for the South China Sea. It is also actively involved in developing regional capacities for non-traditional security threats in the region and is also active in the ASEAN-related organisations.

Japan

Under the Abe leadership, the role of Japan's Self-Defence Forces has been revised and institutional changes effected as detailed above. Under the revised Defence Guidelines, the cooperation with the US is expected to extend to the South China Sea as well, thereby, bringing yet another power to the region to counter China. Japan is also building defence cooperation with the Philippines and Vietnam to strengthen their naval capacity. Its relations with South Korea are at an all-time low, making it difficult for the US to develop a triangular defence cooperation against China. During the two meetings between President Xi and Prime Minister Abe in Beijing (November, 2014) and in Jakarta (April, 2015), the Chinese media stated that both sides agreed to start a diplomatic and security dialogue whilst acknowledging their different positions on the Senkaku/Diaoyu dispute.

The December 2013 Mid-Term Defence Plan envisages acquisition programmes for the 2014-19 period that includes new destroyers, amphibious capability, additional submarines, unmanned aerial vehicles for long-range maritime surveillance, F-35A joint strike fighters and tilt-rotor aircraft; it has, recently, launched its largest ever helicopter-carrying destroyer, *Izumo*. Japan has lifted restraints on arms exports and on joint production under its new policy. It is also planning to install shore-based artillery, mobile launchers and anti-ship cruise missiles on some of the Ryukyu Islands.

North Korea

North Korea has been taking an aggressive stance against South Korea and the US. With China, its relationship, under the new leader, has plummeted as the latter worries as to the prospect of state collapse and its consequences for the balance of power in a strategically critical region. Its recent firing of an SLBM has alarmed the major powers in the region. Its missile firing, in March, 2014, across the UN Command-mandated (1951) Northern Limit Line, evoked a strong response from South Korea.

According to analysts, North Korea continues to advance capability to deliver nuclear warheads by using ballistic missiles. The satellite launch, in December 2012, reflects its efforts for developing capability for inter-continental ballistic missiles even as the current missiles have capability of reaching targets in Japan. Although its defence hardware is quite old, it has made significant advances in missile capabilities; it finds the US-South Korea 'Freedom Guardian' exercise provocative against which it threatens a pre-emptive nuclear strike. A propaganda North Korean film showed sea-skimming, anti-ship cruise missile similar to Russian Uran 3M24 missile – a projected capability against South Korea's coastal defence patrol vessels. Satellite imagery has identified two new helicopter-carrying corvettes and a possible large submarine type vessel – which is twice as large as the existing submarines.

South Korea

As stated above, its military approach towards North Korea has become pre-emptive in terms of the defence of both its land as well as maritime borders. The South Korean leadership, also, envisages that, in the event of state collapse in North Korea, the unification of the Korean peninsula would be under its control.

It has an ambitious maritime programme to include an eventual fleet of nine Son Won-il class (German Type-214) submarines, new frigates and a second helicopter carrier. It is also building deterrent capabilities against North Korea's nuclear missile, conventional and cyber capabilities. It is developing air defence and anti-missile capability, based on the US Patriot surface-to-air missile system which could also, potentially, concern China. Under the new President, power has been delegated to local commanders to respond effectively to North Korea's provocations.

South China Sea littoral countries

Vietnam

Vietnam's relations with China remain most fraught in regard to their conflicting claims on the Spratlys; the former also has the largest number of these islands under its occupation with one of them, Spratly Island, having an airstrip, since 1976, capable of cargo and surveillance flights. On this issue, the Vietnamese nationalism is strong as is evident from its reaction over the recent Chinese placement of a rig for oil exploration in its claimed EEZ. However, it retains strong party-to-party links with China and there are exchanges of visits and delegations between the countries.

Vietnam is making efforts to enhance its naval and air capabilities. Two out of six Kilo class (Project 636) submarines from Russia were delivered in March, 2014. US announced, in October 2014, that it was easing embargo for future transfer of maritime security-related defence items to Vietnam. This announcement, possibly, opens way for P-3C patrol anti-submarine warfare aircraft or even P-8A Poseidon.

The Philippines

Its relations with China have plummeted rapidly under the present leader, President Acquino. The Chinese aggressiveness has led to the Philippines losing control over two Spratlys islands; it has strengthened a pre-existing airfield, with US financial assistance, at its naval station on the Thitu Island (officially named 'Pagasa') about 100 nautical miles from Chinese-held Fiery Cross Reef. Additionally, its surface vessels' acquisitions from Japan,

South Korea and US, are aimed at improving its coastal patrolling capacity. Its first naval exercise with Japan in the South China Sea, on May 12, 2015 was protested by the Chinese foreign office. It is building a naval base at Oyster Bay on the coast for faster access to its Spratlys installations.

It signed with the US, in April, 2014, the Enhanced Defence Cooperation Agreement for rotation and pre-positioning of equipment at selected bases such as, *inter alia*, Subic Bay and Clark air base. This agreement, however, is under challenge before the Supreme Court which had earlier ruled against permanent bases in the country. It is also negotiating with Japan an agreement for possible grant of rotational access to its bases.

Indonesia

Under the new Indonesian leadership, a new maritime future for the country is being projected by emphasising investment in maritime infrastructure and the building of naval and coast guard capabilities. Although its distrust level has gone up in recent times because of Chinese activities, it is also quite positive about the MSR programme which envisages major port-based economic zones infrastructure for the country.

In January, 2013, the Indonesian Defence Minister announced plans for accelerated development of a 'Minimum Essential Force' (MDF). Amongst its most expensive acquisitions are submarines; it has ordered three submarines from South Korea but is also considering Russia's Kilo class submarines. It is looking at acquisition of Corvettes and F-16 C/D fighters from US and of C-130 Hercules transport aircraft. It is also planning to build a naval base at Natuna islands amongst other forward bases around the country's periphery.

Malaysia

Malaysia has, traditionally, prided itself in keeping a stable and close relationship with China which has been reciprocated by the latter. However, repeated patrolling by Chinese naval, including amphibious, ships near the Malaysia-controlled James Shoal, in the Spratlys, has led the government to make rare private demarche to the Chinese. It has embarked on an accelerated modernisation of its army and air force. It is developing a naval base at Bintulu, the closest coastal town to James Shoal. Its modernization plans include the setting up of a Marine Corps.

Singapore

Singapore aims to develop more robust and resilient maritime forces. These plans include acquisition of large helicopter-equipped amphibious ships and submarines from Germany and Sweden. It is also looking for acquisition of long-range strike aircraft. Concerned about the Chinese activities in the South China Sea, it is hosting a US LCS and 311 US troops in support of the US 'pivot' to the East.

Thailand

A part of the pattern, Thailand is also modernizing its maritime capabilities. Its plans for procurement include frigates and the building of submarines. It also hosts 366 US troops as part of its defence relationship. However, due to the US criticism of its recent internal policies, it plans to acquire Chinese submarines.

Australia

Australia is planning for strengthening its complement of maritime surveillance aircraft and has prioritised the replacement of its ageing submarines. The navy is to get three air warfare destroyers by 2016 and two amphibious ships. It also has expressed its interest to continue its maritime patrols in the South China Sea; it has, though, abandoned its earlier commitment to join US in the event of a possible stand-off with China in the Taiwan Strait of the type which took place in 1995-96.

New Zealand

New Zealand has placed orders for naval helicopters and has a perspective plan for procurement of support ships and littoral operations ships. It also plans to replace the existing frigates and maritime patrol aircraft after 2020.

Nature of Regional Naval Modernisation

Profoundly, maritime nature of the geopolitics of the Indo-Pacific region entails a major naval dimension. Naval modernisation, on the part of all countries in East Asia, including the extra-regional powers present there, characterises the strategic scenario today. The salience of naval war fighting capability, in the countries' national military doctrines, is only going to sharpen. It will remain integrated into full-spectrum war fighting capabilities, including "irregular" warfare. The pattern of Asian naval expansion has an action-reaction aspect which portends naval contestations in the foreseeable future given the forward deployment postures; the latter prospect creates the imperative for acquisition of sea-control and access-denial capabilities. The capacity-building for asymmetric naval warfare remains another characteristic of this buildup with the exception of the US Navy; in asymmetric warfare, including "irregular" warfare, submarines are considered, in this thinking, as an essential weapon of choice.

Geoffrey Till (*'Asia's Naval Expansion'*, *IISS Adelphi Paper, December 14, 2012*) has reflected on some thinking amongst naval strategists of comparing the current situation with the Anglo-German naval arms race of 1909-14 which was seen as driven by international rather domestic imperatives, being usually bilateral, intense in effort, rapidity and expression, associated with high levels of political tension, being operationally specific, indicative of high strategic stakes and regarded as such by the main players. He, however, does not find in the current situation identical characteristics but has worries that there are no or few constraints on competitive naval development, that popular nationalism backs naval development, and, that, a naval arms race remains fundamental to the future maritime security of the Asia-Pacific region due to the region's maritime dimension.

Implications for India's Regional Interests

India's interest is growing in the region and the major powers, like US and Japan, as well as the ASEAN want it to be present there. The diaspora linkages, the economic interests, the hydrocarbon and other mineral resources and the safety of navigation concerns are the main reasons for Indian interest in East Asian affairs. In expressing these interests in several ways, including, maritime and naval activities, its power projection capabilities, nevertheless, remain limited with its Andaman and Nicobar infrastructure being able to cover the Straits of Malacca but much less as in so far as the Lombok and the Sunda Straits are concerned. The Chinese naval facilities, at Hainan, are far closer than either India's at Vishakhapatnam or the US's at Guam. These recent developments also signify that the regional, simmering tensions would be driven by the strategic designs originating outside the region; thus, developments taking place outside the region would impact on the regional strategic dynamics. The Indian government, including its various maritime agencies such as the navy, has been active in various ASEAN-related forums where its contribution – and, genuine interest in strengthening ASEAN - is universally recognised. It is also keenly engaged in strengthening bilateral relations with the regional countries, including China. Indian navy has also been an active participant in the WPNS programmes and India's contribution to capacity-building for addressing the regional non-traditional security challenges can be scaled up.

India's concerns about the regional affairs – and, its own foreign policy interests - have led to closer relations, including in their maritime aspects, with US, Japan and Australia; India-Japan-US trilateral dialogue is, now, being complemented by India-Japan-Australia trilateral dialogue which has shades of the 'quad' dialogue and which was abandoned following Chinese demarches to India and Australia in 2007[5]. India's frequent naval deployments and coast guard visits have an impact on the strategic situation, particularly, in the South China Sea, especially in terms of the littoral states feeling it to be some kind of balance against China. India's summit-level statements with US and Japan are perceived by China as a diplomatic signal that their bilateral relations need to be mended and stabilised especially as regards the situation concerning the India-China Line of Actual Control (LAC). Given that all major powers have their own respective agendas, it is important that India should not get sucked into a situation not of its own making: this, definitely, requires nimble diplomacy on India's part as it coordinates its moves with these powers in East Asia. Such challenges are bound to arise as diplomacy around MSR, Spratlys and a China-threatened ADIZ in South China Sea hots up; India's response on these issues can make a strategic impact there. Equally importantly, a strengthened ASEAN is in India's interest. It can assist these countries in building their naval and other aspects of defence capabilities. Sale of weapons and extensive training as well as joint studies in defence conceptual development should be actively pursued; the last named is important in that most of the littoral countries are reworking their defence doctrines.

India has to aim to prevent the Indian Ocean Region (IOR) receiving the spillover of the strategic contestation in East Asia. PLA Navy's power projection capabilities in IOR are limited as its maritime order is heavily skewed in favour of US which suits India's strategic interests too. The Indian Ocean remains relatively benign although it faces the full-spectrum of traditional as well as non-traditional security threats some of which have been triggered by US interventions in littoral countries leading to their destabilisation. To ensure that the great power tension in the Indian Ocean region does not grow as a kind of self-fulfilling prophecy, diverse range of actions are needed to be taken both from security as well as foreign policy point of view. A pro-active 'Act East' Policy, of the Modi Government, with its stronger naval and maritime dimension with a view to strengthening ASEAN-related mechanisms in the South China Sea littoral is – but – one answer.

NOTES AND REFERENCES

1   Blasko, D. (2015). The 2015 Chinese Defense White Paper on Strategy in Perspective: Maritime Missions Require a Change in the PLA Mindset. [online] The Jamestown Foundation. Available at: http://www.jamestown. org/programs/chinabrief/single/?tx_ttnews%5Btt_news%5D=43974&tx_ ttnews%5BbackPid%5D=789&no_cache=1#.VsFSLvl97IU.

2   Martinson, R. (2015). A Salt Water Perspective on China's New Military Strategy | Real Clear Defense. [online] Realcleardefense.com. Available at: http://www.realcleardefense.com/articles/2015/06/02/a_salt_water_ perspective_on_chinas_new_military_strategy_107997.html .

3   LaGrone, S. (2015). New Pacific Russian Nuclear Missile Submarine Facility Could Open by October - USNI News. [online] USNI News. Available at: http://news.usni.org/2015/07/01/new-pacific-russian-nuclear-missile-submarine-facility-could-open-by-october.

4   Crisisgroup.org, (2015). Stirring up the South China Sea (III): A Fleeting Opportunity for Calm - International Crisis Group. [online] Available at: http://www.crisisgroup.org/en/regions/asia/north-east-asia/china/267-stirring-up-the-south-china-sea-III-a-fleeting-opportunity-for-calm.aspx.

5   Pant, H. (2015). Asia's New Geopolitics Takes Shape Around India, Japan, and Australia. [online] The Diplomat. Available at: http://thediplomat. com/2015/07/asias-new-geopolitics-takes-shape-around-india-japan-and-australia/.

5 SOUTH CHINA SEA DISPUTE AND ITS IMPACT ON REGIONAL STABILITY

Kamlesh K Agnihotri

Introduction

China aspires to grow into a dominant player in the maritime domain, in furtherance of its aim to become a global power. It therefore, vehemently seeks to extend its maritime control domain as far away from its shores as possible, starting with its immediate periphery. The South China Sea thus, naturally comes first in its priority of maritime expansion plans. But the above Chinese over-reach renders the maritime security situation in that part of the globe quite fragile, particularly in view of long outstanding territorial disputes. All countries bordering this Sea i.e. China, Philippines, Taiwan, Vietnam, Malaysia and Brunei have claimed some or all of the tiny Spratly islets and the associated maritime spaces. China, Taiwan and Vietnam also lay their claims on the Paracel islands.

In addition to the importance of South China Sea and its immediate vicinity as a major trade and energy lifeline of the world, ongoing exploitation and future potential of rich natural resources – oil, minerals, fisheries etc. – are also at the root of expansive claims of the disputants. China as a major power and a key player in the area, seeks to arrive at a solution on terms which would be most favourable to its own interests. China and Vietnam both, have adopted virtually intractable postures with regards to their claims on various features in Paracel and Spratly chains and their associated maritime zones. Passing of the 2009 baseline bill by Philippines extending its territory to include Huangyan Island (Scarborough shoal) and part of Spratly group of Islands in the South China Sea and associated enlargement of the EEZ has added more complexity to the equation. The American position articulated in various ASEAN Regional Forum (ARF) meets commencing 2010 and its recent strategy to 'rebalance' towards Asia-

Pacific, leaves no doubt about its strategic national interest in the region.

Figure 1 shows the inter-se location of various features in the Spratly Island and the current status of their occupation. Four operational airfields in the area are located at Swallow Reef (Malaysia), Itu Aba (Taiwan), Thitu Island (Philippines) and Spratly Island (Vietnam).

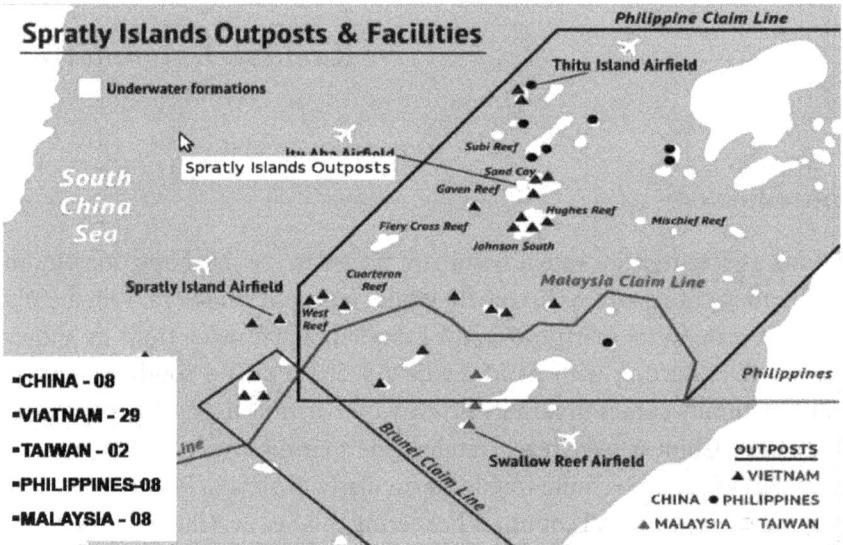

Spratly Islands Outposts & Facilities

Philippine Claim Line
Thitu Island Airfield
Underwater formations
South China Sea
Itu Aba Airfield
Spratly Islands Outposts
Subi Reef
Sand Cay
Gaven Reef
Hughes Reef
Fiery Cross Reef
Johnson South
Mischief Reef
Spratly Island Airfield
Cuarteron Reef
West Reef
Malaysia Claim Line
Philippines
Brunei Claim Line
Swallow Reef Airfield

- CHINA - 08
- VIATNAM - 29
- TAIWAN - 02
- PHILIPPINES-08
- MALAYSIA - 08

OUTPOSTS
▲ VIETNAM
CHINA ● PHILIPPINES
▲ MALAYSIA   TAIWAN

Fig.1. Inter-se location of various features in the Spratly Island
[Source: Asia Maritime Transparency Initiative][1]

This chapter discusses the issues and interests of various disputants in the South China Sea, their ongoing activities to support such interests; and analyses the resultant impact of their interactive dynamics on the regional stability.

Chinese Issues and Interests in South China Sea

In March 2010, the Chinese State Councillor, Dai Bingguo, apparently conveyed to the visiting US Deputy Secretary of State, James Steinberg, that as per the new State policy, the South China Sea was part of the Chinese 'core interests' as regards its sovereignty and territorial integrity. Subsequently, the newfound 'core interest' phrase was bandied about in the Chinese media regularly, and the Chinese public opinion appeared to back Beijing's position. The fact remains that China has always considered the South China Sea as its 'core interest', but it was not officially articulated to the world as such till May 2009, when China officially submitted a map to the UN Commission on the Limits of Continental Shelf (CLCS) and asserted that China "enjoyed sovereign rights and jurisdiction over the islands in South China Sea and the adjacent waters, as well as seabed and sub-soil thereof."[2] China has also internally ensured that this position permeates down to the lowest possible echelons of the Chinese governance and administration.[3]

China has consistently maintained that the South China Sea dispute can be and must be handled bilaterally, and that there is no scope for external intervention. Beijing has been particularly vocal on this stand since the July 2010 ARF meet when the Chinese Foreign Minister advised the US not to internationalise a bilateral issue between China and the individual ASEAN nations. The same position has been reiterated again and again. For instance, in May 2015, the visiting US Secretary of State, John Kerry was told by General Fan Changlong, Vice Chairman of the Chinese Central Military Commission (CMC) that the US as an external entity had no role; hence it should abide by the principle of not taking sides over South China Sea issues.[4]

China has also sought to interpret the UNCLOS and its provisions to stretch its maritime control by adopting its own 'Law on the Territorial Seas and Contiguous Zones 1992' and the 'Exclusive Economic Zone and Continental Shelf Act 1998'.[5] China's position on the Marine Scientific Research (MSR) regime under the UNCLOS is that the use of the EEZ for non-peaceful purposes without its consent is illegal. This includes military exercises by warships of foreign countries, mapping of underwater hydrological conditions, aerial reconnaissance and electronic intelligence gathering activities. These are precisely the activities which the US Navy has regularly been indulging in.

Chinese Activities to Support its Interests

Beijing announced the establishment of Sansha City Prefecture on Woody Island in July 2012 to administer South China Sea islands. At the same time, Hainan Provincial Council issued a Regulation for 'Management of Public Order for Coastal and Border Defence,' effective January 1, 2013. It provides for Hainan's maritime security agencies to board or seize foreign vessels in case they are found to indulge in activities threatening national security on or around the islands under its control.

Large scale reclamation of six features in the Spratly group of islands has been in progress since the beginning of 2014, including the construction of an airfield on the Fiery Cross Reef. Underwater archaeological survey, deep sea oil exploration and rigid access control of Scarborough and Second Thomas shoals to prevent maritime agencies of Philippines from logistically supporting its presence, are the other major activities. Some of these are discussed in brief.

Woody Island (Paracels)

This island lies about 180 Nautical miles (NM) south-east of Hainan Island and is part of the disputed Paracel group. A Sansha military garrison under Hainan's control and Xisha maritime garrison under South Sea Fleet of the PLA Navy were also concurrently set up to look after the defence needs of the islands. Currently there are no aircraft based at the island, but a runway of about 8000 feet length and the logistical infrastructure including ship berthing facilities under development will be highly useful to the PLA Navy and its Air Force in extending aerial coverage by another 200 NM seawards.

Reclamation in Spratlys

Since January 2014, China commenced reclamation work in six features of Spratly Islands under its control, each located within 30 NM from at least one of the others. As of March 2015, China had reclaimed about 500 acres of land on these features, and had progressed from reclamation work to infrastructure development at four sites. These include building of harbours, communication and surveillance systems, logistics support facilities and at least one airfield. The details of reclamation activity feature-wise are mentioned below:[6]

(a) *Fiery Cross (Yongshu) Reef* - Reclamation began in August 2013. Principal landmass construction was finished by November 2014. An airstrip of about 3,110 meters length was under construction since January 2015. Work was also progressing on a port facility.

(b) *Gaven (Nanxun) Reef* - Construction at Gaven Reef began after March 2014. An island measuring approximately 300 by 250 meters with causeways extending from a central islet has been reclaimed since then.

(c) *Mischief (Meiji Jiao) Reef* - Beginning in early 2015, Mischief Reef has undergone extensive reclamation activity along its western rim. Widening of southern entrance to the reef, coupled with sightings of PLA Navy vessels suggests a future role for the reclaimed reef as a naval base.

(d) *Hughes (Dongmen) Reef* - Construction on Hughes Reef began in mid-2014. What was earlier a 380 sq. mts. concrete platform on stilts, has now been expanded to a 75,000 sq. mts. ground through reclamation.

(e) *Subi (Zhubi) Reef* – Intensive reclamation work commenced in July 2014 and more that 3 million sq. meters has been reclaimed, with enough space for a possible 3000 meter runway along its western edge in addition to the standard military and civil installations seen on other features. A 230 meter wide access channel is also being dredged to enable ships to enter the lagoon.

(f) *Johnson South (Zhigua) Reef* - Johnson South Reef is a 7.2 sq. km. submerged reef in the Union Banks. Until early 2014, the only manmade feature on the reef was a small concrete platform that housed a communications facility, garrison building and a pier. This platform is now surrounded by an island that measures 400 meters at its widest, and has an area of about 100,000 sq. mts. China is also expected to build an airstrip on the reef. The infrastructure existing on Johnson South reef as of June 2015 is shown at Table 1:

Table 1. Infrastructure on Johnson South Reef (as of June 2015)

1.	Access Channel	8.	Pre-existing communications facility
2.	Concrete plant	9.	Pre-existing garrison building
3.	Defensive Towers	10.	Pre-existing helipad
4.	Desalination pumps	11.	Roll on/Roll off (RORO) docks
5.	Fuel dump	12.	Pre-existing Military facility
6.	Multi-level military facility	13.	Pre-existing pier
7.	Possible radar facility	14.	Reinforced seawalls

Underwater Archaeological Survey

China built its first underwater archaeology ship in 2013 to enable search, location, mapping and excavation of underwater relics. The ship is now being utilised for underwater archaeological tasks in South China Sea, and is meeting with reported successes. In May 2015, Chinese archaeologists claimed to have recovered Qing Dynasty sculptures from one of the islands in Paracels.[7] This kind of activity helps China in laying claim to various features in the South China Sea, citing historical evidence of Chinese presence in the past.

Deep Sea Oil Exploration in Vietnamese EEZ

On May 2, 2014, Chinese oil rig *Haiyang Shiyou-981*, stationed itself in Vietnam's EEZ, 25 nm east-southeast of Triton Island in Paracel archipelago. China's marine police vessels, tugs and commercial vessels formed a protective cordon around the rig and chased Vietnamese law enforcement ships beyond 10 nm from the rig. The Chinese ships also besieged, rammed and fired water cannons at Vietnamese vessels trying to approach the cordon. Two Chinese aircraft continually swept over the location where the rig was moored. China unilaterally withdrew the rig in July 2014, ostensibly after having completed its survey task.[8]

Access Control over Philippines' Occupied Features

Chinese maritime enforcement agencies have also mounted round-the-clock presence and surveillance missions on either side of the Second Thomas Shoal (Renai Reef), where a Philippines Navy ship remains aground for last 16 years.[9] Similar deployment off Scarborough Shoal also continues, and is also supported by appropriate rhetoric by the Chinese Foreign Affairs Office (FAO) and the Ministry of National Defense (MND).

Vietnam - Issues and Interests in South China Sea

Vietnam has also been preparing the pitch for forcing the issue of legitimate sovereign rights in its EEZ since May 2009, immediately after making its submission to the UN CLCS. Vietnam, as the Chair of the ASEAN Regional Forum (ARF) in July 2010, managed to garner positive endorsement of a majority of participating States over the vexed problem. With the perceived backing of American interest in the South China Sea as suggested by US articulations during various ARF meets –

even though not directly in support of Vietnam's cause – Hanoi may have assessed the current period as the most opportune moment to exercise its rightful position. Vietnam has been steadfastly calling for international involvement, stating that peace, stability, security, and maritime safety in the Eastern Sea (Vietnamese nomenclature for the South China Sea) is in common interest of the countries inside and outside the region.

Vietnam in particular cites the example of 'Binh Minh' incident to illustrate how the situation in South China Sea is precariously poised and can deteriorate suddenly. On May 26, 2011, three Chinese maritime patrol ships ventured into the Vietnamese EEZ and cut off the exploration cables of a Vietnamese seismic survey ship 'Binh Minh 02' engaged in oil exploration, about 116 NM off the Vietnamese coast.[10] Barely five days later, two vessels believed to belong to China, tried to come too close to another Vietnamese chartered vessel, 'Viking 2' which was engaged in seismic exploration in the Vietnamese EEZ. However, they were headed off by timely intervention from a Vietnamese naval ship. Vietnam conducted a live-fire maritime exercise in its EEZ on June 13, 2011, after a series of such maritime incidents started occurring regularly. The exercise, though located well away from the disputed islands and comparatively nearer to the Vietnamese coast, nevertheless lay in the overlapping claims of the two countries' maritime zones.

Vietnamese Activities to Support its Interests

Vietnam promulgated its domestic 'Law on Vietnamese Sea' on June 21, 2012 in order to define and administer its maritime areas and zones. This Law which came into effect on January 1, 2013 brought the Paracels (Hoang Sa) and Spratly (Truong Sa) under its sovereignty and national jurisdiction. It also mandated the Vietnamese maritime law enforcement authorities to ensure the protection of its sovereignty and national jurisdiction.[11]

Vietnam is also carrying out reclamation on two reefs under its control, namely, Sand Cay and West Reef in Spratlys. Between 2011 and 2015, Vietnam expanded the Sand Cay Reef by more than 50 percent, adding extensive defensive structures and improving existing facilities. Vietnam built a lighthouse on West Reef in 1994 followed by some military structures. Beginning August 2012, the West Reef has seen extensive land reclamation and construction of additional facilities including a harbour. China In fact, took the cue from renewed Vietnamese reclamation activities since 2012, but has since left Vietnam well behind in terms of scale, area and speed of reclamation.

There was very also strong opposition to the deployment of Chinese oil rig in the Paracels, with public protest, arson against Chinese businesses and fatalities of Chinese citizens. Vietnam has also been protesting against unilateral fishing ban imposed by China, including in 2015. Vietnam is also procuring *Kilo* class submarines, ships and ASW helicopters from Russia in order to signal its intent, should China try to intimidate it with its naval might.

Philippines - Issues and Interests in South China Sea

Philippines occupies eight features in the Spratly islands, but is finding it hard to fend off the pro-activism shown by Chinese fishermen and the maritime agencies. Since its maritime capabilities are no match against those of China, it seeks to involve other nations of ASEAN and the US in order to explore a multilateral approach to the dispute resolution. The greatest impact of Chinese pro-activism has been felt by the Philippine fishing industry. Chinese vessels have cordoned off most of the fertile fishing spots around these islands by resorting to an 'Onion Peel' strategy, wherein the opposing side continues to encounter layer upon layer of obstructions in its quest for the objective which lies in the centre. Philippines has also flagged environmental concerns arising out of Chinese reclamation activity, which could adversely affect long term fish productivity.

Philippines' Activities in Support of its Interests

In addition to lodging regular protests against Chinese pro-activism, Philippines unlike Vietnam has gone a step further, by seeking international arbitration under article 287 and Annexure VII of UNCLOS, in January 2013. It contends that having exhausted all political and diplomatic means to resolve the disputes bilaterally – and particularly after a three-month stand-off over Scarborough Shoal commencing mid-April 2012 – it was left with no option but to resort to arbitration plea at the international forum. It has sought the following injunctions, from the international tribunal among others:-[12]

(a) Declaration that China's maritime claims in South China Sea based on its so-called nine-dash line are contrary to UNCLOS and are invalid.

(b) Requires China to bring its domestic legislation in conformity with its obligations under UNCLOS.

(c) Requires that China desist from activities that violate maritime domain rights of Philippines in West Philippine Sea. (Philippines' nomenclature for South China Sea)

Philippines government vessels have regularly been confronting Chinese maritime agencies' ships in order to logistically support its presence in Scarborough and second Thomas shoals. Philippines tourism department runs a regular air ferry service to Thitu Island in the Spratly chain. Beijing, in fact, warned Manila not to infringe on its sovereignty, when the Philippines' Ministry of Defence organised an aerial situational awareness tour for foreign journalists to that island on May 11, 2015.[13] Philippines is procuring patrol ships from Japan and UAVs from US for bolstering its maritime law enforcement capability. It has also been actively seeking US advice and also beseeching Washington to intervene in support of its cause.

American Issues and Interests in South China Sea

The Strategic Guidance Review of US titled *'Sustaining US Global Leadership: Priorities for 21st Century Defense'* of January 2012, clearly outlines a realignment of US force deployment away from Europe, towards the Asia-Pacific. This so called 'strategic rebalance' is candidly described as an 'imperative' for America, as that region is strategically too significant for the US, to leave it open to the overpowering influence of China. The US Navy's *'Cooperative Strategy for 21st Century Sea Power'* document of March 2015 also mandates an enduring regional presence in 'Indo-Asia-Pacific' by maintaining a Carrier Strike Group, Carrier air wing, Marine Expeditionary Force and Amphibious Ready Group in Japan; and deploy more attack submarines in Guam.[14]

In line with this strategic direction, approximately 60 percent of its naval force will be based in the region by 2020. Though the potential adversary against whom all this naval hardware is being rearranged has not been named, various American assessments make it more than evident. For instance, successive quarterly Congressional Research Service (CRS) reports to the US Congress have been mentioning the following goals for the PLA Navy modernisation, particularly the last two, being of core concern:-[15]

(a) Asserting China's maritime territorial claims, particularly in most of the South China Sea – claims that overlap with those of other countries and are potentially expansive enough to go well beyond what would normally be supported by international legal norms.

(b) Enforcing China's view – a minority one among world nations – that it has the right to interpret international laws relating to the freedom of navigation in exclusive economic zones (EEZ), which is at odds with that of the US.

(c) Displacing US influence in the Pacific Ocean region.

(d) Asserting China's status as a major world power.

American Activities in Support of its Interests

The July 2010 assertion of the US Secretary of State, Hillary Clinton at the Hanoi ARF meet that the "*US has national interest in the freedom of navigation and open access to Asia's maritime commons, and respect for international law in the South China Sea*",[16] virtually pitched the US formally into the equation. US backed up its stated position by deploying the *George Washington* aircraft carrier and *John McCain* destroyer in Vietnamese waters in August 2010 – a first in more than four decades since the cessation of hostilities between the two countries.

The US Senate also passed a resolution each in 2011, 2013 and 2014 "deploring/condemning the use of force by naval and maritime security vessels from China in the South China Sea; calling for multilateral resolution to maritime territorial disputes in South East Asia, and supporting the continuation of operations by the US Armed Forces to enable the 'freedom of navigation' in international waters and air space in that Sea".[17]

The US Department of Defence report of May 2015 on military capabilities of China, took exception to ongoing Chinese reclamation work in South China Sea, stating that China was attempting to change facts on the ground by improving its defense infrastructure there.[18] US media also highlighted a Pentagon proposal to send naval ships and aircraft to directly contest Chinese territorial claims over artificial islands that it was creating. Though US officials denied any such plans, the flight of a US Navy P-8A reconnaissance aircraft over one of these islands on May 21, 2015, did lend credence to these media assertions.

During the Shangri La Dialogue in June 2015, the US reiterated that maritime security and freedom of navigation remained an issue of particular importance for the region; which elicited a caustic response from China to the effect that freedom of navigation in South China Sea was not threatened for anyone. Washington nevertheless followed up on its stated position by sailing its destroyer *Lassen* within 12 NM of Subi Reef in October 2015, despite vociferous protests from Beijing, before, during and after the ship's movement.

Indian Issues and Interests in South China Sea

India's current issues in the South China Sea could be said to revolve around three elements driven by its specific national interest. These relate to its primary and secondary areas of maritime interest; insistence on freedom of the seas; and its oil exploration and production cooperation with Vietnam. According to Indian Navy's 'Freedom to use the Seas: India's maritime Strategy, 2007' document, India's secondary area of interest extends to South China Sea, and in fact up to Western Pacific Ocean.[19]

Freedom of the Seas

India has always maintained at various multilateral meets that 'freedom of navigation' in South China Sea should not be affected. During 2010 to 2012 ARF meets, India joined others in calling for freedom of navigation in South China Sea. In July 2011, India's Foreign Secretary, Nirupama Rao publically reiterated this stand. The Indian position has been articulated much more clearly since mid-2014, as is evident from the joint statements of the current political leadership.

In a joint statement issued during the visit of Vietnamese Prime Minister to India on October 28, 2014, both the Prime Ministers reiterated their desire and determination to work together to maintain peace, stability, growth and prosperity in Asia and beyond. They agreed that freedom of navigation and over-flight in the East Sea/South China Sea should not be impeded and called the parties concerned to exercise restraint, avoid threat or use of force and resolve disputes through peaceful means in accordance with universally recognised principles of international law, including the UNCLOS 1982. They also welcomed the collective commitment of concerned parties to abide by and implement the '2002 Declaration on the Conduct of Parties in the South China Sea', and to work towards the adoption of a 'Code of Conduct' in the South China Sea on the basis of consensus.[20]

A Joint Statement articulating similar position was made on September 30, 2014 during visit of Prime Minister Narendra Modi to the US, wherein "...the Indian Prime Minister and the US President ... affirmed the importance of safeguarding maritime security and ensuring freedom of navigation and over flight throughout the region, especially in the South China Sea. The Prime Minister and President called on all parties to avoid the use, or threat of use of force in advancing their claims. The two leaders urged concerned parties to pursue resolution of their territorial and maritime disputes through peaceful means, in accordance with universally recognised principles of international law, including the UNCLOS."[21]

INS Airavat 'Non-Incident' in South China Sea

India had an occasion to publically state its 'freedom of navigation' position on South China Sea in September 2011, when the media reported a confrontation of sorts between Indian naval ship *Airavat* and a Chinese vessel off Vietnam. Extract of the statement of Indian Ministry of External Affairs in reproduced below:-

> "The Indian naval vessel, INS Airavat paid a friendly visit to Vietnam between 19 to 28 July 2011. On July 22, INS Airavat sailed from the Vietnamese port of Nha Trang towards Hai Phong. At a distance of 45 NM from the Vietnamese coast in the South China Sea, it was contacted on open radio channel by a caller identifying himself as the Chinese Navy" stating that "you are entering Chinese waters". No ship or aircraft was visible from INS Airavat, which proceeded on her onward journey as scheduled. There was no confrontation involving INS Airavat. India supports freedom of navigation in international waters, including in the South China Sea, and the right of passage in accordance with accepted principles of international law. These principles should be respected by all."[22]

Oil Sector Cooperation with Vietnam

The start-point of the cooperation in oil sector was the signing of a production sharing contract in May 1988 between Hydrocarbon India Ltd (as ONGC Videsh Limited was then called) and Petro-Vietnam. Under that agreement, the Indian company was allowed to explore gas in Block 6.1, which presently contributes about 50 percent of Vietnam's gas requirement. ONGC Videsh Limited (OVL) has been carrying out oil exploration in blocks 127 and 128 since 2007. OVL and Petro-Vietnam signed an agreement of cooperation on October 12, 2011, for developing long term cooperation in oil and gas industry. Some key areas of cooperation relate to new investments, expansion and operation of oil and gas exploration and production including refining, transportation and supply in Vietnam, India and third countries. New agreements for wholesome cooperation in oil exploration, production and distribution were also signed between oil companies of the two countries during the visit of Vietnamese Prime Minister to India in October 2014.

Impact on Regional Stability

In view of the complexity of the issue involving multiple parties, it is considered that an immediate resolution to the South China Sea dispute is unlikely. The disputing parties have varied perceptions of their territorial claims and limits of associated maritime zones. They also interpret the rights and obligations of coastal states and outsiders in these maritime zones differently. It is also obvious that the 2002 'Declaration on the Conduct of parties in the South China Sea'– which entailed all concerned to exercise self-restraint in activities that could complicate or escalate disputes and affect peace and stability – is not being effective due to its legally non-binding nature.

In the meanwhile, China, Vietnam and Philippines are engaging in incremental brinkmanship. But naval strength and maritime law enforcement capabilities of Vietnam are still far below that of China. However, its naval strengthening does seem to suggest increasing aspirations to challenge China's naval might. Promulgation of maritime laws by both sides[23] do provide legal basis for maritime law enforcement agencies to prosecute infringements within their respective jurisdictions. This creates fertile grounds for future skirmishes, if not open conflict. Over-ambitious perceptions of some ASEAN countries about the level and scope of American support with regard to their maritime disputes with China, is also a cause for rising acrimony. The resultant instability, should matters aggravate, would potentially affect vital trade and energy flow on a global scale. Consequent restrictions on 'freedom of navigation' could upscale the crisis from regional to a global one, possibly forcing the hand of international community.

China also opposes research activities of American ships and reconnaissance aircraft in its EEZ. It also advises US not to take sides on territorial disputes. It argues that the US being external power has no *locus standii* in dispute resolution. It criticises American statements on Chinese reclamation activities and has warned that "a confrontation can hardly be avoided if US sends ships or aircraft within territorial waters of the reclaimed islands."[24]

The American diplomatic efforts backed by naval rebalance to bring about a sense of normalcy in the region, seem to meet limited success. Vietnam and Philippines expect the US to favour their positions and support them. On the other hand, Beijing views Washington's overtures as superficial at best, given its clear opposition to the increasing US involvement in regional security affairs. Considering the broader picture in the Western Pacific, Washington thus faces a real dilemma with at least three countries in the area soliciting open support as allies/partners, and others looking on with similar expectations, while it debates on how 'not' to get involved directly.[25]

Conclusion

It is almost a given that China will continue to press its claims with renewed vigour and progressively greater leverage, duly backed by its 'Comprehensive National Power.' The division of the ASEAN Community– which previously presented a united front vis-a-vis China while negotiating the 2002 'Declaration on Conduct of Parties' – into States having a dispute with China and others who don't, has led to further dilution of stance, with consequent advantage for China. The dilemma for Beijing however, is whether to adopt a hard-line approach or offer a more nuanced response bordering on the softer option. But placatory statements apart, China has been leaving no opportunity to press its claims further, to the detriment of other South China Sea disputants.

China would also like to prevent the involvement of the US in the region and it's 'Freedom of the Seas' posture generally favouring the standpoint of other disputants. To that end, China's security-related policies towards the US – whose domination it will have to challenge eventually – can be characterised as a two-sided effort of 'co-option' and 'prevention'. Co-option essentially focuses on maintaining cordial relations with US and prevention seeks to hinder any US initiatives that may be directed towards frustrating the expansion of Chinese capability and influence.

Against this tenuous backdrop, the future 'Code of Conduct' agreement under negotiation between China and ASEAN since 2012 may not suffice to ease the situation, unless it is made legally binding. As for India, it will have to stand by its current position on 'Freedom of Seas'; and also maintain that oil exploration issues with Vietnam are purely commercial ventures under Vietnamese awarded contracts; thus leaving the territorial dispute to be bilaterally resolved between the two parties.

Finally, it would be appropriate to sum up this chapter with two differing perspectives, which are considered to lie at the opposite ends of the spectrum, as far as the possibilities in the South China Sea are concerned:

- *"A thousand mile journey begins with the first step"*–A Chinese proverb quoted by Yang Jiechi, Foreign Minister of China after DOC guidelines were unanimously adopted between China and ASEAN, preparatory to ARF in July 2012.

- *"The south china sea is the future of conflict"*–The title of Robert D. Kaplan's article in *Foreign Policy* Journal of August 15, 2011, wherein the Author convincingly argues that the 21st Century's defining battleground is going to be in these waters.

The global community and the South China Sea littorals in particular, would therefore, do well to understand both these perspectives – the subtle message about longevity of the issue, brought home so aptly by the Chinese Foreign Minister through the first quote; and the second more alarming one, but should not be discounted in a hurry.

NOTES AND REFERENCES

1   Asia Maritime Transparency Initiative, Island Tracker June 16, 2015, available at: Asia Maritime Transparency Initiative, Island Tracker June 16, 2015, available at: http://amti.csis.org/islandracker/, accessed July 30, 2015.

2   The Chinese communication (CML/18/2009 of May 7, 2009) was in response to Vietnamese submission dated May 7, 2009 to the UN Commission on the Limits of the Continental Shelf, available at http://www.un.org/Depts/los/

clcs_new/ submissions_files/vnm37_09/chn_2009re_vnm.pdf, accessed June 19, 2015.

3   Two instances of this manifestation were personally observed by the Author. The map of China in the in-flight magazine of Air China, the official Chinese air carrier depicts the entire South China Sea enclosed by dotted lines and is appended to the mainland Chinese boundary. Exactly the same illustration was again observed in the elementary Chinese language textbook that the Author was studying as part of his formal learning of the Chinese language. The text book incidentally was published in 1986.

4   Chinese Ministry of National Defense Website, 'Chinese military leader urges U.S. to honor commitment on South China Sea', May 16, 2015, available at http://eng.mod.gov.cn/TopNews/2015-05/16/content_4585231.htm, accessed July 31, 2015.

5   These laws were formulated to provide a legal basis for China to exercise sovereignty over its territorial seas and jurisdiction over the adjacent EEZ and continental shelf.

6   Unless otherwise specified, the details of reclamation work have been taken from the CSIS's AMTI Island tracker newsletter of June 16, 2015, available at http://amti.csis.org/ island-tracker, accessed July 30, 2015.

7   Global Times, 'Chinese archaeological team explores Shanhu Island in South China Sea', May 17, 2015, available at http://www.globaltimes.cn/content/922021.shtml, accessed July 30, 2015.

8   Vietnam's Peoples' Army Newspaper, 'China's illegal placement of Haiyang Shiyou-981 oil rig in the exclusive economic zone and continental shelf of Vietnam', July 9, 2014, available at http://en.qdnd.vn/ news/chinas-illegal-placement-of-haiyang-shiyou-981-oil-rig-in-the-exclusive-economic-zone-and-continental-shelf-of-vietnam/310609.html, accessed July 31, 2015.

9   Jeff Himmelman, 'A Game of Shark And Minnow', October 27, 2013,New York Times, available at http://www.nytimes .com/newsgraphics/2013/10/27/south-china-sea, accessed July 31, 2015.

10   VietNamNet, 'Binh Minh ship – another CGX case in East Sea?', May 31, 2011, available at http://english.vietnamnet. vn/fms/special-reports/8557/binh-minh-ship---another-cgx-case-in-east-sea-.html, accessed July 31, 2015.

11   Vietnam News, 'The Law of the Sea of Vietnam', August 7, 2012, , available at http://vietnamnews.vn/politics-laws/ 228456/the-law-of-the-sea-of-viet-

nam.html, accessed July 31, 2015

12 Republic of The Philippines, Department of Foreign Affairs, 'Notification and statement of claim on West Philippine Sea', No. 13-0211, January 22, 2013, available at http://www.dfa.gov.ph/index.php/component/ docman/ doc_download/56-notification-and-statement-of-claim-on-west-philippine-sea?Itemid=546, accessed July 31, 2015.

13 Chinese Ministry of National Defense Website, 'China urges Philippines to stop provocations in South China Sea', May 12, 2015, available at http://eng.mod.gov.cn/TopNews/2015-05/12/content_4584648.htm, accessed July 31, 2015

14 Forward, Engaged, Ready: US Navy's 'Cooperative Strategy for 21st Century Sea Power', March 2015, p. 11.

15   Ronald O'Rourke, 'China Naval Modernisation: Implications for U.S. Navy Capabilities – Background and Issues for Congress', CRS Report for Congress, July 28, 2015, pp. 7-8, available at http://www.fas.org/sgp/crs/ row/RL33153.pdf, accessed July 30, 2015.

16 Kamlesh K Agnihotri, 'Naval Power Dynamics in the Western Pacific Ocean: Impact on Maritime Situation in East and South China Seas', Maritime Affairs Journal of the National Maritime Foundation, Volume 9, No. 2, Winter 2013, p. 14.

17 US Senate resolutions, S. Res. 217 of June 27, 2011; S. Res. 167 of June 10, 2013; and S. Res. 412 of July 10, 2014. The last resolution of 2014 is available at https://www.congress.gov/bill/113th-congress/senate-resolution/412, accessed July 31, 2015.

18 US Department of Defense Annual Report to Congress, 'Military and Security Developments involving the Peoples Republic of China 2015', p. 72

19 The caveat though is that areas of secondary interest will come in where there is a direct connection with areas of primary interest, or where they impinge on the deployment of future maritime forces. India's Primary Areas of Interest include the Arabian Sea and the Bay of Bengal, which largely encompass its EEZ, island territories and their littoral reaches, the choke points leading to and from the Indian Ocean – principally the Straits of Malacca, Hormuz, Bab-el-Mandeb and the Cape of Good Hope; IOR island countries; Persian Gulf which is the source of majority of its oil supplies; and the principal ISLs crossing IOR. See Integrated Headquarters Ministry of Defence (Navy), 'Freedom to use the Seas: India's Maritime Military Strategy', May 2007, pp.

59-60.

20   Indian Ministry of External Affairs, 'Joint Statement on the State Visit of Prime Minister of the Socialist Republic of Vietnam to India', October 28, 2014, available at http://www.mea.gov.in/bilateral-documents.htm?dtl/24142/Join t+Statement+on+the+State+Visit+of+Prime+Minister+of+the+Socialist+Re public+of+Vietnam+to+India+October+2728+2014, accessed July 31, 2015.

21   Indian Ministry of External Affairs, 'Joint Statement during the visit of Prime Minister to USA', September 30, 2014, available at http://www.mea. gov.in/bilateral-documents.htm?dtl/24051/Joint+Statement+during+the+ visit+of+Prime+Minister+to+USA, accessed July 31, 2015.

22   Indian Ministry of External Affairs, 'Incident involving INS Airavat in South China Sea', September 1, 2011, available at http://www.mea.gov.in/ media-briefings.htm?dtl/3040/Incident+involving+INS+Airavat+in+South+ China+Sea, accessed July 31, 2015.

23   These refer to Hainan regulation for the management of public order for coastal and border defense' and Law on Vietnamese sea', both effective January 1, 2013.

24   Global Times, 'Firm response to meet US sea provocation', May 14, 2015, available at http://www.globaltimes.cn/ content/921618.shtml, accessed July 31, 2015. The editorial went on to remind US that 'China was a major power with nuclear weapons, and there was no way that US forces could take reckless actions in the South China Sea.'

25   Kamlesh K Agnihotri, 'Naval Power Dynamics in the Western Pacific Ocean' ibid, p. 17

6 RELEVANCE OF UNCLOS AND OTHER LEGAL INSTRUMENTS IN RESOLVING MARITIME DISPUTES IN THE SOUTH CHINA SEA

Raghavendra Mishra

Introduction

The South China Sea (SCS) has witnessed a series of confrontations, skirmishes, and use or threat of use of force since the early 1970s. Such incidents have become more frequent in the 21st Century and have almost invariably involved China, either as an initiator or as the target. Three recent incidents that could be highlighted are the large-scale land reclamation by China in the Spratlys, the overflight by a United States (US) Navy P8A *Poseidon* long-range maritime reconnaissance (LRMR) aircraft over one of these artificial facilities, and the 'surprisingly robust response' by Malaysia to the Chinese coastguard intrusion in its claimed waters. This trend is viewed as emblematic of the gradual erosion in regional security situation, hardened postures by the direct (claimants) and other stakeholders with strategic stakes in the region, and the increasing tendency to engage in power politics. The statement by Chinese Foreign Minister, Wang Yi that 'changing position on SCS disputes would be akin to shaming the ancestors', is a moot example.[1]

The rich fishing resources, significant though unproven estimates of strategic mineral reserves, such as the offshore gas and oil deposits, besides the large volume of seaborne traffic by value and volume traversing the busy sea-lanes, any disruption in the trade crossing the SCS would have global effects. In essence, it would be appropriate to posit that the South China Sea "presents a problem of economic, diplomatic, environmental and military stability".[2] The importance of the SCS for India can be explained through the tripolar logic:

(a) The vector of India's 'Act East policy' passes through the SCS;

(b) SCS has been designated as one of the 'Secondary Areas of Interest' by the Indian Navy in its strategy and doctrinal documents.[3] Given the regional/global geopolitical developments and the increment in the capacity/capability of the Indian Navy in the interim, this 'secondary tag' to SCS may well undergo a change.

(c) The trend regarding the direction of trade indicates that around one-third of India's commerce by value, both in export and import terms, is to the regions located to the east of the Straits of Malacca (Figure 1).

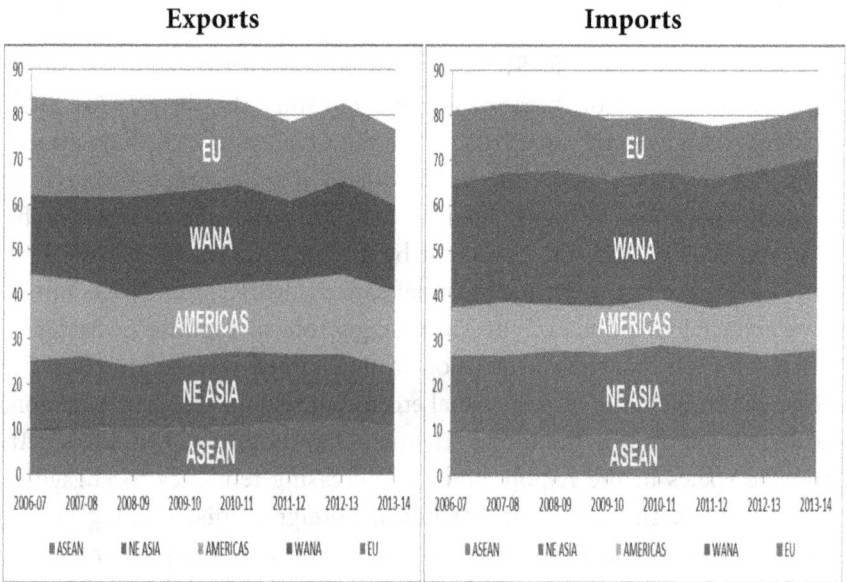

Fig. 1. India's Regional Trade (2006-07 to 2013-14) (By value, in percentage terms)

[Source: *Ministry of Commerce Database*, Authors' compilation]

Law Force and Diplomacy

Drawing upon the recent work by Ken Booth titled "Law, Force and Diplomacy at Sea"[4], this paper analyses the applicability and interpretations of the existing legal framework apropos the SCS disputes. The use of force or its coercive application in the SCS, in true military sense, has been episodic. Force was used by China twice against Vietnam. First, in January 1974 during the clash over the Crescent Group of features in the Paracels, and thereafter in March 1988, during the skirmish over the Johnson South Reef in the Spratlys. The threat of force for coercive purposes was also used by both China and the US during the 1995-96 Taiwan crisis. Interestingly, the recent stand-offs in the SCS among the claimants have generally involved the non-military or para-military assets such as the coast guard and other constabulary maritime management agencies, including proactive use of fishermen for asserting their claim positions, leading to a new conceptual coinage of 'para-gunboat diplomacy'.[5] That said, the use of force for changing *status quo* is considered illegal except for self-defence in accordance with the United Nations (UN) charter.

As far as formal/informal diplomacy for resolving the SCS disputes is concerned, four major initiatives since the 1990s have not yielded optimal results. The first of these was the track two initiative launched by the Indonesian Ambassador Hashim Djalal with support from Canada that faded after a series of meetings, once China refused to commit for a joint development programme in the central part of the SCS, despite agreeing to it in principle.[6] The second initiative was by Stein Tonnenson in 2000 comprising a six-stage plan where all the SCS claimants were expected to engage in 'bilateral, trilateral and multilateral bargains' over the disputed claims related to territory, sovereignty and sovereign rights.[7] Despite considerable initial enthusiasm, the proposal did not receive adequate backing due to two main sticking points, though not overtly stated. The first of these was the long coastline of China, and the apprehensions that the claims of other parties would be adversely affected especially in light of the repeated reference to "land dominates the sea" principle during international arbitrations. The second issue had to do with the growing concerns that China wanted to resolve the SCS dispute by action or coercion through its naval supremacy.[8] The next diplomatic initiative was the 2002 Declaration of Code of Conduct of Parties in the South China Sea (DoC) between China and the Association of South East Nations (ASEAN) member states.[9] The practice and evidence suggests that the norms of DoC - a non-legally binding multilateral diplomatic agreement and hence not a source of public international law, have been virtually ignored by all the parties to the SCS dispute. A similar treatment of the 2011 agreement between China, Brunei, Malaysia, Vietnam and the Philippines over joint management of SCS also indicates that the diplomatic approaches have largely concentrated on the 'management' as against the larger and more desirable aim of 'dispute resolution'. Therefore, with force and diplomacy as unviable means in the foreseeable future, the question arises as to whether the legal framework provides a way ahead for the resolution of SCS disputes.

Geography of SCS, and its Legal Status

The geography of SCS depends on the theme under discussion. For the purpose of this paper, the extent of SCS as defined in the 1953 International Hydrographic Organisation (IHO) publication delineating the limits of various ocean and seas of the world is used.[10] Therefore, while some scholars have included the disputes in the Gulf of Thailand between Malaysia, Cambodia, Vietnam and Thailand as part of the SCS dispute milieu, where some agreements have been achieved although formal resolution is awaited, these have been left out of scope of this paper. The four major features that find reference in the analyses on the SCS dispute are the three island groups of the Spratlys, Paracels and Pratas and one submerged feature of the Macclesfield Bank. The China-Taiwan bilateral sovereignty conundrum despite most of the world aligning itself to 'One China Policy' remains a flashpoint in the SCS. An additional feature that has gained prominence since 1995 in this regional dispute matrix is the increased friction between China and the Philippines on the Scarborough Shoal/Reef. Some features though relevant but not given adequate attention are the four islands controlled by Indonesia are Natuna, Anambas, Badas, and Tambelan. The reason being the generally undisputed status of these features. A cartographic depiction of the relevant geography of SCS is placed at Fig. 2.

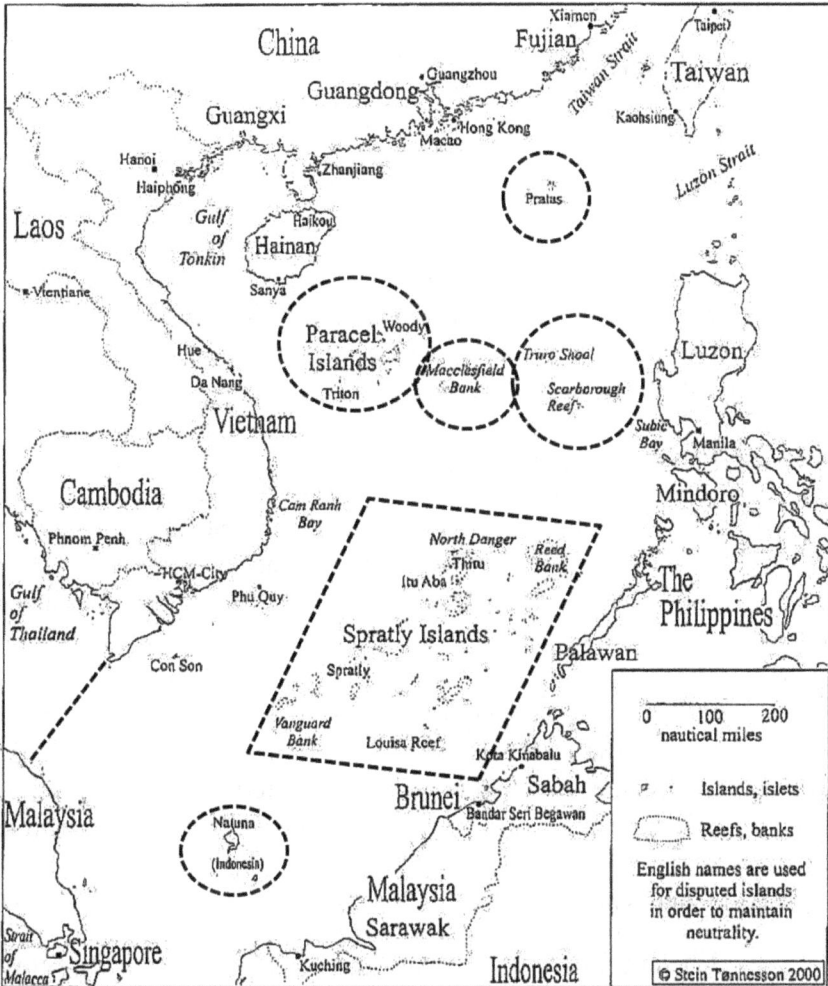

Fig. 2. Major features of SCS disputes

[Source: Tonneson, *Security Dialogue, 2000*]

In legal terms and irrespective of geographic extent used for the analyses, the SCS conforms to the criteria for a 'enclosed or a semi-enclosed sea' as per Article 122 of the United Nations Convention on the Law of the Sea (UNCLOS).[11] The UNCLOS also mandates that the states bordering such seas invite other stakeholders to participate in such efforts to evolve joint cooperative mechanism in exercise of their rights and responsibilities, particularly, towards management of living resources, marine environment and scientific research endeavours.[12]

Claimants, Stakeholders and the Claims

With the defined geographical construct as the point of reference for this paper, the claimants or the directly involved parties to SCS dispute comprise Brunei, China, Indonesia, Malaysia, the Philippines, Taiwan and Vietnam. Of these, China, Vietnam and the Philippines are considered as the more active (and vocal) players with the rest voicing their concerns on an episodic basis, especially so when their claims are infringed upon. Further, the SCS dispute discussions are incomplete without other important, albeit indirectly involved stakeholders like the US that has bilateral security arrangements with the Philippines and Taiwan, Japan, Australia, EU, ASEAN and to some extent India.

The SCS disputes revolves around two critical but distinct categorisations. The first being "who owns what", that is, which land/ maritime feature in the SCS belongs to whom. Such disputes can be categorised as one of 'sovereignty with land connotations'. The second part of the dispute is related to "who gets what" which are related to, but not exclusive of the land sovereignty contextualisation. In other words, such disputes are about the overlap between the various maritime entitlements with 'sovereignty cum territoriality' context, viz., 'Territorial Seas' as well as those of 'sovereign rights' that provide for preferential access to maritime resources under the UNCLOS regimes of the Exclusive Economic Zone (EEZ) and Continental Shelf (CS).

The scholarly/strategic community has discussed the respective assertions by the 'direct claimant community' to the SCS disputes extensively, mostly by examining different themes and particular aspects, thus leading to a fragmentation of the narrative. While space constraints preclude a detailed enumeration of the claim positions and the overlap in the paper as such, these can be found in an excellent analysis by Ramses Amer in 2002.[13] While some of the normative arguments have changed in the interim, the underlying rationale used by the directly involved parties and the extent of their claim positions, except for the land reclamation efforts in the interim - an issue discussed later, has not changed substantially. A synoptic chart depicting the overlap and intersection among the claimants to the SCS disputes is placed at Fig. 3.

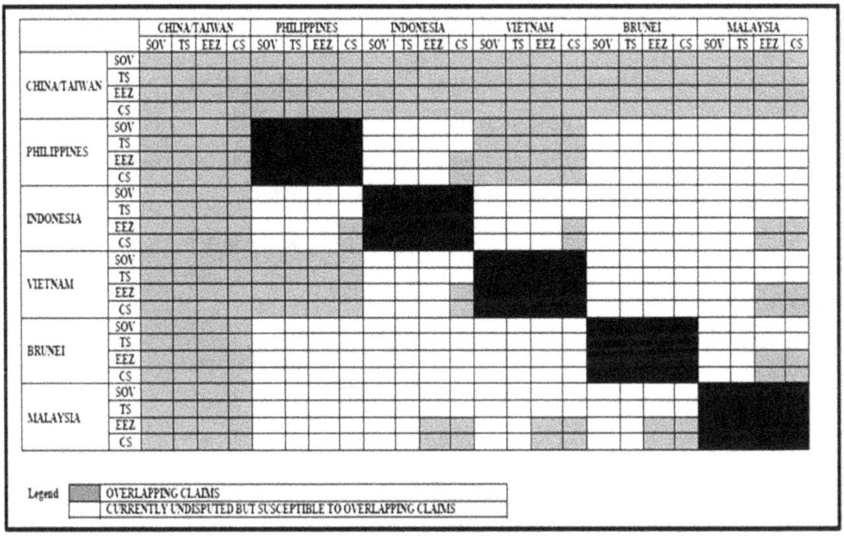

Fig. 3. SCS Dispute Matrix

[Source: Kivimäki, *War or Peace in the South China Sea:* 2002; Authors compilation]

At this stage, it is pertinent to mention that all direct claimants to the SCS dispute are party to the UNCLOS except Taiwan. Since the larger world community affirms the 'One China' policy, the status of Taiwan could be roughly equated to that of an 'entity' by the strict legal interpretation of the UN Charter, therefore it not a party to the UNCLOS. However, it is stressed that Taiwan also accepts the UNCLOS regime as customary public international law.[14]

While a large part of the chart at Fig. 3 seems free of overlapping claims, it is worth considering that none of the claimants has actually sought maritime entitlement from the disputed features. Therefore, 'if, how and, when' the ownership of these features and their 'status' are resolved/ determined, a new series of overlaps would emerge. This is quite apparent from the depiction at Fig. 4. For example, while China claims 'undisputed sovereignty and sovereign rights' within its so called 'nine-dashed line claim' of 2009, it has not made any discrete claims to the EEZ/CS in accordance with the UNCLOS. Some experts believe that China has kept its claim position 'intentionally ambiguous to pursue its strategy of consolidation of its near seas.[15] A section of eminent Chinese publicists, including a sitting judge on UN arbitration panel, are also of the view that China should make more concrete and unambiguous articulations about its claim position in the SCS.[16] In essence, the nine-dashed line claim co-exists with its declared baseline articulation of 1996, where China stated, "[it] will announce the remaining baselines of the territorial sea ....at a later date".[17] Similarly, while Vietnam lays claim to the Spratlys, its current definition of baselines is distinct from the extent of its sovereignty claims.

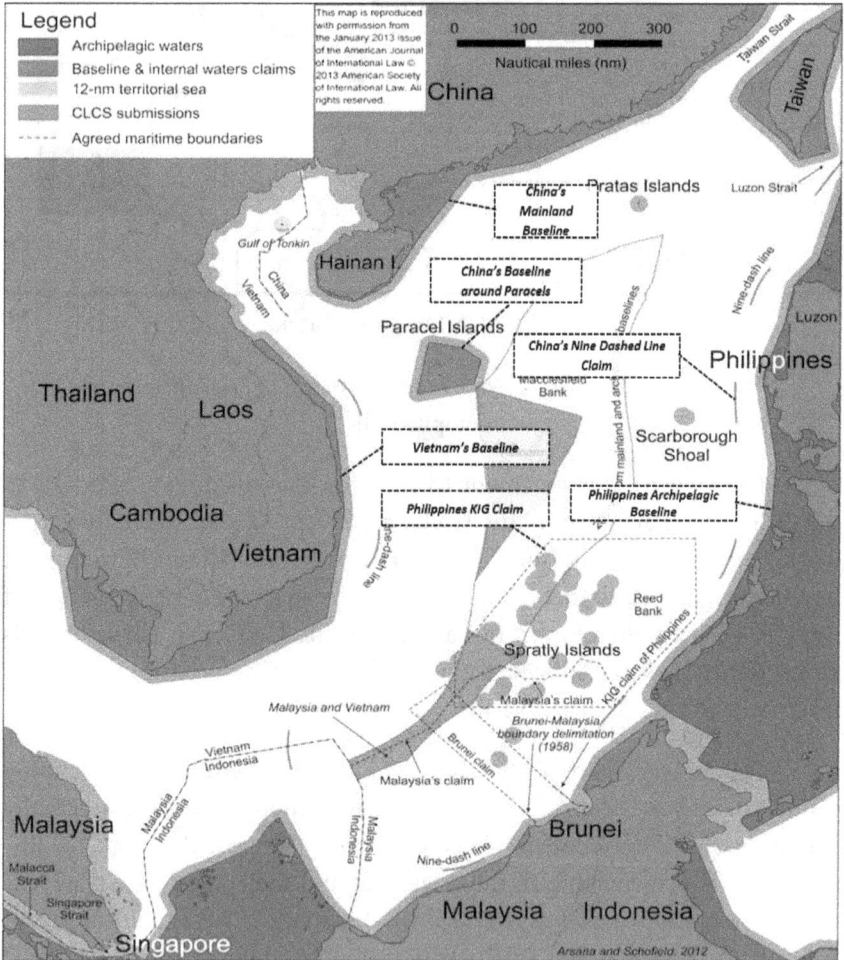

Figure 4: Sovereignty Claims and Baselines in South China Sea

[Source: *American Journal of International Law*, 2013]

To summarise, the SCS dispute consists of two interesting mixes of overlaps and intersects. First, without prejudice to the assertions made by the claimants, each party has simultaneously used 'expansive, narrow and selective' interpretations of ancient as well as contemporary doctrines, principles and norms besides history and cartography in support of their articulations. A recent work makes a pithy (and scathing) analysis of the 'historical' context of parties to this dispute.[18] For example, while China uses the logic of first discovery and uses ancient literature to support its claim position, the selective citation seems evident.[19] Similarly, the conduct and treatment of Thomas Cloma - the so called discoverer and one-time proclaimant of the 'The Free Territory of Freedomland' vis-à-vis the current sovereignty claim by the Philippines over the 'Kalayaan Group of Islands' in the Spratlys make for an absorbing narrative.[20] In a similar vein, while the colonial legacy remains an uncomfortable period with all the SCS claimants, the references to 'successor state' status for asserting their current positions is another example in support of this proposition.[21] The second mix, as explained earlier, is the complex web of overlapping, intersecting and intermeshed nature of these claims with varying degrees of sovereignty, territoriality and maritime entitlement connotations, which in turn raises an important question as which portion of the dispute can be resolved where and who all can participate.

Legal Resolution of SCS Dispute - What, Where and How

The three international legal platforms available for inter-state dispute resolution are:

(a) International Court of Justice (ICJ) uses the UN Charter, the statute establishing the ICJ, and other founding UN documents including the UNCLOS and the dispute resolution mechanism contained therein, depending upon on the contents of the case.

(b) International Tribunal for the Law of the Sea (ITLOS) was established after the UNCLOS came into force as an international legal framework for the management of global maritime domain and, is guided by rules of its founding statute.

(c) Permanent Court of Arbitration (PCA) was established after the 1899 and 1907 Hague Conventions for the Pacific Settlement of International Disputes. In the traditional sense, the PCA is not a court but a permanent framework for arbitral tribunals constituted to resolve specific disputes of both private and public international law. The Rules of Procedure are established individually for each case. For cases involving disputes of territorial and/or maritime connotations, the PCA draws upon the UN Charter, ICJ Statute and the dispute resolution mechanism specified under the UNCLOS for framing these rules, which also depend upon the content of the case 'submitted and accepted' for resolution.

Before answering the question of legal resolution, a brief overview of Public International Law is considered relevant, especially when 'states' (Brunei, China, Indonesia, Malaysia, the Philippines and Vietnam), and an 'entity' (Taiwan) form the core group of claimants to the SCS dispute. Traditionally, the Public International Law was considered the preserve of states but has lately expanded to include international and regional organisations. While the primary and subsidiary sources of Public International Law are well known, this section limits itself to three primary and one subsidiary source, namely the treaty, codified and customary legal frameworks and the case law.[22] While other sources do contribute to the evolution of international law, these are as considered most germane to the SCS dispute. While using case law or past judgments, awards and advisories by the international legal bodies, a clear distinction is to be made between the 'norms or principles', and the 'precedents or general positions'. Norms are contemporary evolved principles for universal application, whereas precedents are an interpretation of a particular aspect of the existing legal framework in a particular case. While 'similarities or correspondence' may exist with another case(s), it is for emphasis that 'virtual congruence or sameness' is near impossible which results in the limited applicability of the "precedents'. Therefore, while parallels can be drawn from the case law, extreme extrapolations may not be the optimal approach.

The continuum of dispute resolution spans three key components of territory-sovereignty-sovereign rights, legal framework-case law, and the various fora available. The legal connotations attached to sovereignty over territory, and maritime entitlements with attached territoriality context, that is, the Territorial Seas require different norms for resolution which are rooted in the principle of unambiguous delineation.[23] For delimitation of territorial seas, the principle of equidistance is used in the absence of historic title and other special circumstances.[24] On the other hand, the maritime entitlements of 'sovereign rights' under the UNCLOS, like the EEZ, Continental Shelf including fishing have more to do with usage of seas and, thus founded on the doctrine of 'equity/equitable delimitation'.[25]

Under international law, five modes by which sovereignty over territory can be acquired are:

(a) Occupation of a *terra nullius*;[26]

(b) Prescription, or the maintenance of effective control for a sufficiently long period of time, also sometimes termed by the ancient Roman principle of *Uti Possidetis de facto*;[27]

(c) Cession, or transfer by treaty termed as the principle of *Uti Possidetis juris* under ancient Roman Law;[28]

(d) Accretion, or growth of territory through acts of nature termed under ancient Roman Law of *Alluvio*, and;

(e) Conquest/Annexation (theoretically, outside the law vide Article 2 of the UN Charter).[29]

As far as disputes of sovereignty over territory are considered even those with linked maritime context, the UNCLOS is not a viable instrument in light of the articulations at Part XV. The relevant text is reproduced (in some detail) for providing the right perspective:

> "Article 298 1. (a) (i). disputes concerning the interpretation or application of articles 15, 74 and 83 relating to sea boundary delimitations, or those involving historic bays or titles, provided that a State having made such a declaration shall, when such a dispute arises subsequent to the entry into force of this Convention and where no agreement within a reasonable period of time is reached in negotiations between the parties, at the request of any party to the dispute, accept submission of the matter to conciliation under Annex V, section 2j and *provided further that any dispute that necessarily involves the concurrent consideration of any unsettled dispute concerning sovereignty or other rights over continental or insular land territory shall be excluded from such submission;*"[30]

It would thus be obvious that UNCLOS cannot be used for deciding the ownership of the disputed features. However, a case on the maritime portion of a hybrid dispute involving both the territorial and maritime connotations, especially about delimitation of maritime entitlements could be resolved under the UNCLOS. At this stage, the case law norm come into play, particularly the principle of "land dominates the sea", first used in the North Sea Continental Shelf dispute in 1969, and emphasised repeatedly thereafter, including in the recent Bay of Bengal maritime dispute legal processes.[31] Further, empirical evidence suggests that all cases with territoriality connotations have been adjudicated at either the ICJ or the PCA. To explain, the 2012 Bangladesh-Myanmar maritime delimitation case was heard at the ITLOS since there was an agreement between the two parties about the position of the land boundary terminal and the dispute was about maritime entitlements under the UNCLOS. On the other hand, since the 2014 Bangladesh-India Case was about the boundary delineation as well as further maritime delimitation, both countries agreed to approach the PCA for arbitration.

In view of the above, the ICJ or the PCA are the appropriate fora with the requisite mandate for a comprehensive resolution of the SCS disputes. However, an overview of the membership of 'direct claimant community' to the SCS reveals two critical issues:

(a) Taiwan is not a member of any of the three international dispute resolution bodies, despite accepting the UNCLOS as customary international law.

(b) While all the claimants have signed and ratified the UNCLOS (except Taiwan), Brunei and Indonesia are not parties to the PCA.

The Philippines-China Legal Imbroglio

All these issues become relevant while considering the ongoing arbitration proceedings initiated by the Philippines in February 2013 against China at the PCA. It is pertinent to mention that this is the first instance where one of the claimants to the SCS dispute has sought recourse to legal mechanism. While exact details of the case are yet to be made public, some of the important issues highlighted by Talmon and Jia. [32]

(a) China's rights in regard to maritime areas in the South China Sea, like the rights of the Philippines, are those that are established by UNCLOS, and consist of its rights to a Territorial Sea and Contiguous Zone under Part II of UNCLOS, to an EEZ under Part V, and to a Continental Shelf under Part VI;

(b) China's maritime claims in the SCS based on its so-called nine-dash line are contrary to UNCLOS and invalid;

(c) Submerged features in the South China Sea that are not above sea level at high tide, and are not located in a coastal states territorial sea. These are a part of the seabed and cannot be acquired by a State, or subjected to its sovereignty, unless they form part of that State's Continental Shelf under Part VI of the Convention;

(d) Mischief Reef, McKennan Reef, Gaven Reef and Subi Reef are submerged features that are not above sea level at high tide, are not islands under the Convention, are not located on China's Continental Shelf; and China has unlawfully occupied and engaged in unlawful construction activities on these features;

(e) Mischief Reef, McKennan Reef are part of the Philippine's Continental Shell under Part VI of the Convention;

(f) Scarborough Shoal, Johnson Reef, Cuarteron Reef and Fiery Cross Reef are submerged features that are not above sea level at high tide, except that each has small protrusions that remain above water at high tide, which qualify as "rocks" under Article 121(3) of the Convention, and generate an entitlement only to a Territorial Sea no broader that 12 M; and China has unlawfully claimed maritime entitlements beyond 12 M from these features;

(g) China has unlawfully prevented Philippine vessels from exploiting the living resources in the waters adjacent to Scarborough Shoal and Johnson Reef;

(h) The Philippines is entitled under UNCLOS to a 12 M Territorial Sea, a 200 M Exclusive Economic Zone, and a Continental Shelf under Parts II, V and VI of UNCLOS, measured from its archipelagic baselines;

(i) China has unlawfully claimed rights to, and has unlawfully exploited the living and non-living resources in the Philippines' Exclusive Economic Zone and Continental Shelf, and has unlawfully prevented the Philippine's from exploiting the living and non-living resources within its Exclusive Economic Zone and Continental Shelf; and

(j) China has unlawfully interfered with the exercise by the Philippine of its rights to navigation under the Convention.

It would be obvious that there are two key questions raised in the case. First, the Philippines seeks 'exact' details from China about the rationale used and the extent of its various maritime entitlements mentioned under the UNCLOS, viz, the territorial seas, exclusive economic zone and the continental shelf regimes vis-à-vis its 'nine dashed line' claim. The second aspect being the request for resolution on the validity of the 'regime of islands' about certain features claimed as such by China in the SCS. The experts and scholars depending on their particular persuasion are divided on the 'validity and applicability' of legal framework, as well as the 'veracity and strength' of the Philippines' claim.[33] China has refused to be party to this legal process by enunciating three major reasons from the very beginning, which were further amplified in its December 2014 position paper. These are:

(a) The arguments used by the Philippines for seeking compulsory arbitration do not come under the ambit of the UNCLOS;

(b) China's formal declaration of 2006 wherein it opted out of the UNCLOS dispute resolution mechanism, and;

(c) The contrarian conduct of the Philippines apropos the 'letter and spirit' of the 2002 DoC.[34]

Further, since the case is under consideration of the PCA, some experts believe that 'intervention' by other stakeholders may not be feasible.[35] As argued elsewhere, the contours of this case remain uncertain and complex; however, the 'what, who and how' of this process could well set the tone and the tenor of the SCS disputes, 'if' the request by the Philippines for arbitration is accepted by the PCA.[36]

Some Interesting Nuances of the SCS Claims

While there a many complex issues related to the SCS disputes, a few of these are discussed as these find mention in the assertions of every direct claimant and could, therefore, be classified as the 'least common denominator'.

History

An overview of the UNCLOS and its correlation with case law indicates that 'historic' rationale can be used for claims to territorial seas and discrete maritime entitlements. While the courts are quite strict about according territoriality/sovereignty based on historicity, they have shown far more positivity in recognising maritime rights as long as the claimant is able to produce adequate evidence, particularly as regards fishing. This proposition, however, does not apply to the upholding of EEZ and Continental Shelf assertions. A large section of the Law of Sea experts are of the view that the 'historic rights/waters' doctrine has become virtually irrelevant in the current context, especially in light of the 'definitive, directive and prescriptive' delimitation norms mentioned in UNCLOS.[37] However, a discrete set of experts and scholars still support the 'historic' regime drawing upon the judgement in *El Salvador V. Honduras* case where three operative principles: formal claim, continuous and effective exercise of relevant jurisdiction, and international acquiescence can be used for claiming 'historic waters and rights'.[38] The issue of 'historic bays' with linked context of 'internal waters' is left out of consideration, since such an assertion has not been made by any of the SCS claimants.

Cartography

Another important issue is the admissibility and cognizance on cartographic information, both historical and contemporary, that each of the involved state has publicised in support of its claims. Considering the accuracy of survey and cartographic skills, which were quite rudimentary earlier, besides the specific purposes for which such maps/charts were prepared, the ICJ in its judgement in the 2007 *Nicaragua V Honduras* case reiterated the 'limited' evidentiary value of maps. This aspect is important as the ICJ reaffirmed this in its earlier judgements during the frontier dispute between *Mali V. Burkina* Faso (1986), *Botswana V. Namibia* (1999) in the Kasikili/Sedudu Island case and, more recently in the *Honduras V. Colombia* (2012), thus providing an established precedent and a norm, which will be crucial for determining ownership (immutable sovereignty) issues. The exact remarks of the court are reproduced here in some detail for providing the right context:

> "The Court recalls that, "of themselves, and by virtue solely of their existence, [maps] *cannot constitute a territorial title,*

that is, a document endowed by international law with intrinsic legal force for the purpose of establishing territorial rights"..... [M]oreover, according to the Court's constant jurisprudence, maps generally have a limited scope as evidence of sovereign title."[39]

Regime of Islands

What constitutes as 'an island' and how it is different from other similar maritime features like the Low Tide Elevation (LTE)[40] is defined under Article 121 of the UNCLOS.

(a) An island is a naturally formed area of land, surrounded by water, which is above water at high tide.

(b) Except as provided for in paragraph 3, the territorial sea, the contiguous zone, the exclusive economic zone and the continental shelf of an island are determined in accordance with the provisions of this Convention applicable to other land territory.

(c) Rocks which cannot sustain human habitation or economic life of their own shall have no exclusive economic zone or continental shelf.

While short and succinct in length, the regime of islands poses considerable difficulties for the expert and courts.[41] Some of the salient phrases that raises critical questions regarding the application and interpretation of this regime are:

(a) Naturally formed – how does one quantify and quantify the 'habitability improvement' and 'environmental protection' measures like the recent controversy over the land reclamation by China in the Spratlys. It is pertinent to mention that all other SCS claimants with control over features have also undertaken similar measures but not at the scale, magnitude and in such a short time frame like China.[42] Brief details of such reclamation in the SCS are appended at Table 1.

Table 1. South China Sea Land Reclamation

Country	Feature	Area reclaimed (sq. metres)
China	Fiery Cross Reef	2,740,000
	Johnson South Reef	109,000
	Cuarteron Reef	231,100
	Hughes Reef	76,000
	Gaven Reef	136,000
	Mischief Reef	5,580,000
	Eldad Reef	Recently started and ongoing
	Subi Reef	3,950,000
Taiwan	Ibu Ata Island	Ongoing
	West Reef	65,000
Vietnam	Sand Cay	21,000
Malaysia	Swallow Reef	2,42,800

[Source: CSIS, *Asia Maritime Transparency Initiative*, July 2015, Authors' Compilation]

(b) Land Area of the 'relevant' feature and qualifying criteria - There is no quantification of the area of the land and no clear demarcation as to whether the economic life and human habitation criteria are to be applied in an 'and/or' manner. It is appropriate to mention that an island with 1 sq. metre is capable of generating an EEZ of 1,25,714 sq km of EEZ at 200 NM, and a continental shelf measuring 3,85,000 sq km at 350 NM, subject to meeting the 'constraint and formula line' conditions. Further, the case law does not provide an established or uniform precedent in the treatment of such features as seen during 2009 while considering the Serpents Island in the Romania Vs. Ukraine case in the Black Sea, and St Martin's Island during both the Bay of Bengal judgements.[43] It is also germane to mention that while the IHO defines a 'small island as an islet' but no concrete criteria are mentioned to differentiate between the two.[44]

(c) High Tide – While the feature considered as an island may lie above the high tide, the UNCLOS specifies 'low water mark' for the delineation of normal baselines, which in effect is the foundation for delimiting the maritime entitlements further to the seaward of a coastal state.[45] Hence, an island with a small area at high water but with a large range of tide may actually expand substantially. A similar effect is also obtained while considering the islands along with the criteria of 'fringing reefs'. [46]

Conclusion

Oceans and seas, as the world's oldest global commons have been witness to an interplay of power, politics and law throughout the course of history. Recent empirical evidence also suggests that despite the current globalised context, which is quite different in its content and context, and despite the so-called 'demise of the traditional state', this axiom is not likely to change. In a similar vein, seas, legal regime and the recourse to law have been intimately related even in a relatively modern context. The fourth and the fifth cases adjudicated by the PCA, namely, the Status of Muscat Dhows (1904-05) and the Grisbadarna case involving the delimitation of a certain part of the maritime boundary between Norway and Sweden (1908-09) had dealt with the legal regime at sea. The first ever case on which the ICJ passed its judgement; the Corfu Channel Case (1949) was about the rights and responsibilities of the coastal states.

The SCS imbroglio is a relevant example of the multi-dimensional and more importantly, the international character of the maritime domain where many factors of international politics constitute the complex web of the dispute with varying degree of cooperation and competition. Therefore, the SCS dispute is neither new nor novel except that there exists a convoluted mix of old and the new, expansive, selective and narrow interpretative logics, with current and future contestations. It has been argued with justification as to whether the law has acted as the driver or helped in the resolution of the SCS dispute, given its complex multilateral nature.[47] Even UNCLOS has come under scrutiny for some inexactness, ambiguity and in certain cases, even voids that have proven problematic not only after 1982 but also before.[48] While these propositions do carry weight, a different argument where the public international law instruments like the UNCLOS are predicated on the twin pillars of 'predictability' and 'flexibility' particularly for the purposes of maritime delimitation. Such an arrangement ensures that while directive and prescriptive principles are available, ample space also exists for devising particular rules and freedom of interpretation so that the 'spirit' of the 'Constitution of the Oceans' is preserved.[49]

With force as an unviable option, diplomacy not yielding the desired results, the discussions in this paper make it obvious that the law also does not provide the 'single point of reference' for the SCS dispute resolution. In fact, it may even be appropriate to describe the SCS dispute as a "story within a story—so slippery at the edges that one wonders when and where it started and whether it will ever end".[50] The pathway to resolution of the SCS conundrum lies through a mixed normative framework of diplomacy and legalese, which goes beyond the *status quoist* standstill options being propagated today. The claimants will have make a choice regarding the conciliation and mediation methodology. Whether the claimants to this interesting dispute 'can and are' really interested in a grand 'give and take'[51] comprising a mix of bargaining, accommodation and avoiding mutually destructive behaviour remains the proverbial big question.

NOTES AND REFERENCES

1   Ben Blanchard, 'China says changing position on sea dispute would shame ancestors', *Reuters*, 27 June 2015, http://www.reuters.com/article/2015/06/27/us-southchinasea-china-idUSKBN0P708U20150627, accessed 29 June 2015.

2   Timo Kivimäki (Ed), *War or Peace in the South China Sea*, Copenhagen, Denmark: NIAS Press, 2002, p. 2.

3   For example, Integrated Headquarters of Ministry of Defence (Navy), *Indian Maritime Doctrine (INBR 8)*, New Delhi: 2009, pp. 65-68; and, Integrated Headquarters of Ministry of Defence (Navy), *Freedom to Use the Seas: India's Maritime Military Strategy*, New Delhi: 2007, pp. 59-60.

4   Ken Booth, *Law, Force and Diplomacy at Sea*. New York: Routledge, 2015, reprint edition.

5   Christian Le Mière, *Maritime Diplomacy in the 21st Century: Drivers and Challenges*. London: Routledge, 2014, pp. 30-47.

6   Hasjim Djalal, 'Indonesia and the South China Sea Initiative'. *Ocean Development and International Law*, vol. 32, no. 2, April-June 2001, p. 97-103; Ian Townsend-Gault, 'Preventive Diplomacy and Pro-activity in the South China Sea', *Contemporary Southeast Asia*; vol. 20, no. 2(August 1998), pp. 171-

189.

7   Stein Tønnesson, 'China and the South China Sea: A Peace Proposal', *Security Dialogue* (2000) 31(3), pp. 307–326.

8   Ralph Emmers, *Geopolitics and Maritime Territorial Disputes in East Asia*. London: Routledge, 2010, pp. 4, 19, 122.

9   The official text of the DoC is available at the Association of South East Nations (ASEAN) website, http://www.asean.org/asean/external-relations/china/item/declaration-on-the-conduct-of-parties-in-the-south-china-sea, accessed 29 June 2015.

10 International Hydrographic Office, *Limits of Oceans and Seas*, (Special Publication No 23), 3rd Edition, Monte Carlo, pp. 30-31.

11 United Nations Convention on the Law of the Sea (hereafter UNCLOS), Montego Bay, Jamaica, 10 December 1982, 1833 *U.N.T.S.* 397. Article 121 defines 'enclosed or semi-enclosed seas' as "For the purposes of this Convention, "enclosed or semi-enclosed sea" means a gulf, basin or sea *surrounded by two or more States and connected to another sea or the ocean by a narrow outlet or consisting entirely or primarily of the territorial seas and exclusive economic zones of two or more coastal States*". Emphasis added.

12 Ibid, Article 122.

13 Ramses Amer, "Claims and Conflict Situations" in *War or Peace in the South China Sea?*, Timo Kivimäki (Ed), Copenhagen, Denmark: NIAS Press, 2002, pp. 24-40. Copyrighted material, used with permission.

14 For example, see, Ministry of Foreign Affairs, Republic of China (Taiwan), 'Declaration of the Republic of China on the Outer Limits of Its Continental Shelf' 12 May 2009, http://www.mofa.gov.tw/EnMobile/News_Content.aspx?s=1DE6A7BA5C27CED3, accessed 30 June 2015.

15 Peter Dutton, 'China's Claims are Unambiguously Ambiguous', 16 June 2015, *CSIS - Asia Maritime Transparency Initiative (AMTI) Brief*, http://amti.csis.org/chinas-claims-are-unambiguously-ambiguous/, accessed 23 June 2015.

16 Ziguo Gao and Bing Bing Jia, "The Nine-Dash Line in the South China Sea: History, Status, and Implications", *The American Journal of International Law*, vol. 107, No. 95, 2013, p. 108; and, Zhiguo Gao, "The South China Sea: From Conflict to Cooperation?" *Ocean Development and International Law* (1994), Volume 25, Issue 3, pp. 345-359. In both articles, the author(s) have opined that the nine-dashed line delineates ownership of islands rather than a maritime boundary in the conventional sense.

17 See, People's Republic of China, 'Declaration on the Baselines of the Territorial Sea of the People's Republic of China of 15 May 1996', http://www.un.org/depts/los/LEGISLATIONANDTREATIES/PDFFILES/DEPOSIT/chn_mzn7_1996.pdf, accessed 30 June 2015.

18 Bill Hayton, *The South China Sea: The Struggle for Power in Asia,* New Haven: Yale University Press, 2014, electronic edition.

19 Ibid, pp. 55-56, pagination as per Adobe Digital Editions reader.

20 Ibid, pp. 75-80. The word 'Kalyaan' in Tagalog translates as the Freedomland.

21 Ibid, pp. 105-107.

22 For more details see, Kelly Vinopal, *Researching Public International Law,* Electronic Resource Guide, American Society of International Law, http://www.asil.org/sites/default/files/ERG_PUBLIC_INT.pdf, accessed 25 June 2015.

23 *The Matter of the Bay of Bengal Maritime Boundary Arbitration between the People's Republic of Bangladesh and the Republic of India, Permanent Court of Arbitration, The Hague, Award, 7 July 2014,* download link: http://www.pca-cpa.org/showfile.asp?fil_id=2705, [hereafter *Bangladesh V. India*], para 191.

24 UNCLOS Note 12, Article 15.

25 Ibid, Articles 59, 74 and 83.

26 Aaron Xavier Fellmeth, and Maurice Horwitz, *Guide to Latin in International Law,* (Oxford: Oxford University Press, 2009), p. 277. The authors define this term as "Nobody's land." Land or territory over which no state exercises sovereignty but that is open to claims of exclusive rights or peaceful occupation by any state with the intention of acquiring sovereignty over it. The continued viability of this concept has been brought into question by modern state practice, at least with respect to lands considered *terra communis* and lands occupied by indigenous peoples. E.g., "In the view of the Court…a determination that Western Sahara was a 'terra nullius' at the time of colonization by Spain would be possible only if it were established that at that time the territory belonged to no-one in the sense that it was then open to acquisition through the legal process of 'occupation.'" Advisory Opinion Concerning the Western Sahara, 1975 I.C.J. Rep. 3, p. 79. See also; Clive Parry, John P. Grant and J. Craig Barker, *Parry & Grant Encyclopaedic Dictionary of International Law,* (Oxford: Oxford University Press, 2009, p. 596. In this case, the term is explained as - "*terra nullius*" was a legal term employed in connection with "occupation" as one of the accepted legal methods of acquiring sovereignty over territory. "Occupation" being legally an original

means of peacefully acquiring sovereignty over territory otherwise than by cession or succession, it was a cardinal condition of a valid "occupation" that the territory should be *terra nullius* - a territory belonging to no-one—at the time of the act alleged to constitute the "occupation".: Western Sahara Case 1975 I.C.J. Rep. 6, p. 39.

27 Aaron Xavier Fellmeth, and Maurice Horwitz, *Guide to Latin in International Law,* supra Note 23, pp. 286-288; and, Clive Parry, John P. Grant and J. Craig Barker, *Parry & Grant Encyclopaedic Dictionary of International Law,* Note 23, pp. 655-656. *Uti possidetis* - An archaic maxim meaning that a state that has acquired possession of territory with intent to annex it has thereby established sovereignty over that territory. Derived from Roman private law, the doctrine was first applicable to Spanish colonies in the Americas, later extended to Brazil and later still to the African continent. The essence of the principle lies in its primary aim of securing respect for the territorial boundaries at the moment when independence is achieved ....[and] the doctrine is of great importance, for it may be relevant to the proper interpretation even of subsequent boundary treaties. Moreover, it aptly enshrines the vital principles of stability of state boundaries. The principle has an application beyond the purely colonial context and was considered in relation to the break-up of the former U.S.S.R. and the former Yugoslavia. *Uti possidetis juris* -["So that you may (rightly) possess]: - A modern principle according to which a change in sovereignty over a territory, especially due to independence following decolonization, does not *ipso facto* alter that territory's administrative boundaries as established by colonial authorities out of respect for succession to legal title by the new sovereign. *Uti possidetis de facto*- (So that you may possess in fact): A principle that was formerly invoked on occasion by postcolonial states to the effect that the boundaries of newly independent states upon decolonization should be defined by the limits of the territory actually administered by the colonial authorities and/or newly independent state rather than the administrative boundaries delimited by the colonizing states.

28 See Note Ibid for more details.

29 Robert Jennings, *The Acquisition of Territory in International Law,* Manchester, University Press 1963, pp. 6-7; and A Burghardt, 'The Bases of Territorial Claims', *Geographical Review,* Vol 63, No 2, 1973, p. 225. Article 2 of UN Charter states 'All members shall refrain in their international relations from the threat or use of force against the territorial integrity or political independence of any state. Nothing contained in the present Charter shall authorise the United Nations to intervene in matters which are essentially within the domestic jurisdiction of any state.'

30   Ibid Article 298, 1 (a) (i), emphasis added.

31   Bangladesh V. India, Note 23, para 279 and; *Dispute Concerning Delimitation of the Maritime Boundary Between Bangladesh and Myanmar in the Bay of Bengal (Bangladesh/Myanmar), International Tribunal for the Law of the Sea (ITLOS), Judgment, 14 March 2012*, available at http://www.itlos.org/fileadmin/itlos/documents/cases/case_no_16/C16_Judgment_14_03_2012_rev.pdf. [hereafter *Bangladesh V. Myanmar*], para 185.

32   The South China Sea Arbitration: A Chinese Perspective, 2013

33   For a largely sceptical perspective, see, Stefan Talmon, and Bing Bing Jia. *The South China Sea Arbitration: A Chinese Perspective.* Oxford: Hart Publishing, 2014. For a pro-Philippines stance see writings by Julain Ku at *Opinio Juris* Blog.

34   Ministry of Foreign Affairs of the People's Republic of China, 'Position Paper of the Government of the People's Republic of China on the Matter of Jurisdiction in the South China Sea Arbitration Initiated by the Republic of the Philippines', 7 December 2014, http://www.fmprc.gov.cn/mfa_eng/zxxx_662805/t1217147.shtml, accessed 29 June 2015.

35   Robert Beckman, 'The Philippines v. China Case and the South China Sea Disputes', presented at the Asia Society/LKY SPP Conference at New York, March 2013, http://cil.nus.edu.sg/wp/wp-content/uploads/2013/03/Beckman-Asia-Society-LKY-SPP-March-2013-draft-of-6-March.pdf   , accessed 30 June 2015.

36   Raghavendra Mishra, 'Complex Road Ahead for Legal Arbitration in the South China Sea', 29 June 2015, http://www.maritimeindia.org/View%20Profile/635711255553119893.pdf, accessed 30 June 2015.

37   Clive Ralph Symmons, *Historic Waters in Law of the Sea: A Modern Re-Appraisal*, (Leiden: Martinus Nijhoff, 2008), pp. 292, 299-300.

38   Ibid, pp. 286, 296-297.

39   *Territorial And Maritime Dispute (Nicaragua V. Colombia), International Court of Justice, Judgment of 19 November 2012*, http://www.icj-cij.org/docket/files/124/17164.pdf, accessed 12 June 2015.

40   See UNCLOS Article 13 for the regime and entitlement applicable for the LTEs.

41   For a detailed examination of the regime of islands as specified under UNCLOS, see, Clive Howard Schofield, 'The Trouble with Islands', Master of Law Thesis, The University of British Columbia, (Vancouver), August 2009.

42 Hayton, *The South China Sea,* supra Note 18, pp. 110-130.

43 *Maritime Delimitation in the Black Sea (Romania v. Ukraine), International Court of Justice at The Hague, Judgement of 3 February 2009,* available at http://www.icj-cij.org/docket/files/132/14987.pdf; and *Bangladesh V. Myanmar ,* Note 31, para 298 -319.

44 International Hydrographic Organization (IHO), *Hydrographic Dictionary,* Part I, Volume I, Special Publication No. 32, Fifth Edition, Monaco: 1994, p. 118.

45 UNCLOS Article 5.

46 Ibid, Article 6.

47 Stein Tønnesson, 'International Law in the South China Sea: Does it Drive or Help Resolve Conflict?', Paper for the Third International Workshop on the South China Sea, Hanoi, November 2011, http://nghiencuubiendong.vn/en/conferences-and-seminars-/the-third-international-workshop-on-south-china-sea/672-internaional-law-in-the-south-china-sea-does-it-drive-or-help-resolve-conflict-by-stein-tonnesson , accessed 25 June 2015.

48 Anastasia Strati, Maria Gavouneli, and Nikolaos Skourtos. *Unresolved Issues and New Challenges to the Law of the Sea: Time Before and Time After.* Leiden: Martinus Nijhoff Publishers, 2006.

49 Yoshifumi Tanaka, *Predictability and Flexibility in the Law of Maritime Delimitation.* Oxford: Hart, 2006. See also, 'A Constitution for the Oceans', Remarks by Tommy T.B. Koh, of Singapore, President of the Third United Nations Conference on the Law of the Sea, http://www.un.org/depts/los/convention_agreements/texts/koh_english.pdf, accessed 20 June 2015.

50 Michel-Rolph Trouillot. *Silencing the Past: Power and the Production of History.* Boston, Mass: Beacon Press, 1995, p. 16.

51 See, Chester A. Crocker, Fen Osler Hampson, and Pamela R. Aall. *Herding Cats: Multiparty Mediation in a Complex World.* Washington, D.C.: United States Institute of Peace Press, 1999; pp. 3-7, and; Thomas C. Schelling, *The Strategy of Conflict.* Cambridge: Harvard University Press, 1980. pp. 4-5.

7 REGIONAL ENVIRONMENTAL CHALLENGES

Kapil Narula

Introduction

An ecosystem is a group of interconnected elements comprising both living organisms and non-living components such as air, water and soil which interact together as a system. Humans live in a physical ecosystem and their survival depends on the health of the ecosystem. However, since the beginning of the industrial age, human society is damaging the planet's ecosystem by excessive resource extraction and untreated disposal of waste, giving scant regard to physical laws of nature, which has resulted in rapid degradation of the environment. The impacts are now beginning to be felt in the form of increasing natural disasters affecting a large number of people, including heavy loss of life and economic damages.

Oceans are the largest ecosystem on this planet as they provide 99 percent of the Earth's living space[1]. They are a major source of economic activity such as shipping, shipbuilding, ports, offshore oil and gas production, thereby contributing significantly to the world's GDP. Eight of the top ten largest cities in the world are located along the coast and around 44 per cent of the world's population lives within 150 km of the coastline[2]. Over three billion people depend on marine and coastal resources for their livelihoods and more than 90 percent of the world's trade is transported via the sea route. The social dimension is equally important as oceans contribute extensively to food security and fisheries are an important source of livelihood. Oceans also drive marine and coastal tourism, recreational and cultural activities and are essential to the society. The environmental facet of the oceans is extremely relevant as they are the primary regulator of the global climate and act as a natural heat buffer. Further, oceans are a large absorber of carbon dioxide and phytoplankton in the seas contribute to around 50 per cent of the world's oxygen. Oceans are also critical for the protection and continuation of biodiversity and have a large intrinsic value. Therefore, healthy oceans are essential for economic, social and environmental well-being of the planet.

Maritime environmental challenges

Environmental challenges can be local, regional or global in geographical scope. The impacts and the threats also increase in the same order and are the largest for global challenges. Coastal pollution may be classified as a local environmental problem as it is restricted to a limited area, around the coast; lowering of fish catch in a heavily harvested area in the high seas is a regional environmental challenge; while climate change and its impact on oceans can be classified as a global environmental challenge. Local challenges, by their smaller geographical scope, fall in the domain of local or national jurisdiction and can be handled in a relatively easier manner. On the other hand, regional challenges require larger resources, involve regional actors such as different countries and require multilateral forums for evolving actions to address these concerns. Global environmental challenges have the largest impact and need coordinated efforts by all countries. They require significantly large resources and global agreements which go beyond the short term interests of individual countries. This chapter restricts itself to regional and global maritime challenges.

Observations on Oceans

Climate change is the single most important environmental challenge for the world today. Following trends have been observed in the oceans:

Increase in Ocean Heat Content

Fig. 1 shows the changes in ocean heat content between 1955 and 2013[3]. Analyses by three different agencies viz. US National Oceanic and Atmospheric Administration (NOAA), Australia's Commonwealth Scientific and Industrial Research Organization (CSIRO), and the Japan Meteorological Agency's Meteorological Research Institute (MRI/JMA) show that the amount of heat stored in the ocean has increased substantially and is continuing to exhibit an increasing trend.

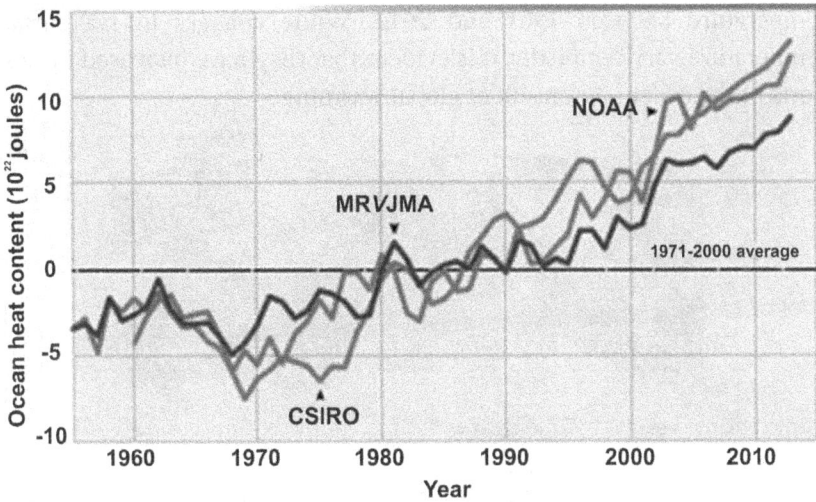

Fig 1. Change in ocean heat content[4]

Increase in Sea Surface Temperature

Fig. 2 shows the average global sea surface temperature[5] from 1880-2013. The global average temperature of 1971-2000 is taken as the reference baseline. Although there is some year-to-year variation, the trend of the overall increase of surface temperatures is clear especially during the past three decades.

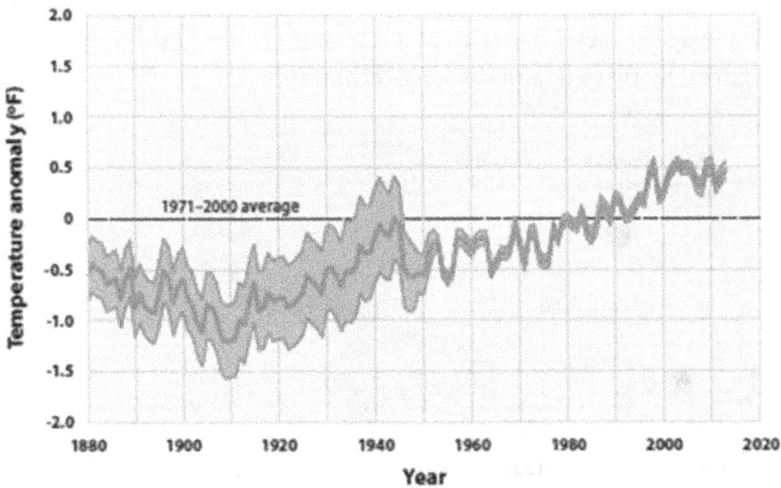

Fig 2. Average global sea surface temperature[6]

Fig. 3 shows the changes which have been observed in sea surface temperature between 1901 and 2012. While changes in sea surface temperature vary regionally, it is evident that they have increased in most parts of the oceans as a result of global warming.

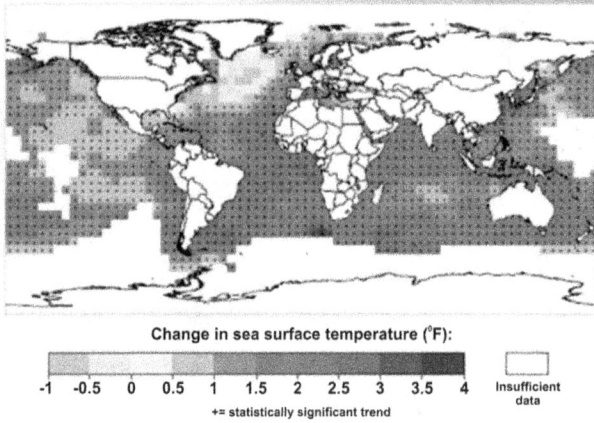

Change in sea surface temperature (°F):

-1 -0.5 0 0.5 1 1.5 2 2.5 3 3.5 4   Insufficient data
+= statistically significant trend

Fig. 3. Change in sea surface temperature between 1901 and 2012[7]

Increase in Sea Level

Fig. 4 shows the change in global average absolute sea level from 1880 to 2013[8]. The increase of sea level is observed to be at an average rate of 0.06 inches per year from 1880 to 2012. While changes in sea level relative to the land, vary from region to region, it has been observed that since 1993, average sea level has risen at a rate of 0.11 to 0.12 inches per year— approximately twice that of the long-term trend.

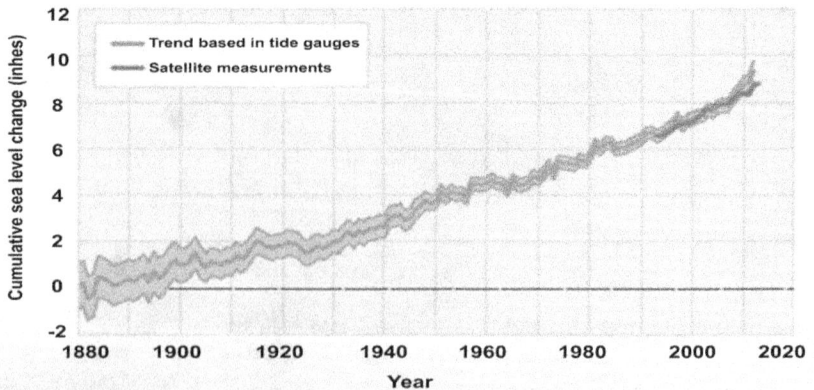

Fig 4. Change in global average sea level between 1880 and 2013[9]

Increase in Ocean Acidification

The ocean absorbs carbon dioxide from the atmosphere and has hence become more acidic over the past few centuries. Geological records suggest that oceanic acidification is the greatest in the last 300 million years. Measurements made over the last few decades have demonstrated that dissolved carbon dioxide levels in oceans have increased. As shown in fig 5[10], the partial pressure of dissolved CO_2 at ocean surface is steadily increasing (shown on left hand scale). This has led to an increase in acidification or a decrease in insitu pH (shown on right hand scale).

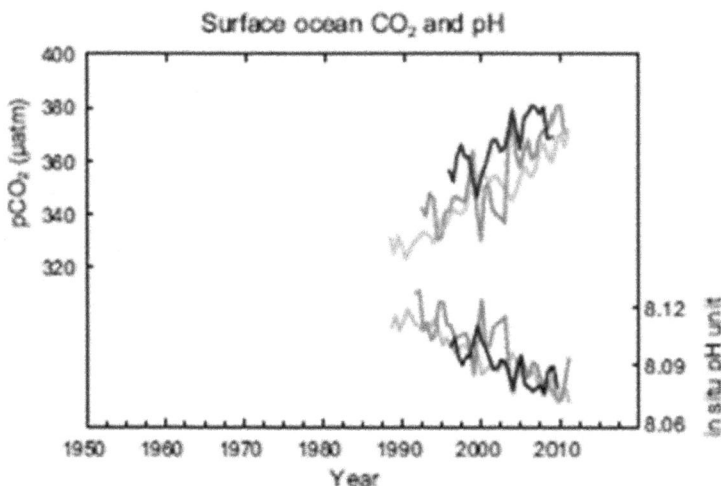

Fig 5. Change in ocean CO_2 and pH[11]

As is evident by various observations, climate change is altering the physical and chemical properties of the ocean, affecting the role of the oceans in the global climate system. This is having a significant impact which is observed in the form of degrading ocean sustainability.

Degrading ocean sustainability

Traditionally, countries have laid great importance on the right to exploit the resources in the Exclusive Economic Zone (EEZ)[12]. However, little attention is paid to the responsibility which a nation has in protecting the oceans. Hence, while overlapping EEZ claims amongst nations and maritime boundaries are regularly in the news, issues related to protection of the EEZ are seldom discussed in public debates.

Monitoring the health of the oceans and seas is a complex task. One of the initiatives in this direction is development of the Global Ocean Health Index (OHI)[13], a tool used to measure the state of world's oceans. It scientifically compares and combines various dimensions of ocean health – biological, physical, economic and social, to provide a snapshot of the health of the ocean. The OHI evaluates the condition of marine ecosystems under ten defined goals, which represent the key benefits that an ocean can deliver in the present as well as in the future. The specific goals along with a detailed explanation, relevance of the goals, average global scores and India's scores for 2014 are listed in Table 1.

Table 1. Goals which comprise OHI, global average and India's OHI scores

S. No.	Areas	Goals	Explanation	Relevance	Global Average Score	India's score
1	Food provision	Harvesting seafood sustainably	This goal measures the amount of seafood captured or raised in a sustainable way.	Seafood helps more than half the world's population meet their need for protein.	33	13
2	Artisanal fishing opportunities	Ensuring access to fishing for local communities	This goal measures whether people who need to fish on a small, local scale have the opportunity to do so.	Half the world's fish harvest is captured by artisanal fishing families.	95	87
3	Natural products	Harvesting non-food ocean resources sustainably	This goal measures how sustainably people harvest non-food products from the sea.	From seashells and sponges to aquarium fish, natural products contribute to local economies and international trade.	31	56
4	Carbon storage	Preserving habitats that absorb carbon	This goal measures the carbon stored in natural coastal ecosystems.	When preserved, carbon is stored in these ecosystems. When destroyed, carbon is emitted into the atmosphere.	74	73
5	Coastal protection	Preserving habitats that safeguard shores	This goal measures the condition and extent of habitats that protect the coasts against storm waves and flooding.	Storm protection by coastal habitats is worth billions of dollars each year.	69	52

S. No.	Areas	Goals	Explanation	Relevance	Global Average Score	India's score
6	Coastal livelihoods & economies	Sustaining jobs and thriving coastal economies	This goal measures how well the identity and livelihoods provided by marine-related sectors are sustained	People rely on the ocean to provide livelihoods and stable economies for coastal communities worldwide.	82	64
7	Tourism & recreation	Maintaining the attraction of coastal destinations	This goal measures the proportion of the total labor force engaged in the coastal tourism and travel sector, factoring in sustainability.	Coastal and marine tourism is a vital part of a country's economy.	39	47
8	Sense of place	Protecting iconic species and special places	This goal measures the condition of iconic species and percent of coastline protected to indicate some of ocean's intangible benefits.	Iconic species and protected places symbolize the cultural, spiritual and aesthetic benefits that people value for a region.	60	39
9	Clean waters	Minimizing pollution	This goal measures contamination by trash, nutrients, pathogens and chemicals.	Water pollution harms human health as well as the health of marine life and habitats.	78	61
10	Biodiversity	Supporting healthy marine ecosystems	This goal estimates how successfully the richness and variety of marine life is being maintained around the world.	People value the intrinsic value of a diverse array of species as well as their contributions to resilient ecosystem structure and function.	85	86

In order to undertake a relative comparison, the OHI calculates the scores (from 0-100) in attaining the ten goals and ranks the countries according to the average of these scores. A high score is given to a region when the oceans is used so that it is able to provide benefits like oxygen and food in the present, and it does not compromise the ocean's ability to deliver that benefit in the future. In 2012 and 2013, the OHI evaluated scores for 220 countries by monitoring areas under the EEZ; however, realizing that more than 60 per cent of the oceans are not covered in this assessment, the score for 2014 have also included 15 regions of the High Seas (also known as the Areas Beyond National Jurisdiction (ABNJ)) and one region of Antarctica and the Southern Ocean along with 220 EEZ regions. A global OHI is also calculated as a weighted mean[14] of all these 236 regions. A close look at the complete list[15] shows that the scores obtained by 236 regions lie within a range of 44[16]-95[17], and the global average OHI for the year 2014 is approximately 67.

The overall OHI score of major countries and high seas in the region are placed at table 2 (a) and (b) respectively.

Table 2 (a). OHI score and rank of countries and High Seas in the region

Areas	Rank	Score
Countries		
Australia	27	76
Bangladesh	71	69
Brunei Darussalam	114	65
Cambodia	195	55
China	150	62
India	181	58
A&N Islands	201	54
Indonesia	149	62
Japan	103	66
Korea North	220	49
Korea South	51	71

Areas	Rank	Score
Countries		
Malaysia	63	69
Maldives	159	61
Myanmar	196	55
New Zealand	19	78
Pakistan	222	49
Papua New Guinea	172	58
Philippines	171	59
Singapore	147	62
Sri Lanka	203	54
Taiwan	199	54
Thailand	76	68
Vietnam	177	58

Table 2 (b). OHI score and rank of High Seas in the region

Areas	Rank	Score
High Seas		
Indian Ocean Eastern	192	55
Indian Ocean Western	15	79
Pacific Eastern Central	100	67
Pacific Western Central	113	65
Pacific Northeast	85	68
Pacific Northwest	208	53
Pacific Southeast	26	76
Pacific Southwest	115	65
Average world score		**67**

The low scores in seas and oceans surrounding South and South East Asian countries are a cause of concern and it is desirable that there is an improvement in these scores.

Main drivers for ocean degradation:

The three main drivers of ocean degradation are discussed in this section.

Climate change

Oceans cover about 71 percent of the Earth's surface and play a major role in regulating the earth's climate. There is a two way relationship between oceans and the climate. On one hand, oceans influence the weather and climate, while changes in climate have been observed to fundamentally affect the oceans. Although the effect of climate change on oceans is slow, it is non-linear and it manifests itself over a longer time frame. These impacts have been highlighted in Section 2 and experts caution that a permanent damage might already have been done as many of these changes may be irreversible[18].

Overexploitation of oceans for resources

Increasing demand for resources and their dwindling stocks on land is leading to enhanced exploration of the oceans. Advances in technology have enabled deep sea fishing, offshore gas and oil production and sea bed mining for biological and mineral resources. Indiscriminate fishing practices have resulted in overfishing and increase in species caught incidentally, leading to loss of biodiversity. Food and Agriculture Organisation (FAO) estimates that about one third of fish stocks in the oceans are over-exploited, while other estimates predict that the proportion is more than half[19]. While the actual numbers may be different in different areas, it is clear that overfishing to meet the increased consumption[20] (17 kg per capita per year in 2012, which is more than five times of 1950 levels) of fish has led to decrease in fish stocks. This overexploitation of oceans for resources is one of the main drivers for degradation of the regenerative capacity of the oceans.

Weak governance structures and inadequate regimes

Weak governance structures and inadequate regime for governing the High Seas is a major factor driving the degradation of oceans. Part 12 of the UN Convention on the Law of the Seas III, 1982 (herein referred to as UNCLOS) spells out the obligations and rights for protection and preservation of the marine environment[21]. According to UNCLOS, countries have the right to set environmental protection laws, regulate and enforce legislation in their territorial waters. Beyond this lies the contagious zone, which extends a further 12 nautical miles into the sea, where the state can enforce laws in pollution control. Under Article 61[22], states have the jurisdiction to protect and preserve marine environment, to determine allowable catch of living resources, to ensure conservation and management and to maintain/ restore population for maximising sustainable yield in the EEZ. Under Article 62[23] which deals with utilization of the living resources, countries have prescriptive and enforcement rights in the EEZ and need to promote optimal utilization of living resources in the EEZ.

Beyond the 200 nautical mile limit lie the 'High Seas'[24], which is considered a part of the global commons. Under the current international law, fishing on the High Seas is open to all countries and the minerals in the seabed are agreed as "the common heritage of mankind". Seabed resources are regulated and controlled by International Seabed Authority (ISA) and shipping activity in the High Seas is regulated by the International Maritime Organization (IMO). Under the rules framed by the IMO, the authority to punish environmentally irresponsible conduct by ships on the High Seas falls on the flag state of each vessel. This has led to the practice of 'flag of convenience' for merchant shipping and is one of the major weaknesses in the environmental regulations. Currently the High Seas are governed by a "patchwork of international regional and sectoral agreements and treaties which overlap and create complicated jurisdictional issues in some of these areas"[25]. Some of the agreements on the 'High Seas' include treaties on protection of species such as whales (International Whaling Commission), regional fisheries agreements such as International Commission for the Conservation of Atlantic Tunas (ICCAT) and UN fish stock agreement coordinated by regional fisheries bodies and FAO, controlling pollution from shipping (by IMO), regulating seabed resources (by ISA) and regional seas convention for convention of biological diversity (by UNEP). As is evident, there are a large number of organizations who are currently responsible for monitoring and enforcement of agreements resulting in an overlapping jurisdiction and this is described as "co-ordinated catastrophe"[26], by the Global Ocean Commission.

Therefore, it is a matter of concern that High Seas which cover almost 50 per cent of the Earth's surface is one of the least protected areas on this planet as they lie in ABNJ and there is no legally binding treaty for the High Seas. Further, less than half a per cent of marine habitats are protected as compared to 11.5 per cent of global land area[27]. Although a few Marine Protected Areas (MPA's) and Particularly Sensitive Sea Area (PSSA) have been established, these are not completely out of limits for activities such as transit of ships, fishing or seabed mining. In essence, there is no comprehensive agreement and no specific organization has the complete authority to act on the High Seas. It is to be noted that with the exception of the international commission that governs the Southern Ocean surrounding the Antarctica region, there is currently no mechanism to establish fully protected marine reserves in the High Seas. The High Seas is therefore a good example of the 'tragedy of commons'[28], where all countries can freely use the resources but the region is unprotected and subject to abuse due to the common ownership.

Increasing threats, risk and vulnerabilities

The above drivers are systematically leading to increasing threats, which are further enhanced due to the existing vulnerability of the nation states. The risk to natural and human systems from these environmental threats is a function of hazards, exposure and vulnerability of a country and the community. Environmental degradation is likely to have a high impact on coastal ecosystems in the region and is projected to affect climate variability, increasing the frequency and severity of storm/tidal surges, tropical cyclones, hurricanes, etc. It is also expected to also cause coastal flooding, erosion, saltwater intrusion into fresh waterways, salinization of soils, and destruction of coastal infrastructure[29]. The impact on coral reefs, seagrass beds, mangroves and coastal wetlands is also expected to be high.

Direct impacts on marine environment

According to the International Programme on the State of the Ocean (IPSO)[30], the scientific evidence that marine ecosystems are being degraded as a result of human activities is overwhelming. The deadly trio of ocean warming, de-oxygenation[31] and acidification of the oceans is leading to de-oxygenation, eutrophication and acidification which are changing the chemical and biological composition of the oceans, thereby making it progressively unfit for aquatic life. The biological consequences of warming include range shifts[32] and species invasions. The report notes that with increasing warming, some physical systems or ecosystems may be at risk of abrupt and irreversible changes and there are early warning signs that both warm-water coral reef and Arctic ecosystems are already experiencing irreversible regime shifts. The report argues that the consequences of the changes in oceans are alarming and cautions that up to 60% of the present ocean biodiversity may be lost. This concern is also shared by the IPCC which cautions that these simultaneous drivers "can lead to interactive, complex, and amplified impacts for species and ecosystems"[33]. IPSO report also states that "the risks to the oceans and its ecosystems have been significantly underestimated and the extent of marine degradation is happening at a pace that is faster than was previously thought to be the case". It concludes that "the threats to the oceans are faster, bigger and closer, as are the consequences".

Unintended impacts of anthropogenic activities on marine environment

Marine pollution is caused from oil spills, domestic sewage, industrial effluents eutrophication (nutrient enrichment) from agricultural and mining runoffs, Persistent Organic Pollutants (POP's), leaching from heavy metals and overburden removal from mining, radioactive substances, and other forms of local pollution from leading to destruction of coastal and marine habitats. Unintended impacts of anthropogenic activities also include pollution at high seas from merchant vessels, floating garbage and plastic waste (e.g. Great Pacific Garbage Patch[34]). It is important to note that upto eighty per cent of all pollution in seas and oceans comes from land-based activities[35] and hence these anthropogenic activities need to be monitored and controlled for limiting the environmental impact on marine environment.

Increasing environmental disasters

The stresses and changes in the environment are now manifesting themselves in the form of natural disasters and its impacts on human security are clearly evident.

Fig. 6 (a). Number of disasters

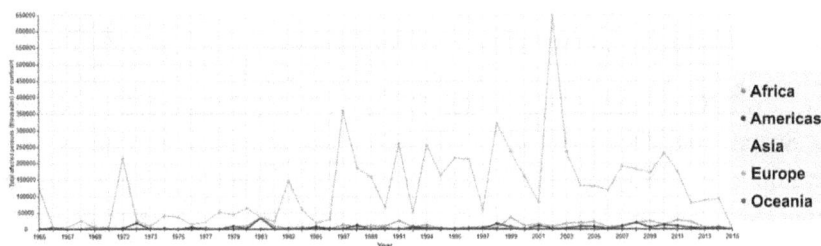

Fig. 6 (b). Total number of affected persons (in thousands)

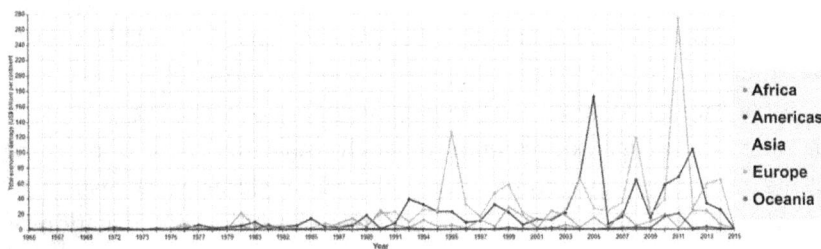

Fig. 6 (c). Total economic damages (billion US $)

Fig. 6 (a) – (c) show the number of disasters, the total number of affected persons and total estimated economic damages from natural disasters over the last 50 years in various continents. Three trends are clearly evident in Asia: the increasing number of disasters during the past 50 years, significantly higher number of affected people (including deaths) and the growing economic damages due to disasters. In the light of the above evidence, it can be concluded that degradation of the natural environment, including coastal and marine environment presents a 'clear and present danger' for the region.

Response strategies and efforts

As oceans play a pivotal role, the call for protection of the oceans has gained considerable momentum and various efforts have been taken in recent years for addressing these concerns. Some of the recent efforts and response strategies are highlighted in this section.

Sustainable Development Goal (SDG) for Oceans

The Rio+20 Conference, 2012 under the aegis of United Nations Conference on Sustainable Development (UNCSD) recommended a process[36] to develop a set of Sustainable Development Goals (SDGs) which would be applicable from 2015 and would extend until 2030. A separate goal 14, "Conserve and sustainably use the oceans, seas and marine resources for sustainable development", has been proposed for the Oceans and has seven targets and specifies three means for implementation. The sub-goals aim to significantly reduce marine pollution, sustainably manage and protect marine and coastal ecosystems, minimize and address the impacts of ocean acidification, effectively end overfishing and illegal, unreported and unregulated (IUU) fishing, implement management plans to restore fish stocks, prohibit certain forms of fisheries subsidies etc. Various means of implementation have also been specified including increasing scientific knowledge, developing research capacities and transfer of marine technology; providing access of small-scale artisanal fishers to marine resources and markets; and ensuring the full implementation of international law for the conservation and sustainable use of oceans and their resources[37].

Sustainable Development Solutions Network (SDSN)[38] is tasked to design an 'Indicators and a Monitoring Framework' for SDGs. Some of these indicators include percentage of fish stocks within safe biological limits, measures of nitrogen concentration in water, nutrients in coastal sea water, area affected by coral bleaching etc. Development of these indicators will help to quantify the targets while making the reporting of parameters uniform. A standalone goal on oceans is important to bring focus on the damage caused by unrestricted human activity at sea. The creation of a SDG goal for oceans would also help in assessing, measuring, monitoring and diagnosing the shortcoming and hurdles and will therefore go a long way in protecting the oceans.

Biodiversity Beyond National Jurisdiction (BBNJ)

Considering that over 60 per cent of the earth's surface which is covered by the high seas is inadequately protected, a UN *ad hoc* open-ended informal working group on 'Biodiversity Beyond National Jurisdiction' (BBNJ) was formed in 2006. It was mobilized to develop a comprehensive possible legal instrument for providing protection to marine life on the High Seas. This gained momentum in 2011, after the G77 and the EU agreed to an 'implementing agreement' under the UNCLOS. The working group[39] addressed five main issues in the proposal:

(a) Marine genetic resources[40], including the sharing of benefits

(b) Area-based management tools, including marine protected areas[41]

(c) Environmental Impact Assessments (EIA)[42]

(d) Building capacity to enable sustainable and equitable development

(e) The transfer of marine technology

The importance and the urgency for framing an agreement got a further boost in 2012, in the Rio +20 conference and September of 2015 was fixed as a deadline for taking a decision on the possibility of development of a new agreement. During the last two years, the UN Informal Working Group has deliberated the scope, parameters and feasibility of a new international instrument under the UNCLOS[43]. This process culminated in the submission of recommendations of the Working Group on the conservation and sustainable use of marine biological diversity in ABNJ in January, 2015. This development presents a major breakthrough, as after eight years of protracted negotiations, the importance of protection of High Seas has been formally recognised and the agenda of Ocean governance has graduated from 'managing the exploitation' of the oceans' resources to 'protection'. This offers a unique opportunity for the global community to integrate the activities of various organizations which govern and regulate fishing, mining and shipping.

These recommendations are likely to be adopted by the United Nations General Assembly by September, 2015[44] to move forward with negotiations for a legally binding agreement under the UNCLOS. It is expected that a preparatory committee[45] would start work in 2016 and submit a report to the General Assembly before the end of the 72nd session, to be held in September 2017. An inter-governmental conference under the auspices of UN will thereafter consider the recommendations of the committee and will evolve the final text of the legally binding instrument within the existing frameworks[46].

Conclusion

Oceans form an integrated component of the earth's ecosystem and the importance of marine environment cannot be over emphasized. Quantification of ocean health over the past few years has highlighted that oceans are witnessing degradation and there are anthropogenic factors which drive the downward trend. Existing governance regimes for protection of marine environment, especially on the High Seas are piecemeal and inadequate for this century. Recent developments such as a standalone SDG for the oceans and a possible agreement on BBNJ are progressive steps towards protecting the oceans but impetus and support is required for quicker implementation of these proposals. As oceans are essential for the well-being of the entire planet, international cooperation on ocean governance is critical for overcoming marine environmental challenges. However, the slow pace of evolving mechanisms to address these growing concerns suggests that the drivers will continue to further degrade marine ecosystems, and will pose a significant challenge to the marine environment, unless considerable action is taken immediately. It can be concluded that environmental challenges pose substantial risks to human and natural systems, which significantly increase the vulnerability of countries. Hence there is a strong case for international cooperation for overcoming regional and global environmental challenges in the maritime domain.

NOTES AND REFERENCES

1   Save the Sea. "Interesting Ocean Facts." http://savethesea.org/STS%20ocean_ facts.htm (accessed Nov 10, 2014).

2   UN Atlas of the Oceans. "Human Settlements on the Coast". http://www. oceansatlas.org/servlet/CDSServlet?status=ND0xODc3JjY9ZW4mMzM9Ki YzNz1rb3M~ (accessed Nov 20, 2014).

3   The baseline for reference is the average temperature for 1971-2000.

4   U.S. Environmental Protection Agency. 2014. Climate change indicators in the United States, 2014. Third edition. EPA 430-R-14-004. pp 47. (Abbreviated as CC Indicators in US, 2014) Available at www.epa.gov/climatechange/ indicators.

5   The shaded band shows the range of uncertainty.

6   CC Indicators in US, 2014, pp 48.

7   Ibid. pp 49.

8   The shaded band shows the likely range of values based on the number of measurements and the precision of the methods used.

9   CC Indicators in US, 2014, pp 50.

10 Three datasets are shown in different colours.

11 SPM-WG3, AR5, pp 10.

12 An Exclusive Economic Zone (EEZ) was adopted at the Third United Nations Conference on the Law of the Sea (1982) which gives the right of resource exploration and jurisdiction in the area to a specific country. The EEZ comprises an area which extends from the seaward boundaries of the constituent states (12 nautical miles, in most cases) to 200 nautical miles off the coast.

13 The OHI is a collaborative effort, of more than 65 experts on marine science, economics and sociology from leading universities, laboratories and government agencies and uses more than a hundred global databases for developing the index.

14 Ocean Health Index, "Methods - A framework for understanding." http:// www.oceanhealthindex.org/About/Methods (accessed Jan 03, 2015).

15 Ocean Health Index, "Index by Region." www.oceanhealthindex.org (accessed Jun 03, 2014).

16 Saint Vincent and the Grenadines located in the Caribbean and is ranked 236

17 Howland Island and Baker Island located in the Pacific Ocean and is ranked 1

18 Science Daily, "Experts call for urgent defence of Deep Ocean", May 15, 2014. http://www.sciencedaily.com/releases/2014/05/140515153947.htm (accessed Mar 03, 2015).

19 The Economist, "Governing the High Seas - In Deep Waters." http://www.economist.com/news/international/21596990-humans-are-damaging-high-seas-now-oceans-are-doing-harm-back-deep-water (accessed Feb 22, 2015).

20 BBC, Gaia Vince, "How the world's oceans could be running out of fish". Sep 21, 2012 http://www.bbc.com/future/story/20120920-are-we-running-out-of-fish (accessed Mar 03, 2015).

21 Article 192 defines the general obligation: States have the obligation to protect and preserve the marine environment. Article 193 deals with the sovereign right of States to exploit their natural resources: States have the sovereign right to exploit their natural resources pursuant to their environmental policies and in accordance with their duty to protect and preserve the marine environment. Article 194 lists the measures to prevent, reduce and control pollution of the marine environment: States shall take, individually or jointly as appropriate, all measures consistent with this convention that are necessary to prevent, reduce and control pollution of the marine environment from any source, using for this purpose the best practicable means at their disposal and in accordance with their capabilities, and they shall endeavour to harmonize their policies in this connection.

22 United Nations. "United Nations Convention on the Law of the Sea of 10 December 1982, Overview and full text- Part V, Exclusive Economic Zone". http://www.un.org/depts/los/convention_agreements/texts/unclos/part5.htm

23 Ibid

24 The 'High Seas' belong to all countries of the world, including land locked states and is not subject to national appropriation.

25 The Pew Charitable Trust. "Protecting Ocean Life on the High Seas-Fact Sheet". Article posted on November 24, 2014, http://www.pewtrusts.org/en/research-and-analysis/fact-sheets/2014/11/protecting-ocean-life-on-the-

high-seas (accessed Feb 10, 2015).

26　The Economist, "Governing the High Seas - In Deep Waters." http://www.economist.com/news/international/21596990-humans-are-damaging-high-seas-now-oceans-are-doing-harm-back-deep-water (accessed Feb 22, 2015).

27　Save the Sea. "Interesting Ocean Facts." http://savethesea.org/STS%20ocean_facts.htm (accessed Nov 10, 2014).

28　This is an economic theory propounded by ecologist Garrett Hardin in 1968. It states that individuals act independently according to their self-interest, but this behavior is contrary to the best interests of the whole group as it often leads to depleting some common resource such as air, land and water sources.

29　Nirmalie Pallewatta. Impacts of Climate Change on Coastal Ecosystems in the Indian Ocean Region In *Coastal Zones and Climate Change* edited by David Michel and Amit Pandya. The Henry L. Stimson Center, Washington, DC, 2010.

30　The State of the Ocean 2013: Perils, Prognoses and Proposals. Available at http://www.stateoftheocean.org/pdfs/IPSO-Papers-Combined-15.1.14.pdf

31　It is estimated that there could be a 1–7% decline of oxygen in the oceans by 2100.

32　It is estimated that marine fish are moving polewards by 30–130 km each decade, and up to 3.5 m deeper.

33　SPM-WG2, AR5, pp 17.

34　The Great Pacific Garbage Patch is a collection of marine debris in the North Pacific Ocean. It spans from the West Coast of North America to Japan. National Geograph ic," Great Pacific Garbage Patch". http://education.nationalgeographic.com/education/encyclopedia/great-pacific-garbage-patch/?ar_a=1 (accessed Feb 01, 2015).

35　Save the Sea. "Interesting Ocean Facts." http://savethesea.org/STS%20ocean_facts.htm (accessed Nov 10, 2014).

36　Outcome document of the United Nations Conference on Sustainable Development (Rio+20) "The future we want". United Nations General Assembly, Resolution A/RES/66/288* adopted on 27 July 2012. http://www.un.org/ga/search/view_doc.asp?symbol=A/RES/66/288&Lang=E (accessed Nov 14, 2014).

37 United Nations. "Open Working Group proposal for Sustainable Development Goals". https://sustainabledevelopment.un.org/content/documents/1579SDGs%20Proposal.pdf (accessed Sep 14, 2014).

38 Sustainable Development Solutions Network. "Indicators and a monitoring framework for Sustainable Development Goals". http://unsdsn.org/wp-content/uploads/2014/07/140724-Indicator-working-draft.pdf (accessed Sep 20, 2014).

39 United Nations General Assembly, "Recommendations of the Ad Hoc Open-Ended Informal Working Group to study issues relating to conservation an sustainable use of marine biological diversity beyomd areas of national jurisdiction and co-chairs summary of sessions" (June 2011), http://www.iilj.org/courses/documents/ailunit3adhocopenendedwgrecs.pdf. (accessed Nov 20, 2014).

40 The status of marine genetic resources beyond national jurisdiction, particularly aspects related to access and distribution of benefits from these resources. These resources are already being exploited with no regulatory constraints.

41 There are limited examples of high seas marine protected areas in the Antarctic Ocean and the North East Atlantic but these are only binding on member states of the relevant treaty regimes.

42 A system for prior EIA and cumulative impact assessment over time of activities that pose a threat to marine biodiversity. While there are some provisions for prior environmental impact assessment deep seabed mineral exploration, the majority of activities on the high seas are not subject to such assessments.

43 IUCN. "Progress towards a legally-binding treaty to safeguard the ocean beyond national boundaries - Background information". (accessed Feb 21, 2015). http://cmsdata.iucn.org/downloads/towards_a_high_seas_treaty__background_information.pdf

44 As per resolution A/69/L.43, adopted on 29 December 2014, the UN Summit on the Post-2015 Development Agenda will take place from 25-27 September 2015, in New York, US. The process of intergovernmental negotiations on the post-2015 development agenda, which will prepare for the UN Summit, began with a stocktaking session on 19-21 January. As adopted in decision A/69/L.44, the subsequent sessions will take place as follows: 17-20 February (Declaration); 23-27 March (SDGs and targets); 20-24 April (MOI and Global Partnership for Sustainable Development); 18-22 May (Follow up and review);

and 22-25 June, 20-24 July, and 27-31 July (intergovernmental negotiations on the outcome document).

45 The committee will include member states, specialized agencies and invited observers to deliberate and to make substantiative recommendations

46 "Outcome of the Ad Hoc Open-ended Informal Working Group to study issues relating to the conservation and sustainable use of marine biological diversity beyond national jurisdiction". Statement 23 Jan http://www.un.org/depts/los/biodiversityworkinggroup/documents/ahwg-9_report.pdf (accessed Feb 23, 2015).

8 CHINA IN THE INDIAN OCEAN: FOREIGN POLICY AND MARITIME POWER

Gurpreet S Khurana

> *"Where the enemy advances, we retreat. Where the enemy retreats, we pursue."*
>
> – Mao Zedong

Introduction

Over the past decade or so, China has been increasing its 'visibility' in the Indian Ocean Region (IOR). It ranges from China's politico-diplomatic and economic engagements with the regional countries to its naval operations in the Indian Ocean, for diplomatic, constabulary and benign missions. These have drawn sombre attention of the countries worldwide – particularly the major powers – that have stakes in the region. Each one is assessing the emerging developments, and extrapolating into the future, the 'rising' China's unprecedented forays beyond its immediate maritime periphery. However, since the assessments are being made by the various stakeholders under the lens of their respective national-strategic interests, these fall short of presenting the 'big-picture'. Besides, the developments relating to China's forays into the Indian Ocean are merely 'tail-end' manifestations of its foreign and economic policies, and its maritime-military strategy. A disparate examination of each one of these developments is inadequate for a comprehensive assessment. The aim of this chapter is to undertake a comprehensive assessment of China's diplomatic and maritime posturing in the region, beginning with an inquiry into China's broader objectives and imperatives, and its national strategy in the Indian Ocean; and to deduce the salient implications for India

CHINA IN THE INDIAN OCEAN: FOREIGN POLICY AND MARITIME POWER

Ascertaining China's intent and national strategy in general, and for the IOR in particular, is a major challenge. China's policy articulations are not always helpful; and at times, these may even be misleading. The major reasons are China's well-known lack of transparency and its propensity to project a benign image. The latter flows from the current geopolitical imperatives of a 'rising global power'; besides, as a China analyst indicates, due to China's unique culture tempered by past geopolitical experiences, which have led to its palpable 'humanitarian activism' in recent times.[1] Hence, for a more realistic assessment, the official documents and statements emanating from Beijing and the Chinese media may need to be 'read between the lines', and these examined in the context of the emerging developments and events.

National Objectives/ Imperatives

Economics

China's 'Blue Book' on Indian Ocean published by an authoritative Chinese think tank in June 2013 is considered to be closest to an official articulation.[2] It says that China's interests in the Indian Ocean are only economic and commercial. This articulation is well supported *inter alia* by the 'Maritime Silk Road' (MSR) initiative of President Xi Jinping,[3] and other port-building initiatives preceding it, such as in Hambantota (Sri Lanka) and Gwadar (Pakistan). Hence, 'economics' is clearly China's primary objective in the IOR and thus the main 'driver' for its national strategy for the region.

The above stems from China's insatiable quest to enhance its Comprehensive National Power (CNP), which is necessary for it to challenge the United States, and to regain the stature of the 'middle kingdom'. Economic power would play the key role in enhancing China's CNP. However, China's 'adverse geography' poses a major challenge. Most of China is continental, far away from the locus of economic activity – the sea. The case may be appreciated better by its 'coast versus land' ratio, which is amongst the least in the world. China is thus severely disadvantaged in this regard. A comparison of 'coast-land' ratios of select major/middle regional and global powers is tabulated in shown in Table 1.

Table 1. Coast-land Ratios of Select Major/ Middle Global and Regional Powers

Country	Length of Coast (km)	Land Area (sq. km)	Coast-Land Ratio
Japan	29,751	364,485	81.60
U.K.	12,429	241,930	51.40
Indonesia	54,716	1,811,569	30.02
South Korea	2,413	96,920	24.90
France	4,853	640,427	7.58
Germany	2,389	348,672	6.85
Australia	25,760	7,682,300	3.35
India	7,000	2,973,193	2.35
South Africa	2,798	1,214,470	2.30
Russia	37,653	16,377,742	2.30
United States	19,924	9,161,966	2.17
China	14,500	9,569,901	1.52
Brazil	7,491	8,459,417	0.89

[Source: The World Factbook]

From Kashghar, the capital of China's Xinjiang province, the distance to the Arabian Sea through Gwadar port in Pakistan is only 2,000 kilometres, but its distance to its nearest Chinese sea port Guangzhou is 4,000 kilometres. From southern part of Tibet, the Bangladeshi ports overlooking the Bay of Bengal are only 600 kilometres away, whereas the Chinese Pacific coast is more than 2,000 kilometres away.

Also, while nature has bestowed China with a fairly long coastline, its maritime frontier lies far away from the major sources of hydrocarbons and other natural resources of West Asia and Africa. Furthermore, China's shipping routes to these countries lie across maritime choke-points of the Indian Ocean, which are often insecure due to various reasons. For Chinese exports, the emerging markets of the IOR are also too distant. Notwithstanding, the dilation of China's economic dependence on Indian Ocean seems unavoidable. An analysis of the trends over the past decade indicates in a steady increase of the proportion of China's trade flows via the Indian Ocean vis-à-vis its total foreign trade. (Fig. 1).

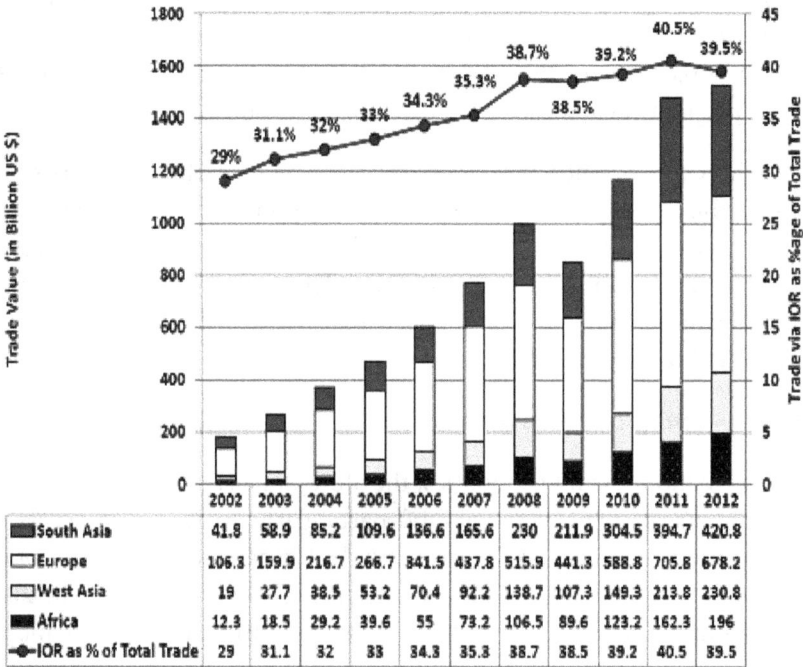

	2002	2003	2004	2005	2006	2007	2008	2009	2010	2011	2012
South Asia	41.8	58.9	85.2	109.6	136.6	165.6	230	211.9	304.5	394.7	420.8
Europe	106.3	159.9	216.7	266.7	341.5	437.8	515.9	441.3	588.8	705.8	678.2
West Asia	19	27.7	38.5	53.2	70.4	92.2	138.7	107.3	149.3	213.8	230.8
Africa	12.3	18.5	29.2	39.6	55	73.2	106.5	89.6	123.2	162.3	196
IOR as % of Total Trade	29	31.1	32	33	34.3	35.3	38.7	38.5	39.2	40.5	39.5

Fig. 1. Trends - China's trade through IOR (2002-12)
[Source: Author/ WTO]

China's phenomenal economic growth over the past three decades has led to widening of per capita GDP between its more prosperous east (that is closer to the coast) and its underdeveloped west, thereby making China's 'adverse geography' more palpable.

In recent years, China's geographical adversity is aggravated by the US rebalance strategy. In May 2014, Singapore's Foreign Minister K Shanmugam stated that "the Trans-Pacific Partnership (TPP) must form the centrepiece of the US economic rebalancing to the region."[4] The TPP is likely to be perceived by Beijing as its 'economic containment'.[5] To counter it, China must forge economic bonds beyond East and Southeast Asia in the IOR. This leads to China's policy of 'March West',[6] which is probably the 'prime mover' of the MSR initiative.

Geopolitics

China's geopolitical imperatives in the IOR are closely related to economics. Money does bring along geopolitical influence and leverages. A non-*status quo* power like China earnestly seeks such influence to meet its core national objectives of territorial consolidation, and also to reorient the global geopolitical and economic order in its favour.

The US 'rebalance' strategy poses a strong geopolitical adversity for China. The 'rebalance' strengthens the US support for China's opponents in the maritime-territorial disputes in the western Pacific, and serves to 'displace' Beijing in the western Pacific. China must, therefore, enhance its engagement with the IOR to offset these 'losses'. The MSR is the latest instrument of such engagement.

Military-Strategic Considerations

Besides economics and geopolitics, the aforesaid adversities also translate into China's strategic vulnerability, particularly in terms of access to hydrocarbon resources. In the past decade, China's total oil consumption has nearly doubled from 5.77 million barrels per day (mbpd) in 2003 to 10.76 mbpd in 2013.[7] Its total oil import in 2013 stood at 7.67 mbpd, which was 71.3 percent of its consumption.[8] An analysis of the region-wise proportion of its total oil imports is depicted in Fig. 2.

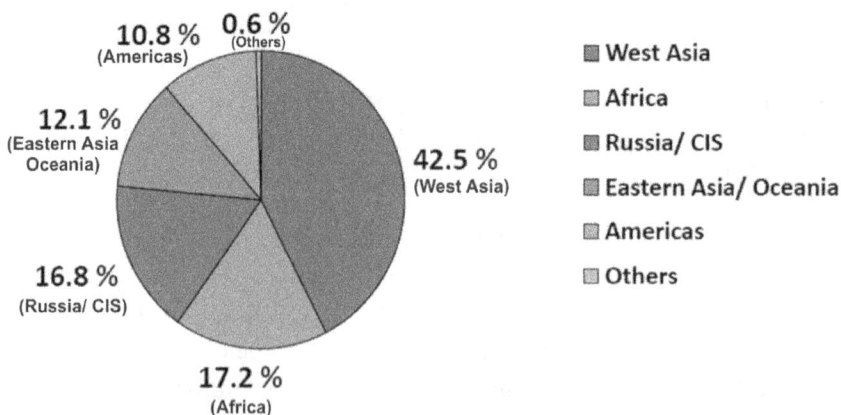

Fig. 2. Region-wise Proportion of China's Oil Imports (2013)

[Source: Author/ BP]

The analysis reveals that in 2013, nearly 60 percent of China's oil imports sourced from Africa and West Asia transited via the Indian Ocean. The African component of this oil (17.2 per cent) needs to transit one of the Southeast Asian straits, with some of it sourced from North Africa crosses through the strait of Bab-el-Mandeb as well. The West Asian component (42.5 per cent) needs to transit the Hormuz Strait in addition to the Southeast Asian straits. Therefore, notwithstanding that Chinese official strategy articulations are mute on the IOR or a maritime military strategy for the region, it is inconceivable that a professional navy that Beijing professes to nurture has not planned for adverse 'security' contingencies that could potentially impinge upon its increasing economic and other vital stakes in the region.

Furthermore, China's increased naval activities in the IOR seem to have revealed another element of China's 'latent' maritime-military strategy in the region. These activities are likely to be a response to the US 'rebalance' strategy. From the Chinese perspective, the US 'rebalance' seeks to contain China's military power by limiting its strategic depth in the western Pacific. In response, China's 'March West' policy could effectively serve as a means of 'strategic distraction' for the US.

National Strategy

Altering Geography

To meet its national objectives, China seeks to alter geography in its favour. Among the planned measures are the overland oil and gas pipeline projects (in Myanmar and Pakistan) and the multi-modal Bangladesh-China-India-Myanmar (BCIM) economic corridor, which is meant to provide maritime access to China's western regions to the Indian Ocean.

Enhancing Regional Stakes

As mentioned earlier, China is a major stakeholder in the IOR, particularly in terms of its critical economic and energy interests, leading to its strategic vulnerability. Its efforts to 'change geography' can contribute only marginally to mitigate this vulnerability. In such a scenario, China's enhancement of its stakes in the IOR seems paradoxical, but is based on sound reasoning. It would not only assist China's economic growth, but also enhance its profile as a stakeholder in IOR, thereby increasing its role in regional multilateralism and legitimizing its 'military presence' in the Indian Ocean.

Since mid-1990s, China has increased its trade with IOR substantially, and has encouraged Chinese business investments in Africa.[9] In 2011, China signed a 15-year contract with the International Seabed Authority (ISA) for seabed mineral exploration in the southwest Indian Ocean ridge.[10] Earlier in 2001, China had obtained similar exploration rights in the central Pacific Ocean. Notably, the area lies barely 500 nautical miles south of Hawaii that houses the US Pearl Harbour military base. In April 2014, China signed another 15-year contract with ISA for seabed exploration in the western Pacific.[11] The area lies only 600 nautical miles east of the US military hub of Guam. Similarly, China's increasing stakes in the IOR are likely to be driven by geopolitical and strategic factors.

Foreign Policy Posture

Over the years, China politico-diplomatic engagements with the IOR countries have been growing steadily, particularly since the launch of the MSR, with increased visits by the Chinese to the IOR countries at all levels, ranging from the apex leadership to government officials and scholars. Trends indicate that Beijing is likely to have developed a foreign policy approach that prioritizes its engagement with certain regional countries that are crucial to meet its national-strategic objectives in the IOR. India, Pakistan, Indonesia, Iran and Sri Lanka are among these countries, for various reasons as enumerated below.

(a) India is important to China, notwithstanding the rivalry. The latest empirical evidence is the MSR. It is necessary for Beijing to 'enrol' New Delhi into the MSR initiative,[12] not because its participation is critical for the success of MSR's economic agenda, but to wean it from Washington's tightening embrace. For the same reason, in April 2015, China proposed to India a joint seabed mining venture in the Indian Ocean. The US does not subscribe to the prevailing global understanding on seabed mining and this presents it an opportunity for China to build bridges.

(b) Indonesia is likely to play a pivotal role in the geopolitics of the Indo-Pacific region. Besides, the archipelagic Indonesia and its choke-points are important for China and its naval forces to have access to the Indian Ocean.

(c) Iran's value to China lies in its geopolitical divergence with the West.

(d) Pakistan is crucial to China both for its endeavours to 'change geography' and to maintain leverage against its regional rival – India.

(e) Sri Lanka is bestowed with a geo-strategic 'centrality' in the IOR vis-á-vis China's maritime energy 'lifelines'. Notably, the Chinese President Xi Jinping called Sri Lanka as the "hub" of MSR.[13]

Sales of Defence Hardware

China's rationale for defence hardware exports to the IOR goes beyond economics; it is meant to create security dependence and accrue military-strategic dividends. In May 2015, a Chinese Yuan-class submarine made a week-long port call at Karachi[14] and Pakistan is likely to purchase eight of these boats. Its week-long halt at Karachi – too long merely for replenishment – is likely to have been utilised to train Pakistani personnel to operate the submarine, and to evaluate its machinery and weapon systems, particularly the Sterling Air Independent Propulsion (AIP) system. Beijing also plays on the advantage of its ability to 'sweeten' the terms of its bids. For example, the contract for selling three submarines to Thailand was sealed by China since it offered not only a relatively low price, but also a soft loan, and technology transfer and training as part of the package.[15]

Security Multilateralism

Lately, China is seeking an increasing representation in IOR's two nascent multilateral security forums – the *Indian Ocean Rim Association* (IORA) and the *Indian Ocean Naval Symposium* (IONS) – even if as a 'tier-two' participant. It has secured for itself the status of a 'dialogue partner' in IORA and an 'observer' in IONS. To be a part of these forums, Beijing has leveraged the 'inclusive' approach of the regional countries. Such approach welcomes the role of major extra-regional powers, not only to tide over the region's capacity constraints to ensure maritime security, but is also necessary for maintaining a stable balance of power and geopolitical 'hedging'.

China's approach is driven by four imperatives: symbolism/ influence, policy shaping, access to information and seizing opportunities.[16] Being a part of IOR multilateralism is necessary for Beijing to buttress its claim to the status of a global power. As a 'tier-two' participant, China cannot 'make' policy, but it could 'shape' policy to make it more favourable for itself. It could do this by altering the behaviour of participants by putting forth its perceptions and views. It would also be aware of the multilateral transactions, including the official position of the ('tier-one') members, in order to lookout for opportunities to further its interests in the region.

Security multilateralism in the IOR is a recent phenomenon, which China sees as an opportunity to be seized. It implies that no other major power – the US included, notwithstanding its major contribution – possesses the advantage of a 'head-start' or primacy in regional security affairs. On the other hand, if Beijing plays its cards deftly in terms of engaging the regional countries, it could attain a degree of eminence, if not primacy. Notably, the US has not yet been admitted as an observer in IONS due to the objections raised by Iran. Has China played its cards through Iran?

Maritime-Military Strategy

China's maritime-military strategy in the Indian Ocean presents a puzzle. China's 2013 'Blue Book' on Indian Ocean says the China has no maritime strategy for the region. Yet, it adds that "if India or the US impede the attainment of its objectives (in the Indian Ocean), it would not desist from resorting to confrontation."

The MSR initiative is much about sea-trade, but avoids any reference to maritime security or safety of shipping and seafarers. Notably, in 2015, China conducted a combined counter-terrorism exercise with the Sri Lankan Army called "Silk Road Cooperation-2015".[17]

On 26 May 2015, China released its Defence White Paper of 2014 titled 'China's Military Strategy'. The document contains no explicit mention of the Indian Ocean; neither in terms of its security interests nor its strategy.[18] Yet it refers to the need to protect "strategic Sea Lines of Communication (SLOCs)". The emphasis on adjective "strategic" indicates that China's considers itself vulnerable to the interdiction of its energy SLOCs in the Indian Ocean.

The inference is that the aforesaid 'omissions' are well-considered and deliberate. It is highly unlikely that the PLA Navy has not catered for adverse contingencies to secure its interests in the IOR. The various facets of China's maritime-military strategy for the Indian Ocean are examined below.

(a) Fungible Missions and Capabilities

Since 2008, China has been actively articulating and demonstrating its emphasis on PLA Navy's 'Military Operations Other than War' (MOOTW) missions such as counter-piracy, search and rescue, and hospital ship deployments. Such missions are useful for presence and surveillance, familiarising the PLA Navy with these waters, and furthering diplomatic engagement with the regional countries.

China's pitch for MOOTW missions is not unusual, since all navies do this. However, as China's Defence White paper of 2014 indicates, PLA Navy's "presence in relevant sea areas (and) capacity for MOOTW missions" is likely to be dovetailed with preparing for 'wartime' operations. This needs to be understood in the context of deployment of China's Song-class submarine in the Indian Ocean in September 2014, which Beijing stated was on a counter-piracy mission. While its rationale was operationally unviable to naval analysts in India and elsewhere, this represents China's doctrinal thought. It also implies that China intends to develop multi-mission capabilities optimised equally for peace and war.

It is pertinent to mention that China already possesses advanced civilian technologies and research vessels for underwater mapping, which also have military applications. In December 2014, its deep-sea manned submersible 'Jiaolong' carried out its first dive in the seabed mining area allotted to China in southwest Indian Ocean.[19] Such capabilities may be used by China to collate hydrographic data for submarine operations in the Indian Ocean.

(b)　Sea Control and Power Projection

As implicit reference to its naval strategy for the Indian Ocean, China's 2104 Defence White Paper indicates a shift in PLA Navy's focus from "offshore waters defence" to "open seas protection" of China's "overseas interests".[20] Along with China's ongoing aircraft carrier programme, this indicates an evolving strategy for 'sea control'. However, this indicates China's doctrinal intent. Given that the operationalisation of China's aircraft carrier task force is still at a relatively nascent stage, it is unlikely that the PLA Navy will be able to establish carrier-based sea control westwards of the Malacca Straits, until at least a decade from now.

Furthermore, "open seas protection", in conjunction with emphasis on protection of "strategic SLOCs and overseas interests" (as stated in the White Paper) implies that as part of naval operations in military role,[21] the PLA Navy seeks to undertake wartime maritime power-projection missions in the Indian Ocean. Until the PLA Navy develops the capability for establishing carrier-based sea-control in the IOR, it could project limited military power projection in the region through its nuclear attack submarines (SSNs) as part of its 'deterrence-by-punishment' strategy. Notably, Chinese media reports indicate that the PLA Navy is likely to commission upgraded versions of its six existing Type 093 SSNs.[22] Armed with land-attack-cruise missiles, these SSNs are optimised for distant power-projection.

(c) Sustenance of Naval Forces

The 2014 Defence White Paper also hints at PLA Navy's strategy for the 'sustenance' of the forward-deployed naval platforms through "strategic prepositioning". Lately, China has been seeking hub-and-spoke logistics support agreements with the IOR states.[23] Whether called 'String of Pearls', or fructified through 'MSR', China is obtaining overseas access facilities in the Indian Ocean, but these are for peace-time use, and not 'military bases'. India too, has such arrangements with many countries, including some in the western Pacific.

However, something that has not been noted is China's likely intent to sustain its naval forces in the Indian Ocean through the concept of 'sea-basing'. China has begun developing 'Mobile Landing Platforms' (MLP) used by the U.S. expeditionary forces, and Logistic Support Ships with roll-on, roll-off (ro-ro) design and bow and stern ramps.[24] The numbers of PLA Navy's Type 903A advanced underway replenishment ships are also increasing.[25] With eight of these vessels added to the older fleet tankers, the PLA Navy is clearly being given the means to support distant missions in the IOR.

The PLA Navy's integral capability is being augmented by the state-owned commercial capacity. In June 2015, the Chinese government approved the new guidelines called *"Technical Standards for New Civilian Ships to Implement National Defense Requirements", which lay down not only the provisions* to requisition civilian ships for naval missions, but also *how* future construction of Chinese merchant vessels would need to adhere to naval specifications.[26] These commercial vessels are numerous. About 2,600 ships are capable of ocean transport,[27] which represents an element of asymmetry with any major navy operating in the Indian Ocean. The US Navy's 31 Maritime Prepositioning Ships (MPS) of its Military Sealift Command (MSC) pales in comparison.

It is also pertinent to mention China's increasing defence exports to the IOR countries. Over the medium to long term time-frame, this may supplement China's military 'sea-basing'. The Chinese-origin hardware being operated by IOR countries would accrue strong military-strategic dividends for China in terms of the sustenance of its naval forces in the Indian Ocean through overseas technical and ordnance support, virtually akin to overseas military bases.

Implications

China seems to be synergising all its instruments of national power effectively to meet its national-strategic objectives in the IOR. China and India being two major powers in Asia, the interplay between the former's emerging strategy of 'March West' and the latter's reinvigourated policy of 'Act East' bears significant ramifications for the two countries, and at the regional and global levels. New Delhi would continually assess the manifestation of China's strategy in the Indian Ocean since the related developments have immense policy relevance for India on many fronts ranging from foreign policy to national security strategy.

Since the 1962 China-India armed conflict, the nature of their bilateral relations is characterised by an adversarial potential. Assuming that the current 'trajectory' of the relationship does not deviate substantially in the foreseeable future, China's increased politico-military presence in the Indian Ocean is likely to enhance bilateral geopolitical and strategic discord further, mainly on three counts.

Geopolitical Adversity

First, the reinforcement of China's sphere of influence within India's geo-strategic frontiers could potentially induce the countries therein – particularly those in its immediate neighbourhood – to pit New Delhi against Beijing. This would severely constrain India's foreign policy options and would impinge on its relations with these neighbours. The ramifications would be particularly severe for Indo-Pak relations. Pakistan is likely to become more intransigent, particularly in context of its proxy-war strategy against India. Pakistan's hardened stance would hem India within the subcontinent, which may encourage China to further increase its politico-military assertiveness against India, at international forums and across the land border.

National Security

Second, given the persisting China-India territorial dispute and the lack of Beijing's demonstrated will to resolve it, China's established military presence in the IOR directly impinges on India's national security. It adds a maritime element to India's military strategy vis-a-vis China, and opens an additional seaward flank. Even if the PLA Navy is unable to establish carrier-based sea-control in the Indian Ocean in the next few decades, the strategic assets and infrastructure in India's littoral would be vulnerable to its SSN-based (albeit limited) power-projection capability. India would hence need to cater for the worse-case; a two-front (China-Pakistan) conflict scenario.

Even in peace-time, Indian naval forces are likely to face unintentional encounters at sea with the PLA Navy units, which is a complex proposition considering that the IOR security architecture has not yet evolved to establish a code of conduct to regulate such encounters. Also, India would need to contend with the Chinese merchant ships and marine research vessels deployed in the Indian Ocean – particularly in the maritime zones of India – to collate strategic and operational intelligence. Furthermore, while Chinese ballistic missile submarines (SSBNs) may not be deployed in the Indian Ocean, its non-strategic naval platforms are likely to encounter (and may even trail) India's SSBNs in its sea-based nuclear bastion in the Bay of Bengal.[28] In India's western operational theatre, China's technological assistance to Pakistan to base its tactical nuclear weapons at sea could also lead to further insecurities.[29]

Regional Stability

Third, the IOR is known be an inherently volatile on account of political instabilities and socio-economic disparities in many 'fragile states'. Until recently, the strategic interests of all major Indian Ocean powers were broadly congruent, which ensured regional stability (albeint with some temporary aberrations). Although China has lately demonstrated its will and capability to contribute to regional security and stability, it is a non-*status quo* and revisionist power, whose overarching national-strategic objectives are divergent with the 'mainstream'. As and when China's becomes an Indian Ocean power, any contingency involving instability in a regional country may lead to China and the established western powers to undertake a hasty politico-military intervention to pre-empt the rival. This would make IOR more unstable, thereby impinging on India's national interests that are closely enmeshed with the IOR.

Conclusion

Given the above, it may be necessary to bear a broader view in mind. Despite the rather serious irritants in India's relations with China, the latter's primary geopolitical and strategic contention is against the United States, and by extrapolation, against the US allies in Asia, not India. Hence, in terms of its larger national objectives, while the Indian armed forces may need to 'keep the powder dry', India need not embroil itself in the intensifying geopolitical tussle between China and the United States, which could well potentially spill over from the Western Pacific into the Indian Ocean. This would need to be factored in India's policymaking vis-a-vis China, by both its foreign policy and security establishments.

NOTES AND REFERENCES

1   The Chinese school of humanitarianism is all-encompassing in nature, which includes any activity ranging from economic to military endeavours. See Antara Ghoshal, 'China's Humanitarian Activism', *NMF Issue Brief*, 22 May 2015, at http://www.maritimeindia.org/CommentryView.aspx?NMFCID=8504

2   'Development Report in the Indian Ocean', *Chinese Academy of Social Sciences* (CASS), 6 Jun 13

3   'Speech by Chinese President Xi Jinping to Indonesian Parliament', *ASEAN-*

China Centre, 3 October 2013, at http://www.asean-china-center.org/english/2013-10/03/c_133062675.htm

4   'TPP must form centrepiece of US economic rebalancing: Shanmugam', *Channel News Asia*, 16 May 14, at http://www.channelnewsasia.com/news/business/international/tpp-must-form-centrepiece/1109400.html

5   Gurpreet S Khurana, ' Economic Dimension of US 'Rebalance': A 'Back Door' to China's Containment?', Experts View, *National Maritime Foundation*, New Delhi, 29 May 14, at https://www.academia.edu/7756661/Economic_Dimension_of_US_Rebalance_A_Back_Door_to_China_s_Containment

6   Yun Sun, 'March West: China's Response to the U.S. Rebalancing', *Brookings*, January 31, 2013, at http://www.brookings.edu/blogs/up-front/posts/2013/01/31-china-us-sun

7   BP Statistical Review of World Energy, 2014, p.9, at http://www.bp.com/content/dam/bp/pdf/Energy-economics/statistical-review-2014/BP-statistical-review-of-world-energy-2014-full-report.pdf

8   China's 'net' total oil import, however, amounted to 6.2 mbpd (57.6 percent of its total consumption). BP Statistical Review of World Energy, 2014, p. 18, at   http://www.bp.com/content/dam/bp/pdf/Energy-economics/statistical-review-2014/BP-statistical-review-of-world-energy-2014-full-report.pdf

9   Howard W. French, 'High Stakes in Africa: Can the U.S. Catch China?', *Bloomberg Business*, July 31, 2014, at http://www.bloomberg.com/bw/articles/2014-07-31/how-the-u-dot-s-dot-can-rival-china-in-africa

10 Amitav Ranjan, 'China set to mine central Indian Ocean, Delhi worried', *Indian Express*, July 31, 2011, at http://www.indianexpress.com/news/china-set-to-mine-central-indian-ocean-delhi-worried/824900/0

11 'China Ocean Mineral Resources Research And Development Association(COMRA) and ISA Sign Exploration Contract', *International Seabed Authority* (ISA) website, at https://www.isa.org.jm/news/china-ocean-mineral-resources-research-and-development-associationcomra-and-isa-sign

12 In March 2014, the Chinese Ambassador to New Delhi proposed to merge MSR with the India's projects 'Mausam' and 'Spice Route'. "China seeks India's 'Spice Route' link with its 'Silk Road'", *Times of India* (New Delhi), March 6, 2015, p.13

13 "China hopeful of Colombo Project as Sri Lanka backs Silk Road", *India Today*, March 26, 2015, at http://indiatoday.intoday.in/story/president-maithripala-sirisena-president-xi-jinping-maritime-silk-road-initiative/1/425874.html (Accessed March 28, 2015)

14 'Exclusive: Chinese submarine lurked past Indian waters, docked in Karachi?', *India Today*, June 27, 2015, at http://indiatoday.intoday.in/story/chinese-submarine-indian-navy-karachi-indian-ocean-pm-modi/1/447505.html

15 Prashanth Parameswaran, 'How Did China Just Win Thailand's New Submarine Bid?', *The Diplomat*, June 26, 2015, at http://thediplomat. com/2015/06/how-did-china-just-win-thailands-new-submarine-bid/ Also see, 'Beijing offers sweetener for Thailand to buy Chinese subs', *Want China Times*, April 08, 2015, at http://www.wantchinatimes.com/news-subclass-cnt. aspx?id=20150408000108&cid=1101 The deal was later suspended, reportedly owing to its adverse effect on Thailand's relations with the United States. Michelle FlorCruz, 'Thailand-China Submarine Deal Suspended Following Concern Over Jeopardizing Ties With Washington', *International Business Times*, July 19, 2015, at http://www.ibtimes.com/thailand-china-submarine-deal-suspended-following-concern-over-jeopardizing-ties-2012291

16 Based on the analytical framework propounded by Nick Bisley and Brendan Taylor, 'China's Engagement with Regional Security Multilateralism: The Case Study of the Shangri-La Dialogue', *Contemporary Southeast Asia* (ISEAS), Vol.37(1), 2015, pp.29-48.

17 'China, Sri Lanka hold "Silk Road Cooperation-2015" joint drill, *PRC Ministry of National Defence*, March 31, 2015, at http://eng.mod.gov.cn/ DefenseNews/2015-03/31/content_4577899.htm and 'SriLanka : China military exercise concluded', *LankaSri News*, July 14, 2015, at http://www. lankasrinews.com/view.php?224OlX2acV5YK04ecyMCd02eAmB2dd2fBm A3030gAm2e4cY5L3ca4lO4b3

18 'China's Military Strategy', *The State Council Information Office of the People's Republic of China*, May 2015, Beijing, at http://eng.mod.gov.cn/Database/ WhitePapers/

19 'China deploys submersible in Indian Ocean to explore metals', *Economic Times*, December 23, 2014, at http://articles.economictimes.indiatimes. com/2014-12-23/news/57350099_1_international-seabed-authority-polymetallic-indian-ocean

20 'China's Military Strategy', The State Council Information Office of the People's Republic of China, May 2015, Beijing, at http://eng.mod.gov.cn/Database/ WhitePapers/ It is pertinent to note that on 01 July 2015, China passed a new domestic law that confers upon the PLA Navy the duty to defend these "overseas interests", through military action if necessary. Minnie Chan, 'PLA tasked with protecting 'overseas interests' under new China security law', *South China Morning Post*, July 02, 2015, at http://www.scmp.com/news/ china/diplomacy-defence/article/1831564/chinas-national-security-law-gives-pla-mission-protect

21 Naval operations in military role is referred to in China's 2014 Defence White Paper as "Preparation for Military Struggle" (PMS).

22 Zhao Lee, 'Navy to get 3 new nuclear subs', *China Daily*, April 03, 2015, at http://usa.chinadaily.com.cn/china/2015-04/03/content_19989106.htm

23 'Strengthening Exchange, Deepening Cooperation and Building the Safe and Harmonious Indian Ocean', Presentation by Rear Admiral Li Yunqing, Vice Chief of Logistic Department of PLA Navy, at 3rd IONS Conference at Cape Town, South Africa, April 2012, at http://ions.gov.in/sites/default/files/Presentation%20by%20China.pdf (accessed 12 Jul 14)

24 The first MLP was delivered to the PLA Navy in end-June 2015. Andrew Tate, 'China building mobile landing platform, new ro-ro PLA support ship', *Jane's Navy International*, June 3, 2015, at http://www.janes.com/article/51984/china-building-mobile-landing-platform-new-ro-ro-pla-support-ship

25 In June 2015, China launched its fifth Type 903A replenishment ship. 'PLA's 5th 'Super Nanny' Type 903A replenishment ship launched' *Want China Times*, June 10, 2015, at http://www.wantchinatimes.com/news-subclass-cnt.aspx?cid=1101&MainCatID=11&id=20150610000066

26 Zhao Lei, 'New rules mean ships can be used by military', *China Daily*, June 18, 2015, at http://usa.chinadaily.com.cn/epaper/2015-06/18/content_21042373.htm

27 According to 2014 statistics from China's Ministry of Transportation. Zhao Lei, 'New rules mean ships can be used by military', *China Daily*, June 18, 2015, at http://usa.chinadaily.com.cn/epaper/2015-06/18/content_21042373.htm

28 Iskander Rehman. *Murky Waters: Naval Nuclear Dynamics in the Indian Ocean* (2015: Carnegie Endowment for International Peace, Washington D.C.), pp.42-47.

29 Ibid.

9 INDIA AND MULTILATERAL SECURITY ARCHITECTURE

Anurag G Thapliyal

Introduction

The topic 'India and Multilateral Security Architecture' contains two keywords 'Multilateral' and 'Security' and how India sees itself in this arrangement. A historical perspective, especially with respect to the interplay of events, past and present would also be discussed to understand the security dynamics in the region.

The region has mostly had grouping of nations primarily based on their geographical locations. So while we have the SAARC (South Asian Association for Regional Cooperation) in the West with membership of eight South Asian countries (Afghanistan, Bangladesh, Bhutan, India, Maldives, Nepal, Pakistan, Sri Lanka), there is ASEAN (Association of South East Asian Nations) in the East with its ten members (Malaysia, Thailand, Philippines, Indonesia, Brunei, Singapore, Vietnam, Cambodia, Myanmar, Laos) located around the China Seas, with larger grouping such as IORA (Indian Ocean Rim Association) with 20 nations as members (Australia, Comoros, Indonesia, Iran, Madagascar, Mauritius, South Africa, Oman, Tanzania, UAE, Bangladesh, India, Seychelles, Kenya, Malaysia, Mozambique, Singapore, Sri Lanka, Thailand and Yemen), six Dialogue Partners and two Observers and the ARF (ASEAN Regional Forum) with 27 members (Australia, Bangladesh, Brunei Darussalam, Cambodia, Canada, China, Democratic People's Republic of Korea, European Union, India, Indonesia, Japan, Lao PDR, Malaysia, Mongolia, Myanmar, New Zealand, Pakistan, Papua New Guinea, Philippines, Republic of Korea, Russia, Singapore, Sri Lanka, Thailand, Timor-Leste, United States and Vietnam). A host of other smaller multilateral groupings in the form of 'Councils' and 'Forum' also exist in the region and serve specific purposes or denote the level of participation as evident from their very names.

The end of the Second World War created a bipolar world and brought independence to a large number of Asian nations. As expected both the USA and Soviet Union soon thereafter left no stone unturned to establish their respective zones of influence and proxies the world over. The cold war kept the region fragmented and saw the emergence of various initiatives by countries in the region so as to have a collective voice in managing the affairs that directly impacted their growth and well-being. The region also witnessed creation of alliances and groupings which indicated their allegiance to a specific bloc. Efforts, however, over the past six decades have continued to establish cooperative and collaborative mechanisms to address the economic development of the region while addressing the myriad of security and stability issues.

South East Asia

For ease of understanding the region can be seen to comprise South Asia which includes countries in the IOR and SE Asia including countries to the East of Philippines. While South Asia has been a 'hot spot' for long due to the territorial disputes between two nuclear capable neighbours, the ongoing developments in the SE Asia region, especially the rapid rise of China, both economic and military, as also its growing assertiveness with regards to its territorial claims in the South China Sea and East China Sea have been a matter of concern. The linkages of this sub-region with the major powers within and outside the region are crucial in the overall security dynamics of the region. Further, the American 'Rebalance to Asia' amply highlights the nature of competition that presents itself in the region and would impact the overall security and development of the nations within the region and their trading partners.

The South East region has not been integrated with common rules or customs. The landscape has been notable for its small - scale, sub regional identities. Due to limited interaction amongst its groups and areas, the individual characteristics were preserved. The traditional rulers of South East Asian nations, even when faced with external threats posed by the European colonial powers in the 20th century, met the challenges individually and not collectively. The colonial era established and strengthened important 'cultural and historical' ties amongst the nations of the region. The maritime character of the region coupled with the baggage of the past and consequent historical claims over areas and territories remain a source of friction. The reasons for various maritime disputes and potential flashpoints due to regional insecurities have also been discussed.

Security Collaboration

Nonetheless over the past fifty years, there have been substantial efforts by the nations in the region to create multilateral structures and institutions that would bring all the key stakeholders together and through dialogue, discussions and consensus resolve contentious issues as also find solutions to the common issues that impact the security and the development of the nation's collectively and individually.

Security is now defined in a more comprehensive manner than before. These new and holistic conceptions of security have led to new forms of security collaboration between nations. New concepts like environment security, food security, energy security, water security, information security and security of navigation have emerged in strategic discourse. Natural disasters and mass epidemics are now being looked upon as security threats, as they can often disrupt our lives and societies much more dramatically than military threats. Security collaboration between nations in times of tsunamis and earthquakes in the form of Humanitarian Assistance and Disaster Relief (HADR) has been witnessed in recent times. Major industrial accidents or oil spills in the ocean can be hugely disruptive, and would require concerted response from all nations in the neighbourhood. So, while earlier, countries used to secure themselves from traditional military threats by adopting forms of neutrality or by aligning themselves in mutual defence arrangements with other countries, in our age, a new form of security cooperation based on regular, structured dialogue between different nations has been evolved rather than formal alliances.

Multilateral Arrangements

Multilateral arrangements represent the collective will of the member nations and binds them together in friendship and cooperation and expects, that through joint efforts and adjustments, their governments will secure for their people and for posterity, everlasting peace, freedom and prosperity. The vision of multilateralism also looks at deriving synergy from the combined natural resources, population, technical means and other strengths that could be collectively brought to bear against any negative influence from outside the region. Differences in outlook amongst the member countries are overcome through understanding, goodwill, faith and realism. Success of any multilateral organisation requires the member states to align national thinking with regional thinking and requires making adjustments to many existing practices, even when considered outside the comfort zone.

A multilateral organisation should be responsive to the needs of its times and should be appropriately equipped to assure its members that such arrangement would provide an environment and conditions of stability, efficient progress of development work and timely completion of the task. It also demands a give and take, and a spirit of equality and partnership. In simple words it paints a picture of a 'win - win situation' where every stakeholder has something to take home to show the efficacy and usefulness of the alliance.

The history of the origin of the various multilateral institutions created in the region is briefly presented ahead.

South East Asia Region

In September 1954, under the US flag the first international organization SEATO or the South East Asia Treaty Organization with eight members (USA, France, Great Britain, New Zealand, Australia, Philippines, Thailand, and Pakistan) was established. The objective was to have defensive collaboration amongst the newly independent nations of the region as a safeguard against the spread of communism. It, however, failed due to lack of agreement and unanimity to pursue a policy or express a stance on an issue, such as Vietnam's invasion of Cambodia. SEATO was formally disbanded in 1977.

The Association of Southeast Asia or ASA was established in July 1961 and comprised then Malaya, Philippines and Thailand. Originally, the Philippines and Malaya had sought an organization similar to the European Economic Community (EEC), but they assented to Thailand's request of an association with a loose structure and obligations. However, outsiders, especially Indonesia, a large country, saw ASA as politically aligned to the West and as a supporter of non-alignment, did not wish to join any organization that was either too strong in its political stance or which Indonesia had no role in creating.

Around the same time Indonesia initiated a new regional grouping known as MAPHILINDO - a combined name of Malaya, Philippines and Indonesia. This was formally established on July 1963 in Manila. The grouping was an attempt to draw together the Malay people but MAPHILINDO could not work well due to different interests of the participating nations. Philippines and Indonesia were put off at the thought of formation of a Federation of Malaysia since each of them had territorial disagreements with Malaya. Consequently, MAPHILINDO was shelved.

Several other organizations such as the Asian Pacific Council (ASPAC), or the Southeast Asian Association for Regional Cooperation (SEAARC) were created, which all ended with not much success. The lukewarm response to membership of such multilateral organizations due to scepticism of many countries over the allegiance of such organizations necessitated one to presume that the era called for a new, effective organization.

ASEAN, or the Association of South East Asian Nations comprising Indonesia, Malaysia, Thailand, Philippines and Singapore came into being on 08 Aug 1967, primarily as an upshot of the American containment strategy. The road to creation of ASEAN was not easy especially since certain disputes were already simmering between Philippines and Indonesia and Malaysia. Also, this was the time when the Vietnam conflict was raging and the US forces were firmly entrenched in Indochina. However, the founding members exercised flexibility and went beyond the ASA membership by including Singapore and used foresight by keeping the association membership open to all SE Asian nations who agreed to the objectives and principles of the Association. The ASEAN Declaration, also known as the Bangkok Declaration, spelt out the aims and purposes of the Association as cooperation in the economic, social, cultural, technical, educational and other (scientific, administrative etc) fields and in the promotion of peace and stability through abiding respect for justice and the rule of law and adherence to principles of the UN charter. Thus, ostensibly, ASEAN was not a security organisation, but the anti-communist grouping in a volatile region made it deal with security issues too.

ASEAN survived due to the charged situation in the region at that time and the threat of communism spreading from Indochina. Four out of the five founding nations of ASEAN had security linkages with the US. US military was already present in Philippines, US had a security treaty with

Thailand and as members of FPDA, Malaysia and Singapore were covered under the agreement. ASEAN thus, provided regional balance even after the defeat and exit of the United States from Indochina. Later, Vietnam emerged as the virtual leader of Indochina and the Chinese attack on her, altered the strategic equation resulting in Vietnam cosying up to the Soviet Union, and also offering base facilities to the Soviet naval fleet. The Chinese ultimately benefitted from this situation and got leverage to get involved in the security affairs of SE Asia directly with the endorsement of ASEAN.

The number of member states from the initial five went up to 10 with Brunei Darussalam joining in 1984, Viet Nam in 1995, Lao PDR and Myanmar in 1997 and Cambodia in 1999. Even today ASEAN is considered a very successful inter-governmental organisation in the developing world and is continually evolving.

Over the years ASEAN has entered into several formal and legally binding instruments, such as the 1976 Treaty of Amity and Cooperation (TAC) in SE Asia and the 1995 Treaty on the SE Asia Nuclear Weapon Free Zone. In 1997, ASEAN adopted VISION 2020 which an outward was looking shared vision aiming at peace, stability and prosperity in the region bonded together in partnership. In 2003, the leaders agreed to establish the ASEAN community and through the Cebu Declaration in 2007 fixed the deadline of end 2015. The three pillared community was to comprise of the 'political security community', the 'economic community' and the 'socio-cultural community'. The ASEAN charter was also brought into force on 15 Dec 2008 and is a legally binding document amongst the member states and serves as a foundation towards achieving the ASEAN Community by providing the legal status and institutional framework to the security dimension of ASEAN.

Established in 1994, the ASEAN Regional Forum (ARF) is a key forum for security dialogue in Asia, complementing the various bilateral alliances and dialogues. Represented at the Foreign Ministers level annually it provides a setting in which members can discuss current regional security issues and develop cooperative measures to enhance peace and security in the region. The ARF is characterised by consensus decision making and minimal institutionalisation. The concept paper set out a three-stage, evolutionary approach to the ARF's development, moving from confidence-building to preventive diplomacy and, in the long term, towards a conflict resolution capability. It draws together 27 members including 10 ASEAN nations, 10 dialogue partners, and seven observers.

At the apex level yet another important multilateral grouping of 18 nations is the East Asia Summit (EAS) which is a regional leaders' forum for strategic dialogue and cooperation on key challenges facing the East Asian region. The inaugural EAS was held on 14 December 2005. The EAS discusses regional and global political and security developments, including maritime security and suggestions to enhance practical cooperation to address a range of traditional and non-traditional security issues, and to deepen regional trade and economic integration. Besides the 10 ASEAN nations eight others (Australia, New Zealand, Japan, Republic of Korea, China, India, the United States and Russia) are members. The 18 EAS member countries represent collectively 55 per cent of the world's population and accounted for around 56 per cent of global GDP (in PPP terms for 2012).

The ASEAN Defence Ministers Meeting or ADMM was established in 2006 as per ASEAN Security Community (ASC) Plan of Action and the first meeting was held in May 2006. This is the highest defence consultative and cooperative mechanism in ASEAN and aims to provide mutual trust and confidence through greater understanding of defence and security challenges as well as enhancement of transparency and openness. It also encourages dialogue and cooperation in the field of security and defence with the ASEAN members as also between ASEAN and its Dialogue Partners. The ADMM was also entrusted with the responsibility of establishing the ASEAN Security Community, a key pillar in the community.

The transnational security challenges faced by the region resulted in establishment of ADMM PLUS in 2010. Since its formation the ADMM has been open to an outward looking philosophy. The PLUS countries were full-fledged Dialogue partners of ASEAN and were already having interactions with the ASEAN defence establishments. ADMM PLUS provides a platform to discuss, deliberate and suggest measures to strengthen security and defence cooperation for peace, stability and development of the region. During the inaugural ADMM PLUS in Vietnam in Oct 2010 five areas of cooperation were agreed upon by the Defence Ministers. These included maritime security, counter terrorism, humanitarian assistance and disaster management, peacekeeping operations and military medicine. Experts Working Groups (EWGs) have been established and on ground cooperation is moving apace.

In Sep 2007, to promote cooperation in the area of maritime security ASEAN established the AMF or the ASEAN Maritime Forum. Besides exchanging ideas on maritime security issues and other broader cross cutting subjects such as marine environment, illegal fishing, smuggling and maritime transportation, issues involving enclosed and semi-enclosed seas and concerns of the larger archipelagic nations are addressed by the AMF. Once again, keeping the transnational nature of maritime security issues required larger participation of countries in the wider East Asia region. Hence, in 2011, like the ADMM PLUS, the AMF was also enlarged and designated Expanded ASEAN Maritime Forum (EAMF) as a Track 1.5 dialogue.

Then there are a few other multilateral arrangements as Track 1.5 or 2.0 involving non-governmental bodies. The Council for Security Cooperation in the Asia Pacific or CSCAP, a non-governmental body was formed in 1993 as an offshoot of the ARF and is a Track 2 initiative to 'discuss political and security issues and challenges facing the region'. It currently has 21 member council and one observer. Institute for Defence Studies and Analyses (IDSA) is an associate member of CSCAP and India too became a full member in 2000. The Western Pacific Naval Symposium (WPNS), a US Navy initiative is a platform where leaders of the Western Pacific navies exchange knowledge, share experiences and collaborate to discuss vital maritime security issues. Another important multilateral grouping established in 1989 is known as Asia-Pacific Economic Cooperation forum or APEC is strictly an economic grouping, with the primary purpose of facilitating economic growth and prosperity in the region, and a vision to create a seamless regional economy.

Indian Ocean Region

By contrast, the Indian Ocean Region has limited multilateral structures. The geography of the region and attendant constraints have been the primary reason for the absence of the same. While some nations are tiny dots of islands in the Indian Ocean, other are landlocked and hence, their global or regional outlooks and security concerns are very different.

Further, territorial disputes between two of the major players in the region, which are also nuclear weapon equipped states, has stymied the growth of any worthwhile multilateral arrangement.

The South Asian Association for Regional Cooperation (SAARC) is an organisation of eight South Asian nations and plays the role of a guiding force for the members. It is not a security related arrangement. The first SAARC summit with seven members was held in December 1985 and Afghanistan joined the organization later. The focus has been on improving the quality of life by way of promoting "welfare economics" and "collective self-reliance" among members and yet "accelerating economic growth" and cultural development.

In 1997, the Indian Ocean countries established the Indian Ocean Rim – Association for Regional Cooperation (IOR-ARC), a regional grouping comprising 20 countries across Asia, Africa and Australia, six dialogue partners and two observers. Later rechristened as Indian Ocean Rim Association or IORA the region is characterised by glaring diversity in terms of nature of governance, religious practices, economic strength, languages and cultures. The member States range from Small Island States to G-20 members. During the past few years the growing incidents of piracy in the Gulf of Aden area have prompted IORA to address security issues too. Since maritime safety and security are vital for trade and economic development of the region, and Indian Ocean serves as the lifeline to bind the member states, these have been included as key areas in the agenda.

Since 1993, the Indian Navy has been hosting the biennial 'MILAN' exercises which bring together navies from the Asia Pacific region to Port Blair in the Andaman & Nicobar Islands where participants engage in exchange of views on issues of common interests and also undertake naval exercises to address non-traditional security threats and challenges.

In 2008 the Indian Navy initiated a specialised multilateral forum IONS or the Indian Ocean Naval Symposium, which seeks to address common security threats and challenges confronting the Indian Ocean states in order to enhance co-operation among the regional navies. Similar to the WPNS the IONS is a maritime security construct and has 35 navies of the region as members.

India and its Linkages with Multilateral Institutions

India, much before its independence had historical linkages with the SE Asia region. It's involvement in the SE Asian affairs since ancient times, are amply testified by the religious, cultural and linguistic influences evident even today in the nations of the region. India supported the freedom struggle of the SE Asian nations and was a member of the Asian Relations Conference in March 1946 and post-independence as a member of the Special Conference on Indonesia in Jan 1949. India was also a major force in convening the first Afro - Asian Conference in Bandung, Indonesia in Apr 1955 which was to show solidarity with the newly independent nations. Thus in the 50s, India was actively involved with the affairs of SE Asia. India was also the Chairman of Neutral Nations Repatriation Commission in 1953 in Korea and International Control Commission in Vietnam set up after the 1954 Geneva Accord.

India's interest in the region, however, diminished after the Bandung Conference. Post 1962 Sino-Indian war, Indian foreign policy became more inward looking to serve its immediate security concerns. Malaysia was the only country to oppose the Chinese aggression in 1962 and the Malaysian Prime Minister visited New Delhi during the war to express solidarity with India. Vietnam, on the other hand supported China. A few years later, during the 1965 Indo-Pak war, Indonesian President Sukarno offered to help Pakistan creating the Jakarta - Peking - Hanoi axis which may have acted as a catalyst for India's disinterest in the region. India was obviously disappointed by the attitude of these countries whose independence struggles India had championed.

Nonetheless, during this period, India supported all regional moves towards building a stable SE Asia such as the formation of the Malaysian Federation in 1963 and later separation into Malaysia and Singapore in 1965, the founding of ASEAN in 1967 and ASEAN's declaration of ZOPFAN or Zone of Peace, Freedom and Neutrality in 1971.

The 60s and 70s were also the time of super-power rivalry in this volatile region of the world and possibly India did not want to get embroiled and seen to be taking sides. Economic exigencies in the 70s disassociated India from the region. Oil requirements, remittances from Indian workers in the Middle East and involvement of Indian firms in the economic development of the oil rich gulf countries were more important tasks at hand. It was only in the 80s that India started looking at the SE Asia region seriously and established strategic equation with Vietnam. Malaysia was keen to make India a dialogue partner in 1980 itself but relations with ASEAN got estranged due to India's recognition of the Vietnam installed puppet regime in Cambodia. Obviously, India was looking at a strong Vietnam as a bulwark against China but failed diplomatically by not sharing its concerns with ASEAN members.

India did not have direct stakes in the SE Asian region and no serious problem with any of the nations except Indonesia under Sukarno for a brief period. It never threatened or interfered in the internal affairs of any country. However, major power rivalry in the Indian Ocean and the expansion of the Indian Navy in the 80s did ruffle a few feathers amongst nations in SE Asia, especially Indonesia, and to some extent Malaysia, with the former perceiving it as a threat to Northern Sumatra and the latter as an alarming development.

Initiated in 1991 during the tenure of Narasimha Rao government, India's 'Look East' policy marked a strategic shift in India's perspective of the world (This has now been upgraded to 'Act East' policy). The policy was rigorously pursued by the successive governments of Mr Vajpayee and Dr. Manmohan Singh. As a result the 90s saw a sharp decrease in the rhetoric against the Indian Navy by ASEAN countries due to increased interaction and defence cooperation initiatives with selected SE Asian nations.

In the closing phase of the last century and the 21st century, India has built bridges with the nations on its East, particularly SE Asian countries. Starting with ASEAN, the most visible multilateral institution, the ASEAN-India dialogue relations have grown rapidly from a sectoral dialogue partnership in 1992 to a full dialogue partnership in December 1995. For India, the centrality of ASEAN is an important part of its vision for an open, mutual, inclusive and rules-based security architecture in the Asia-Pacific region, where disputes are resolved through dialogue and diplomacy rather than by unilateral show of force. The relationship was further elevated with the convening of the ASEAN-India Summit in 2002 which is now an annual feature. At the ASEAN-India Commemorative Summit held on 20 December 2012 the Leaders adopted the ASEAN-India vision statement and elevated the partnership to a strategic level. It could thus be seen that the existing institutions and organisations in SE Asia region are generally meeting the purpose for which they were created in the first place.

However, recently there have been proposals for creating a new maritime security architecture in East Asia. A Japanese think tank IIPS or the Institute of International Policy based in Tokyo has argued that East Asia still does not have a permanent organisation or regional body to address maritime security issues. The President of the Institute has proposed that given the recent meeting of Japan with China and the USA, the establishment of a new grouping to be named the Asia Maritime Organization for Security and Cooperation (AMOSC) would be very timely. The central objective of this organisation would be to prevent and manage existing maritime disputes between countries by enhancing domain awareness, improving capacity-building, and enacting confidence-building measures. It argues that maritime competition and territorial disputes in the region are a reality today. Keeping in view the history of the plethora of institutions created in the past it is doubtful whether such institutions, can really help manage such prickly territorial disputes at all. One needs to remember that institutions like the ARF and the ADMM Plus already address the maritime security issues in some form or the other. The EAMF further focuses on maritime issues more narrowly.

Asian diplomats dealing with these growing institutions have increasingly emphasized harmonizing them to avoid duplication. At the same time it is also a fact that under the current arrangement, wherein the grouping such as ASEAN prefers consensus and 'in turn' comfort, makes it difficult to initiate timely action especially on contentious issues. So it seems that more than the absence of the institutions, it is the lack of political will that is preventing the resolution of disputes in the region. Further, based on its close monitoring the developments in the region, IIPS is convinced that the speed at which China is pushing its agenda to change the 'status quo' on ground in its favour by large scale land reclamations, construction activities and mobilisation of its military forces to show presence, needs an equally strong policy and response that the new organisation can provide.

Conclusion

For most Asian countries to continue their rapid growth, they will require assured access to energy resources and other commodities. The same can increasingly be said of global value chains. Ensuring freedom of navigation at seas is thus essential for maritime security. For India, freedom of navigation on the seas has always been an important one, since its history has been shaped by the constant inflow of goods and people between India and other countries in Asia and Africa. India is determined to build on its maritime traditions to foster security, cooperation, prosperity and safety from nature's fury, and for all those countries to which it is connected by sea.

India has always opposed the threat of unilateral force to resolve maritime territorial disputes, as this can disrupt normal trade flows, threatening the economic security of all countries that depend on free flow of trade and commerce. Indian has always urged all parties to such disputes to abjure military solutions and to rely on diplomacy and international maritime law to come to a mutually acceptable outcome. Freedom of navigation and energy security is also threatened by piracy in crowded sea lanes. Cooperation between countries on exchange of information on white shipping and creation of marine domain awareness has acquired a new salience to prevent such threats at sea.

Having seen that the countries from both the Asia Pacific and the Indian Ocean region possess a culture of working through multilateral institutions based on common interests, concerns and challenges, more so the nations in the Asia Pacific region, it is opined that these arrangements are there to stay. The region, and its unique maritime geography and character has dictated the need for multilateralism aka Europe. Though the 'multilateral security cooperation' in Asia Pacific vis-a-vis Europe is still lagging behind, there has been relative peace in the region since the end of Cold War. Of course, the near permanent military presence of U.S. and its ongoing policy of rebalancing as also the military-to-military cooperation between nations in the region has been an important stabilising factor.

India's relations with most of the SE Asian nations have remained good and has been build up gradually. A certain level of trust and mutual understanding does exist at various levels of interaction. But since many of the SE Asian nations perceive China as a major long term threat and a sizable number of them have territorial issues with China especially in the SCS, India stands a better chance of playing a key role in the region. This would not be easy keeping its adversarial relations with China in mind. Revival of Japan's militarism is another fearful possibility and the nations of SE Asia are closely watching these developments. The countries in the region, have learned from the past that security is best served with major powers counter-balancing each other.

It has become quite clear, that the time has also come to add some teeth to the key multilateral organisations like ASEAN as done by reshaping India's 'Look East' policy to 'Act East' policy. More recently, India has demonstrated an increased willingness to exert greater impact in shaping the South China Sea dynamics. The specific mention of the situation in the South China Sea for the first time in the September 2014, through the Joint Statement issued with US President Barak Obama by the Indian Prime Minister Modi, both sides expressed their concern about "rising tensions over maritime territorial disputes" in the region. In conclusion, there appears to be an overkill in the realm of formal multilateral initiatives in the SE Asian region and, as brought out elsewhere, there is serious thinking on whether so many institutions or organisations are really required or not.

10 INDIA'S ACT EAST POLICY: ADDING SUBSTANCE TO STRATEGIC PARTNERSHIPS

Shankari Sundararaman

Introduction

This chapter focuses on India's Act East Policy with particular emphasis on the strategic partnerships which it is developing with its immediate Eastern neighbours. While looking at the emerging maritime dynamics in the Eastern Indian Ocean Region and the Western Pacific Ocean region, it is important to first address the issue of conceptualizing this region. Today this vast maritime connect is being referred to as the Asia-Pacific, the Indo-Pacific or the Indo-Asia-Pacific interchangeably. The debate over the use of the term Indo-Pacific is becoming more focused around the rise of China and how the regional matrix is changing with this transition taking shape. Added to this dimension is the fact that, recent US rebalancing has brought back the focus on great power rivalry in the region. This credibly alters the manner in which the regional balance is poised where the focus of major power rivalry is once again visible in the region of the Asia-Pacific or the Indo-Pacific.[1] The two terms are not really geographically contiguous areas to be identified as regions. The Asia-Pacific is a term that was used to connote a region that did not cover South Asia. Given the dynamics of the cold war this theatre remained significant for a long time. However, with the changes that are visible in the post-cold war period, China's emergence and India's rise, the linking of the maritime extents of the Indian and Pacific Oceans is more likely to be the focus of great powers in the years to come. While there is huge diversity in this notion of the Indo-Pacific, it also highlights the critical issues that bind the wider region together.[2] The very fact that the region is drawing the attention of both China and the United States credibly adds to the complex mix of issues that have emerged in the regional balance. In fact a former Commander of the US Pacific Command described the US area of operations as extending from "Hollywood to Bollywood and from penguins to polar bears", thereby reiterating the expanse that the region covers.[3]

This chapter seeks to look at the manner in which India's relations with its Eastern neighbours has expanded over a period of time. Moving from a focus on economic integration, India is today looking at the opportunity to add more substance to the strategic partnerships that it has initiated with all of the ASEAN countries. This theme is critical given the changes and developments that are shaping this region today –the importance of the Indian Ocean has been in the discourse over the past decade. Robert Kaplan's March 2009 article titled *"Centre Stage for 21st Century: Power Plays in the Indian Ocean"*, published in Foreign Affairs, highlights that the Indian Ocean will be critical given the recent incidents of piracy off the coast of Somalia and the Mumbai terror attacks of November 2008.[4] Kaplan identifies both the Arabian Sea and the Bay of Bengal as critical points that can be affected by 'dramatic changes in the countries that bound these waters.'[5] Moreover, the rise of India and China has also led to a change in perceptions on how they view the maritime extents around this region. The efforts of regional powers to vie for more maritime space is actually highlighting a dramatic shift towards the seas and securing these dynamics are not going to be easy for any single country, but needs to be dealt with in a concerted manner.[6] In this context India's own views particularly as it expands its interaction with East Asia will critically need to focus on the Bay of Bengal. This importance has also been clearly emphasized in terms of the need to build capacity in this region. The plan to upgrade the tri-service command located at the Andaman and Nicobar Islands, through infrastructure development highlights some of the domestic components of furthering the defence ties with the eastern neighbours. The region which is also identified as the Eastern Indian Ocean, is significant to India's maritime concerns and also to the other countries which are littoral states. Countries such as Myanmar, Thailand and Indonesia are significantly focused on issues in the Straits of Malacca.

Critical to this understanding is also the need to look at the changes that have occurred recently in the Western Pacific ocean region – which includes the extents of the South China Sea (SCS), the East China Sea and the Philippines Sea – merging into the South Pacific. This area which is a crucial link between Asia and the Americas acts as a pivot through which much of the global trade flows. Added to this the potential for resource exploration makes the region a potential conflict zone where competing interests of nation-states that bound these waters are vying for control over these waters. China's recent spurt of activities in this regard has been of concern to the countries that are also claimants to the SCS disputes. The Paracel and Spratly islands which are contested regions have been in the centre of conflict among the regional players with China staking claims to these areas on the basis of "historical claim dating back to antiquity".[7] While the Chinese have remained ambiguous on the exact coordinates which they are claiming, there is no doubt that the claims over the area that falls under the nine-dash line of the Chinese comprises nearly sixty to eighty percent of the total area and is based on 'indisputable sovereignty', over all the features in the adjacent waters'.[8] This position of the Chinese has made the Western Pacific ocean a region of impending conflict which has also raised the threat perceptions of other claimant countries. Further to this, the importance of Sea Lanes of Communications (SLOC's) which run right through the region of Southeast Asia make these countries vulnerable to armed hostilities in the region. The area bound by the two adjacent oceans is likely to be one of the most critical maritime zones in the years to come.

Southeast Asia as the Core of the Indo-Pacific

Lying at the core of the Indo-Pacific is the region of Southeast Asia – with China to the north, India to the west and Australia to the south. Southeast Asia as a region has been seen as 'strategically quiet' for more than two decades.[9] This strategic quietness identified by Martin Ott, states clearly that the last inter-state war in the region was the Third Indo China Conflict (Cambodian war) triggered by Vietnamese intervention into Cambodia. However, following the 1991 Paris Peace Accords and the subsequent expansion of the ASEAN to include the ten member countries in the region, this grouping and the ASEAN have been focused on expanding regional mechanisms to bring in major players.[10] Interestingly ASEAN since its inception has been averse to major power rivalry in its immediate region. This was because in the aftermath of the Second World War, Southeast Asia was emerging from the colonial period. The newly independent countries had conflicting expectations with regards to how they perceived both their domestic and external security relations. First, at the domestic level, as a result of protracted communist insurgencies within the state, countries looked to secure their domestic security by addressing economic disparities and with reduced focus on individual freedom and more tightly controlled political processes. In order to address communist insurgencies, member states of the ASEAN even considered the possibility of a multilateral arrangement to fight communism. By 1976, the original members of ASEAN were exchanging intelligence and information on communist insurgencies to assist each other to address domestic concerns.[11] Second, at the external level, the focus of the ASEAN was to ensure that major powers did not have a role in undermining the potential to create regional autonomy for the ASEAN members. This assertion towards establishing regional autonomy was to ensure that there was no place for competing major power interests to undermine the position of the ASEAN which sought to engage through diplomatic means within the region. However, achieving this was easier said than done, given that the regional countries were themselves tied up in various security arrangements even prior to ASEAN formation in 1967.[12]

Both Philippines and Thailand were members of the Southeast Asia Treaty Organization (SEATO). Malaysia and Singapore were part of the Five Power Defence Arrangement (FPDA), which has been viewed as merely a 'consultative forum and not a formal alliance'. [13] However, this arrangement has continued to prevail through the regional changes and is today carrying out joint military exercises in the SCS too.[14] The fifth original member of ASEAN was a founding member of the Non-Aligned Movement (NAM) and following the 1965 coup which ousted President Sukarno, the Suharto regime began to show closer military ties with the United States and was receiving assistance under the US International Military Education and Training (IMET). This military assistance was suspended following the human rights abuse by militia groups following the East Timor violence in 1999. The military assistance was started again in 2002.[15] Other ASEAN members like Vietnam were closely associated with the Soviet Union, while Cambodia and Myanmar were closely linked to China for years. Such a situation among the ASEAN countries has not really helped to achieve the degree of strategic autonomy that the grouping needs to tackle the issues of major power rivalry in the region.[16]

This factor underpinned much of the ASEAN discourse throughout the cold war. In the aftermath of the cold war, ASEAN regionalism became more broad-based to include several members within its fold in the attempt to maintain the centrality of the ASEAN principles within regional mechanisms. This was in fact an argument put forward by several constructivist scholars that the ASEAN was seeking to 'socialize' other member countries into following the ASEAN way that would remain at the core of the institutional mechanism across the wider Asia-Pacific. And true to this view for nearly two decades following the cold war this was the case – the emergence of forums like the ASEAN Regional Forum (ARF), the East Asia Summit (EAS), the ASEAN Defence Ministers Meeting Plus (ADMM+) and the ASEAN Maritime Forum (AMF) are all examples of regional mechanisms that were based on the core principles of ASEAN itself. Almost from 2003 onwards there have also been proclamations about ASEAN being able to move towards a European Union like structure that will eventually lead to the evolution of the ASEAN Community – with its three pillars – the ASEAN Politico-Security Community, the ASEAN Economic Community and the ASEAN Socio-Cultural Community. These initiatives however remained inadequate in terms of bringing more binding aspects of membership and were to be loosely adhered to, not really changing the format of the regional mechanisms. While several scholars have written about the success of the ASEAN format, it left huge gaps in how to bring errant members to follow a more order based system. Also given the lack of uniformity in terms of the economic development of many of the smaller ASEAN members, the potential for them to be under the influence of major powers is a factor that needs to be borne in mind. This was amply demonstrated during the 2012 ASEAN summit when for the first time the ASEAN members were unable to come up with a joint communiqué on the security concerns related to China's role in the SCS.

This shift in the region's power play is factored in due to the rise of China and the US rebalancing to Asia which has impacted the shifts within the ASEAN countries that are looking towards other states for closer partnerships particularly on issues of common security concerns. In that sense, there is a visible regional shift which has resulted from China's rise, not just in terms of challenging the regional order but the global order as well. The US preoccupation with Europe and West Asia, is now credibly shifting to the Pacific once more with its rebalancing and pivot to Asia policy which has again brought the balance of power into the region.

India's Act East Policy

India's Look East Policy which began in 1991 under Prime Minister Narasimha Rao, was distinctive - it began to look primarily at the possibility of extending India's foreign policy engagement to a wider regional ambit. From 1998 onwards the Annual Reports of the Ministry of External Affairs have been highlighting the logic of increasing India's interaction across an `extended neighbourhood', which was seen as a shift from the focus on South Asia, with an emphasis on Pakistan and China.[17] What began primarily as an economic integration today has moved beyond economics to deepening partnerships with the wider region.

Several factors prompted the shift towards a Look East Policy – first, given that the cold war ended, the political dynamics gave way for possibilities of more integration with less ideological baggage to worry about. India's own policy of Non-Alignment recalibrated the changes that were occurring and took a more nuanced position towards integration with other states at the political level. Second, on the economic front the changes that drove India's liberalization necessitated the need for greater economic integration at the global level. Added to this the region of Southeast Asia where India began its Look East Policy had been historically and culturally connected to India. Added to this towards the end of the colonial period, India and these countries had shared a common period of nationalism in which history once again tied the region together. China's rise and its move towards closer integration with Southeast Asia had shown successful results economically and with the opening up of India's economy this seemed to be the way to move forward.[18] Even as India began to Look East, the ASEAN expanded its membership to include several new members from the region. Myanmar's inclusion in 1997 brought Southeast Asia closer to India by connecting the regions through a land route – India's shared land boundary with Myanmar brought the logic of connectivity into sharp focus making this another factor that drove the Look East Policy forward.

One of the significant milestones in the India ASEAN ties was the establishment of the summit relationship at the ASEAN Plus One level – ASEAN-India summit, which was established within a decade of starting the Look East Policy. The first India-ASEAN summit was held in November 2002 in Phnom Penh, Cambodia[19], during which India and ASEAN agreed to move towards a Comprehensive Agreement on establishing a Free Trade

Area (FTA) across several parameters – basically focusing on consolidating trade and investment links.

Through the second decade of the Look East Policy, the shift towards establishment of ties with other countries across East Asia and Australia began to be more visible. India's membership into the East Asia Summit (EAS) was initially contested by China on the grounds that it did not belong to East Asian region. However, the ASEAN countries played a clear role in the decision to bring India into the format which endorsed the fact that India was being seen as a long term partner in the move towards realizing a long term vision for larger regional integration mechanisms in the wider region. Endorsing the role that ASEAN played in the centrality of India's larger regional integration with the East Asia and the Pacific, Indian Foreign Minister Yashwant Sinha at a speech at Harvard emphasized that ASEAN was at the core of India's expansion to the East and Australia.[20] He also stressed that in the growing ties with China and Japan, Indian foreign policy shift was clearly indicating the need to further its role in the regional dynamics.[21]

After nearly two and half decades of the Look East Policy, trade between India and Southeast Asia today stands at a volume of approximately US $ 80 billion. Interestingly while Southeast Asia remained at the pivot of the Look East Policy, India's economic integration also expended with other East Asian countries such as China, Japan and South Korea, as well as with the Pacific countries like Australia and New Zealand. India's trade with China expanded to the tune of US $ 66.4 billion in 2012, making it the number one trading partner for India and this is targeted to reach US$ 100 billion by 2015.[22] Moreover, with the expansion of India's ties to the Pacific, particularly both Australia and New Zealand, this Look East policy has been able to expand further east pushing this initiative into its second decade.

In May 2014, the government of Prime Minister Narendra Modi assumed office, following which there has been greater focus on India's foreign policy towards the wider Asian and Pacific regions. In the initial days of Prime Minister Modi taking office, there was a view that the importance given to the Look East Policy was not visible – this was particularly because of the move in calling all the South Asian neighbours for the swearing in ceremony of the Prime Minister. The choice to leave Myanmar out of this process was debated by many, but Myanmar's position as a Southeast Asian state was considered to be the key factor. Added to which India's relations with Southeast Asian states were already robust and stable, while the tensions within South Asia were more difficult to address. In November 2014, when Prime Minister Modi visited Myanmar for the India ASEAN summit he identified the shift in the Look East Policy as the Act East Policy. Under the Act East Policy there is a growing impetus given to the deepening and strengthening of India's strategic level ties with the countries of Southeast Asia, East Asia and Australia.

Strategic Dimension of the Act East Policy

While the first phase or decade of the Look East Policy primarily focused on the economic aspects, almost from its inception, security level ties have also been critical. The expansion of India's defence and security ties in the region has also occurred as a result of other extraneous factors – primary among which is the rise of China. While China is still the number one economic partner, the region views China's rise with concern. Particularly, China's military modernization is an issue that is worrisome and there is a view that the spate of military modernization in Southeast Asia is triggered by this insecurity. Some scholars attribute this military expansion including addition of submarine capability which is being proclaimed by countries like Singapore, Indonesia, Malaysia and Vietnam, with the Philippines following suit.[23] While balancing China is one of the factors, the region has seen an increase in the procurement of arms since 1992. There was a lull in the activity following the Asian Financial Crisis in 1997, but arms procurement is once again on the rise. Even domestic factors such as economic capability and the availability of such military hardware have been cited as factors for the build-up.[24]

In the case of India, development of security relations were not offset by serious political problems and historical animosity, in fact quite the contrary. The absence of territorial conflicts and political stresses between India and its Southeast Asian neighbours made the process of evolving security ties that much easier.[25] In this regards the first defence cooperation agreement was between India and Malaysia in 1993 which was initiated through the MIDCOM – Malaysia- India Defence Cooperation Meetings. In 2003, India and Singapore signed a Defence Cooperation Agreement that addressed training for military personnel and joint exercises such as SINDEX (Between the Republic of Singapore Air Force (RSAF) and the

Indian Air Force (IAF)) and SIMBEX (Singapore India Maritime Bilateral Exercise).[26] Similarly with both Thailand (2005) and Indonesia (2002), India has signed defence agreements. The coordinated patrols (CORPAT) with both Indonesia and Thailand have been commendable efforts and are capable of being enhanced in the future. Both the MILAN and the IMBL patrol are also credible examples of the maritime cooperation dimensions that India has progressed with Southeast Asia.

More recently the ties with both Myanmar and Vietnam have also been moving ahead in areas of defence cooperation. One of the areas where Myanmar showed a keen interest was in procuring off-shore patrol vessels from India. In 2013, India agreed to develop four off-shore patrol vessels for Myanmar, bringing maritime cooperation to the forefront of the defence cooperation.[27] While the proposal had met with delays during a recent visit of Myanmar's military chief to India in July 2015, this was further discussed especially the possibility of further coordination in the area of maritime security.[28] Simultaneously the defence cooperation with Vietnam has also been stepped up in the recent years. While Vietnam and India have always shared close ties due to India's historical support to Vietnam during the cold war, there is no doubt that regionally Vietnam is emerging as a credible link in the ASEAN chain. During the visit of the Vietnamese premier to India in October 2014, India reiterated the rights of the littoral states in the SCS region to find a lasting solution to the conflict. While India does not have a direct role in the conflict the statements on the rights of passage and freedom of navigation which have been highlighted by the Indian Prime Minister in his speech at the UN are clear indicators that India will not hesitate to expand is ties and opportunities with the regional countries.[29] India's cooperation with Vietnam is also seen in the US$ 100 million line of credit given to Vietnam for Indian patrol boats. Also agreements to boost ties on defence and coastguard cooperation have been agreed during the visit of the Vietnamese Defence Minister in May 2015.

Apart from this, Vietnam also is critical from the Indian view point especially with regards to the SCS where the potential for joint exploration has been underway. Chinese opposition to this is an important factor that has actually pushed India and Vietnam closer. In the context of the SCS conflict, Vietnam and Philippines stressed on India to take a position at the 2013 ADMM+ in support of the ASEAN states in the SCS Conflict – but

India remained hesitant stating that it was not a claimant and therefore would refrain from taking a position. [30] However, in recent statements from within the Indian political establishment, the reference to the freedom of navigation and the right of passage has been oft repeated, in addition to the support India has given to the United Nations Convention on Law of the Seas III, 1982 (UNCLOS). [31]

India's own response to the growing presence of major powers within the Indian and Pacific Ocean region has been indicated through the establishment of strategic partnership agreements with its immediate neighbours in Southeast Asia. During the 2012 India ASEAN Commemorative Summit, the two sides decided to broaden the scope and content of their relations to a strategic partnership agreement that would deepen the regional economic integration between India and Southeast Asia. [32] The purpose of this summit was to elevate "ASEAN-India Dialogue Relations across the whole spectrum of political and security, economic, socio-cultural and development cooperation". [33] One of the significant areas of this focus was the maritime domain which was becoming critical with the growing assertions of China in the SCS.

One of the most critical aspects of the security and strategic environment is the maritime dimension that has become increasingly relevant. With the importance given to the Sea Lines of Communications (SLOC's) the waters that connect the Indian and Pacific Oceans dominate the security concerns of all regional players and the maintenance of freedom of navigation for trade transport is an important factor. For India too, this is a critical factor given that approximately 55 percent of trade moves through the Malacca Straits. In case any country attempts to dominate these passages the loss would be very high for most countries. Thus there would be attempts by India to navigate the strategic relations in the region more carefully to avoid any form of competition from other countries. [34]

Over the last two decades Chinese efforts to increase its presence in the Indian Ocean region has been of concern to India. China's growing presence in the region has been a factor that has tested the security environment in the Indian Ocean. Its access to ports like Hambantota, Gwadar and other off-shore islands in Myanmar, such as Coco islands, Hainggyi islands and Kyaukpyu islands are important catalysts that have factored in India's security calculations. Added to this, China has been showing increasing assertiveness in the manner in which it has handled its claims to the `maritime territorial disputes in the East and SCS, prompting Asia-Pacific nations to look towards India to play a balancing role'.[35]

As an outcome of the India-ASEAN Commemorative Summit of 2012, the move towards India expanding its maritime cooperation through the ASEAN Maritime Forum (AMF) and the Expanded ASEAN Maritime Forum (EAMF) are clear indicators of the shift towards addressing the maritime threats in the wider region. Issues relating to piracy, Search And Rescue (SAR), safeguarding of fisheries are increasingly becoming relevant to all member countries of the regional institutional mechanisms. More recently, there has been an emphasis on the need to protect freedom of navigation and reaffirming the tenets of the UNCLOS.[36] While India in the second phase of the Look East Policy was keen on forging regional security level ties, its role as a security guarantor to the region was still debatable. [37]

The actual mandate of the Act East Policy extends to both Japan and Australia. India's relations with these two countries have also expanded under the Modi government particularly following the visit of the Prime Minister to Japan and Australia. The ties with Japan have been upgraded to a special strategic and global partnership. While in terms of the economic ties, there is a greater focus on issues relating to infrastructure development and the manufacturing sector. This is particularly in line with the focus that the Modi government has launched with the `Make in India' initiative. In terms of security relations, both India and Japan have upgraded their defence cooperation agreement and have signed a pact on regional stability. One of the areas of increased interaction on defence related matters pertain to the possible sale of Japanese US -2 amphibious aircraft which India is seeking.[38] Second, the importance attached to the sale of uranium from Japan to India is also critical in this regards. This is an area where both India and Japan have to acknowledge the fact that they may have divergent views on issues relating to more stringent codes and safeguards for the use of nuclear technology.[39] Finding headway in this matter will lead to strengthening the ties that are currently in place. In the arena of maritime security, both India and Japan have already initiated the Japan India Maritime Exercise (JIMEX) which has been in place since 2012. This is along the same lines as the SIMBEX which is a bilateral exercise with Singapore. The extension of this format to include Japan is a significant step in the military ties which India is fostering with Japan.

India has also furthered its ties with Australia. The visit of Prime Minister Tony Abbot to India in September 2014 and the visit by Prime Minister Modi to Australia during the G-20 Summit in November 2014 show the manner in which ties are being shaped.[40] On the economic front the visit moved towards the Comprehensive Economic Cooperation Agreement (CECA) with Australia that would push for the India Australia Free Trade Agreement. While this was to be concluded by the end of 2015 there have been delays in the negotiation process and it is yet to be finalised. The second issue which has made considerable headway is the sale of uranium to India. Australia was one of the countries which had been reluctant to accept the Indian nuclear tests of 1998. In 2008 the Australian parliament did not agree to sell uranium to India on the basis that India was not a signatory to the NPT. This decision was overturned in 2012 under the leadership of Prime Minister Gillard which culminated in the India-Australia Civil Nuclear deal.[41]

The Indian Ocean region will be vital to both India and Australia. In fact the Trilateral Dialogue on Indian Ocean (TDIO) between India, Indonesia and Australia provides a significant platform for these three countries to coordinate on issues of mutual concern to take the Indian Ocean Rim Association (IORA) initiative forward. Interestingly in May 2015 the Indian Navy's Eastern Fleet plied the waters of Southeast Asia and Australia – making both port calls and conducting joint exercises.[42] Added to this in June 2015 India, Japan and Australia held the first trilateral dialogue which centered on maritime security issues, with particular reference to freedom of navigation in the SCS and trilateral security cooperation in the Indian and Pacific Oceans. One of the clear signals that emerged from this was that it was not directed against any particular state, given that earlier when a quadrilateral dialogue was envisioned on the side lines of the Malabar exercise of 2007, China had strong reactions that it was an anti-China grouping.[43] India and Australia have also held its first bilateral maritime exercise, AUSINDEX in September 2015, which is an indication of the growing defence relations between the two countries.[44]

Simultaneously the ties with China have also been expanding. While China's presence in the Indian Ocean region is a critical factor that propels other states to move towards greater bilateral and multilateral cooperation, China too has been putting in place several new ideas and policies. With 70 per cent of its oil supplies and 80 per cent of its trade moving through the

Indian Ocean China's 'Maritime Silk Road' (MSR) and the 'One Road One Belt' (OROB) policies are both economically and strategically focused with concerns for the region.[45] Both the trading routes and the energy demands are vital aspects of China's efforts to maintain a primary position in the Indian Ocean.[46]

The domestic compulsions and problems relating to the unsettled border issues with China are critical in determining the course of India's wider engagement with China. Despite India's concerns over 'strategic encirclement' propounded by the 'string of pearls' theory, India's relations with China have also expanded considerably under the Look/Act East Policy. Since Prime Minister Modi's government took office there have also been high level interactions with China – President Xi Jinping's visit in September 2014 led to some progress on the economic front, particularly in the setting up of infrastructural projects.[47]

On the security front the presence of Chinese submarines in the Indian Ocean has caused concern to not just India but to other regional countries as well. Indonesia's plan to move towards establishing both global maritime fulcrum or the *'poros maritime dunia'* and the growing emphasis on the *'dua samudera'* or the two ocean policy are all pointing towards the critical linking of the Indian and Pacific Oceans.

Conclusion

One of the most important milestones in the Indian Foreign policy has been its Look East Policy. There has been bipartisan support for this from the political establishment within India and the economic and security level advances that have been made are truly striking. The changing dynamics in the region are critically moving towards a stage when India's engagement will have to be far more critical in its willingness to act as a major security provider for the region. While Southeast Asia has always recognised China s its potential economic partner, it still looks upon the US as the major security provider. However, both regional players and major powers are increasingly pushing India into a more responsible role. For the Southeast Asian region, growing Chinese assertion will necessitate looking towards India to act in more concrete fashion towards maintaining regional balance by becoming a more active player. These factors will clearly necessitate more focus on India's willingness to Act East.

NOTES AND REFERENCES

1   For details see Shankari Sundararaman, India and the Indo-Pacific: Semantic Change or Strategic Shift, in Gauri Khandekar (ed.), EU-India Strategic Partnership: Facing the Foreign Policy Divide, Lenin Media Pvt Ltd., New Delhi, 2015, pp. 127-140.

2   Ibid.,

3   Keynote Speech by Admiral Harry B. Harris Jr. Commander of the US Pacific Fleet at the 2014 US-Japan Council Annual Conference on 10 October, 2014 at the website http://www.usjapancouncil.org/admiral_harry_harris_s_keynote_speech_2014_annual_conference (accessed on July 1 2015). Also cited in Andrew S. Erickson and Gabriel Collins, Dragon Tracks: Emerging Chinese Access Points in the Indian Ocean Region, at the website Asian Maritime Transparency Initiative (AMTI),at the website http://amti.csis.org/dragon-tracks-emerging-chinese-access-points-in-the-indian-ocean-region/ (accessed on 2 July 2015).

4   Robert Kaplan, Centre Stage for the Twenty-first Century: Power Plays in the Indian Ocean, Foreign Affairs, vol. 88, no. 2, March/April 2009, pp. 16-32.

5   Ibid.,

6   Ibid.,

7   Subash Kapila, Paracel and Spratly Islands Conflict resolution Impeded by China – Analysis, Eurasia Review, 27 June, 2014 at the website http://www.eurasiareview.com/27062014-paracel-spratly-islands-conflict-resolution-impeded-china-analysis/ (accessed on 4 July, 2015).

8   Carlyle A. Thayer, Strategy and Maritime Power in a Contested Environment: National, Military, Maritime Strategy and the South China Sea, Presentation to the 66th Current Strategy Forum, U.S. Naval War College, Newport, Rhode Island, June 16-17, 2015, p. 2-3, at the website https://www.scribd.com/doc/269074004/Thayer-Strategy-and-Maritime-Power-in-a-Contested-Environment-The-South-China-Sea (accessed on 2 July 2015).

9   Martin C. Ott, The Geo-Political Transformation of Southeast Asia, February 2013, Foreign Policy Research Institute at the website http://www.fpri.org/articles/2013/02/geopolitical-transformation-southeast-asia (accessed on 23 January, 2015)

10   Ibid.,

11 For Details see ASEAN Security Problems: Issues and Responses, Adelphi Paper Special Issue, A New Regional Order in Southeast Asia: ASEAN in the Post-Cold War Era, vol. 33, no. 279, IISS, 1993, pp. 17-40.

12 Amitav Acharya, Constructing a Security Community in Southeast Asia: ASEAN and the Problem of Regional Order, Routledge London, New York, 2001, pp. 51-56

13 Cited in Carlyle Thayer, Five Power Defence Arrangements: The Quiet Achiever, Security Challenges, vol. 3, no. 1, February 2007, p. 79.

14 Ibid.,

15 Indonesia-US Military Ties, Indonesia Briefing, International Crisis Group, 17 July, 2001, at the website http://www.crisisgroup.org/~/media/files/asia/south-eastasia/indonesia/indonesian%20us%20military%20ties.ash

16 For detail see, David Martin Jones and Michael L.R. Smith, Making Process Not Progress: ASEAN and the Evolving East Asian Regional Order, International Security, vol. 32, no. 1, Summer 2007, pp. 148-184.

17 Priya Chacko, The Rise of the Indo-Pacific: Understanding Ideational Change and Continuity in India's Foreign Policy, The Australian Journal of International Affairs, vol. 68, no. 4, April-July 2014, pp. 438-41, accessed online at http://dx.doi.org/10.1080/10357718.2014.891565 on 8 January, 2015.

18 Danielle Rajendram, India's new Asia-Pacific Strategy: Modi Act's East, Lowy Institute Analysis, December 2014, pp. 2-3, at the website http://www.lowyinstitute.org/files/indias-new-asia-pacific-strategy-modi-acts-east.pdf (accessed on 22 June, 2015)

19 Shankari Sundararaman, India and ASEAN, The Hindu, 19 November, 2002, Chennai.

20 Speech by External Affairs Minister Shri Yashwant Sinha at Harvard University, September 29, 2003, at the website http://mea.gov.in/Speeches-statements.htm?dtl/4744/Speech+by+External+Affairs+Minister+Shri+Yashwant+Sinha+at+Harvard+University   (accessed on 29 January 2015)

21 Ibid.,

22 Dilip Kumar Satapathy, India China Bilateral Trade projected at $ 100 billion by 2015, Business Standard, New Delhi, April 15, 2013 at the website http://www.business-standard.com/article/economy-policy/india-china-bilateral-

trade-projected-at-100-bn-by-2015-113041500358_1.html (accessed on 2 July 2015)

23 Mathew Ribar, Explaining Southeast Asia's Force Build Up, The Diplomat, January 14, 2015 at the website http://thediplomat.com/2015/01/explaining-southeast-asias-force-buildup/ (accessed on 17 June 2015)

24 Ibid.,

25 C Raja Mohan, Samundra Manthan: Sino-Indian Rivalry in the Indo-Pacific, Oxford University Press, New Delhi, 2012, p. 101.

26 For details on this see Pankaj Jha and Rahul Mishra, Defence Cooperation: A Case Study of India and Singapore, Air Power Journal, vol. 5, no. 2, Summer 2010 (April –June), pp. 73-96.

27 Vivek Raghuvanshi, India Boosts Defence Ties with Myanmar, Defence News, July 30, 2013, at the website http://archive.defensenews.com/article/20130730/DEFREG03/307300009/India-Boosts-Defense-Ties-Myanmar (accessed on 2 July 2015).

28 Prasanth Parameswaran, India and Myanmar Eye Future Defence Cooperation, The Diplomat, 28 July 2015, at the website http://thediplomat.com/2015/07/india-myanmar-eye-future-defense-cooperation/# (accessed on 24 November, 2015).

29 Increased Economic Engagement Focus During Vietnam Premier's Visit, The Economic Times, 24 October 2014.

30 C Raja Mohan, An Uncertain Trumpet: India's Role in Southeast Asian Security, India Review, vol. 12, no. 3, July-September 2013, p. 134.

31 US-India Joint Statement, 30 September, 2014, at the website https://www.whitehouse.gov/the-press-office/2014/09/30/us-india-joint-statement (accessed on 5 January, 2016).

32 Vision Statement of ASEAN India Commemorative Summit, 21 December, 2012 at the website http://www.asean.org/news/asean-statement-communiques/item/vision-statement-asean-india-commemorative-summit (accessed on 24 May, 2015)

33 Ibid.,

34 David Scott, India's Role in the South China Sea: Geo-Politics and Geo-Economics at Play, India Review, vol. 12, no. 2, May 2013, p. 55.

35 Danielle Rajendram, n. 18, p. 3.

36 Vision Statement of ASEAN India Commemorative Summit, 21 December, 2012 at the website http://www.asean.org/news/asean-statement-communiques/item/vision-statement-asean-india-commemorative-summit (accessed on 24 May 2015)

37 C. Raja Mohan, n. 30, p. 134.

38 For details see Shamshad A Khan, Deconstructing "Tokyo Declaration" 2014: Takeaway's from Indian Prime Minister's Japan Visit, ICWA Issue Brief, 24 September, 2014, at the website http://www.icwa.in/pdfs/IB/2014/ DeconstructingTokyoDeclaration2014.pdf (accessed on 31 January 2015)

39 Ibid.,

40 Barton Deakin Brief: Australia India Economic Relationship, 18 November, 2014 at the website http://www.bartondeakin.com/wp-content/ uploads/2014/11/Barton-Deakin-Brief-Australia-India-Economic-Relationship.pdf (accessed on 2 July 2015)

41 Ibid.,

42 Scott Cheney-Peters, India's Maritime Acts in the East, Asian Maritime Transparency Initiative, 18 June 2015, at the website http://amti.csis.org/ indias-maritime-acts-in-the-east (accessed on 27 June, 2015)

43 Prasanth Parameswaran, India, Australia, Japan Hold First Ever Trilateral Dialogue, The Diplomat, 9 June 2015, at the website http://thediplomat. com/2015/06/india-australia-japan-hold-first-ever-trilateral-dialogue/ (accessed on 4 July, 2015).

44 Prasanth Parameswaran, Australia India to Hold First Ever Naval Exercise Amid China Concerns, The Diplomat, 1 September, 2015, at the website http://thediplomat.com/2015/09/australia-india-to-hold-first-ever-naval-exercise-amid-china-concerns/# (accessed on 29 December 2015)

45 Brahma Chellany, What are Chinese Submarines Doing in the Indian Ocean? Huffington Post, 19 May, 2015 at the website http://www.huffingtonpost. com/brahma-chellaney/chinese-subs-in-indian-ocean_b_7320500.html?ir=I ndia&adsSiteOverride=in (accessed on 5 July 2015).

46 Danielle Rajendram, n. 18, p. 5

47 Tanvi Madan, Indian Prime Minister Modi Visits China, Upfront Brookings, 13 May, 2015 at the website http://www.brookings.edu/blogs/up-front/ posts/2015/05/13-modi-china-visit (accessed on 7 January 2016).

11   SEMINAR TAKEAWAYS

Antara Ghosal and Kapil Narula

The theme of the seminar 'Maritime Dynamics in the Eastern Indian Ocean Region and the Western Pacific Ocean Region' aptly captures the growing importance of the region. The objective of the seminar was to explore the emerging geopolitical trends and developments in the region vis-à-vis India's own maritime and strategic interests. Based on the views of the paper presenters and discussions by the panellists following were the key takeaways from the seminar.

China's rise and regional responses

The biggest development in recent years is China's foray in the Indian Ocean Region and the concurrent development of ports and support infrastructure as part of its flagship Belt and Road Initiative (BRI). China, on one hand, has prioritized its bilateral engagements with the IOR countries, while on the other hand, has sought to pursue security multilateralism through inclusion in the Indian Ocean Rim Association (as a dialogue partner) and the Indian Ocean Naval Symposium (as an observer). Presently, China is focusing on increasing its presence in the IOR, adding to surveillance capacity, increasing its port calls, and developing familiarity with blue water naval operations. However, its long term intent may be sea control and power projection in the IOR. This is being sustained by 'strategic prepositioning', such as by building access facilities in various countries and enhancing the reach of its naval arm. Although economics is considered as the main driver for China's international initiatives, given the lack of transparency, it is difficult to ascertain China's real intent and national strategy.

It was noted during the discussions that although China is a reluctant maritime power, it is increasingly being pushed by economic factors to look seaward. It is evident that notwithstanding China's efforts in building pipelines to bypass several chokepoints, China would continue to depend significantly on the seas for its energy needs. In other words China's 'Malacca Dilemma' is far from getting resolved, and its renewed thrust on Indian Ocean to protect its Sea Lines of Communication (SLOCs) may lead to competition with other resident powers in future. It emerged that the possibility either of trade warfare (i.e. for trade protection), either offensive or defensive cannot be ruled out.

In this backdrop, it was important to map the responses of other countries in the region to this evolving security scenario. Given the fragile nature of the existing strategic equilibrium in the region and the uncertainties prevalent on account of great power rivalries, security alliances, and rogue state behaviour in East Asia, all states in the region have begun to increase their maritime capabilities so as to improve their leverage against other countries which is signalled by their postures. The evolution of the terminologies like the 'Indo-Pacific' and 'Indo-Asia-Pacific' is symbolic of the growing conflict between paradigms of *status quo*-ism and revisionism playing out in the region.

The U.S. being the biggest player in the region, its policy of 'Pivot to Asia' merit attention. It was noted that the U.S.'s 'Pivot' has two main drivers, viz.

(a) Global economic shift to the East and

(b) Increasing military expenditure of Asian nations

The Pivot is not about containing China but about engaging China - be it peacefully or in a hostile way. The U.S. is carrying out the rebalancing in three main ways

(i) Diplomatic, through building strategic ties with Japan, Korea and Philippines

(ii) Economic, by forming trade framework like Trans Pacific Partnership (TPP)

(iii) Military, in terms of its Air Sea Battle (ASB) concept

The shifting strategic alignments of South East Asian nations are also important developments. It emerged that countries which were close to China like Malaysia, Brunei, Singapore, Indonesia are moving towards the U.S. to balance China's "assertive posture". Nations like Philippines, which do not share a very pleasant history with the U.S., are increasingly getting aligned to the U.S. It is only Laos and Cambodia which still remain Chinese stronghold, while Thailand, is slowly aligning with China after the military coup.

Maritime Disputes and Potential Flash Points

Some of potential flashpoints in the region are located in the disputed maritime areas and islands in the South and East China Seas. This long outstanding maritime dispute has two interesting mixes - firstly, the combination of history, cartography, and varying interpretations of norms for inter-state delimitation by each claimant. The second is the complex web of overlapping, intersecting and intermeshed nature of these claims with varying degrees of sovereignty, territoriality and implications of maritime entitlement. It was noted that since beginning of the 21st century, the actions as well as articulation by different stakeholders in the South China Sea (SCS), i.e. those directly involved (claimants) and some with strategic stakes (indirectly), have become particularly assertive. This has resulted in a few occurrences of skirmishes between nations, deteriorating the regional security environment. This may become a major focal point of future conflict if issues are not resolved with due maturity, when the environment is relatively peaceful.

In such a scenario, United Nation Convention on the Law of the Sea III, 1982 (UNCLOS) and other legal instruments becomes instrumental in tackling the South and East China Sea dispute. The panellists delved deep into the philosophy, spirit and applicability of public international law, especially the UN Charter and UNCLOS, the ambit and jurisdiction of various legal mechanisms like the Permanent Court of Justice (PCA), International Court of Justice (ICJ) and the International Tribunal for the Law of The Sea (ITLOS).

It was also observed that the South China Sea dispute is so complex that neither diplomacy nor legality alone may be able to provide the right solution and the solution has to emerge from within the parties involved. Compromises have to be made by all and it is only though a mix of diplomacy and legality suiting the South China Sea that a binding code of conduct can be reached.

Economics and Environment as Potential Areas of Cooperation

In spite of existing challenges and disputes, there is a growing trend of integration among the nations in the region especially in the realm of economics and environment. The initiatives like the Trans-Pacific Partnership (TPP), an expanded East Asia Summit (EAS) grouping, the Asian Infrastructure Investment Bank (AIIB) mechanism and the Maritime Silk Route (MSR) indicate a changing institutional and grand strategy architecture unfolding across the region where nations are moving towards a deeper economic integration with Beijing while relying on the security cover provided by Washington.

At another level, environmental challenges driven by global warming are also having an increasing impact on the region. The threat of sea level rise, frequent natural disasters, over-exploitation of marine resources and its effect on coastal sustainability is emerging as a serious cause of concern for the entire region. This common vulnerability to environmental hazards has the potential to bring all parties together to cooperate against environmental degradation.

India's Role in the Region

Chinese maritime and diplomatic posturing in the IOR is one of the biggest geopolitical and national security challenges for India. This not only implies greater concerns for the Indian Navy and India's sea-based nuclear deterrent, but also has the potential to complicate New Delhi's relations with its neighbours who facilitate China's foray in the IOR.

While India is directly not a part of the Asia Pacific region, it does have economic and strategic interests in that region and many of South East Asian and other Asia Pacific nations are its trade and strategic partners. India, therefore, has stakes and would thus like to remain relevant in the overall dynamics of the region, even to the discomfort of certain nations.

India's upgrading its 'Look East' policy to 'Act East' is thus an apt way of underscoring its interest and commitment to the changing dynamics of the region. Under the new policy, India has moved from solely focusing on economic integration with the nations of the region to a larger strategic engagement with its extended neighbourhood. India has always maintained good political and diplomatic relations with countries of the region especially Japan, Vietnam, Singapore, ROK, Indonesia, Thailand and Philippines. Furthermore, with large markets, huge pool of talent and an open democratic system India has a potential to enhance its appeal in this region.

Conclusion

The seminar highlighted the growing importance of the region for India and the following action points can be inferred as policy recommendations for enhancing India's national interests and increasing its engagement in the region in accordance with its 'Act East Policy'.

(a) India should continue to support freedom of navigation in the South/East China Sea without getting into the territorial disputes.

(b) South East Asia is the gateway to Indo-Pacific region. India needs to engage more extensively with SE Asian nations for reaching out to the Indo-Pacific. Therefore, India needs to continue its involvement in the region in the form of bilateral and multilateral engagements with SE Asian Countries.

(c) India can also refurbish its historical, cultural-religious linkages with SE Asia, along with positioning itself as a provider of large pool of skilled workforce, extensive domestic markets and its democratic values to project its appeal in its extended neighbourhood.

(d) Cooperating with the Indio Pacific countries in tackling environmental challenges can also help build positive image for India as a responsible global power

(e) Along with its outreach to SE Asia, India should also strive to maintain its edge in the IOR and to assume a leadership role in the region.

CONTRIBUTORS

Admiral Arun Prakash (Retd.)

Admiral Arun Prakash retired as the 20th Naval Chief and Chairman Chiefs of Staff Committee in end-2006. A naval-aviator by specialization, he commanded a fighter-squadron and four ships including the carrier *Viraat*. In flag-rank he commanded the Eastern Fleet, the National Defence Academy, the Andaman & Nicobar Joint Command and the Western Naval Command. He headed the Aviation and Personnel branches of the navy and was Vice-Chief before taking over as Chief of the Naval Staff in 2004. He is a graduate of the IAF Test Pilots School, the DSSC and the US Naval War College. During the 1971 war he was awarded the Vir Chakra while flying with an IAF fighter squadron. Post-retirement, he served two-terms on the National Security Advisory Board and was Chairman of the National Maritime Foundation; which he had helped found. He lives in Goa and writes and speaks on maritime and strategic issues.

Rear Admiral K R Menon (Retd.)

Admiral Menon was a career officer and a submarine specialist in the Navy and retired in 1994 as the Assistant Chief of Naval Staff (Operations). His published work includes, *Maritime Strategy and Continental Wars'*, a standard text for the Staff College. His second book *'A Nuclear Strategy for India'* is recommended reading for the Indian Strategic Force. His third book *'The Indian Navy: A Photo Essay'* is the official gift of the navy. He is the editor of the book *'Weapons of Mass Destruction: Options for India.* Admiral Menon was a member of the Arun Singh Committee and of the National Defence University Committee. He is a visiting lecturer at all institutes of higher study of the Indian armed forces and the Foreign Office. He has recently retired as the Chairman of the Task Force on Net Assessment and Simulation in the National Security Council, and is a distinguished fellow in the Institute of Peace and Conflict Studies and the National Maritime Foundation.

Vice Admiral Anup Singh (Retd.)

Commissioned on 01 Jul 1973, Vice Admiral (Retd) Anup Singh served the Indian Navy till superannuation on 31 Oct 2011. His last seagoing appointment was that of Flag Officer Commanding Western Fleet. His last assignment in the Service was that of Flag Officer Commanding-in- Chief, Eastern Naval Command from Aug 2009 till Oct 2011. A keen sportsman and adventurer, his interests include golf, riding and sailing. He is a regular speaker in seminars and holds the following honorary assignments with institutions:-

- Member, Executive Council, IDSA;

- Member, Armed Forces Historical Research Board, USI;

- Director (Strategic Studies) and Managing Editor, Society for Indian Ocean Studies (SIOS) and;

- Advisor (History), Indian Navy

Ambassador Yogendra Kumar (Retd.)

Yogendra Kumar is a postgraduate in history and was in the diplomatic service for nearly 35 years. He retired in 2012 in the rank of secretary (equivalent to vice minister) to the Government of India. At retirement, he was serving as Ambassador to the Philippines with concurrent accreditation to the Western Pacific island countries of Palau, Federated States of Micronesia and the Marshall Islands. He has served as High Commissioner (Ambassador) in Namibia and as an Ambassador in Tajikistan. He has served in Indian diplomatic missions in Moscow, London, Tashkent, Islamabad and Brussels and, at headquarters, in divisions handling Sri Lanka and the Maldives, the Soviet and Central Asian affairs. He has also been on the faculty of the National Defence College of India. He has contributed to various journals and books on foreign affairs. After superannuation, the Philippines Government conferred their national honour, the Order of Sikatuna, for endeavours to build friendship between the people of India and the Philippines.

Commander Kamlesh K Agnihotri

Kamlesh K Agnihotri is presently working at the Maritime Doctrine and Concepts Centre, Mumbai. Prior to this appointment, he was heading the China Centric 'Red Cell' at Maritime Warfare Centre, Visakhapatnam. He was also a Research Fellow at the China cell of the National Maritime Foundation (NMF) from 2009-2014, wherein he published several articles on maritime security issues, and extensively presented papers related to China in India and abroad. He has authored a book titled "The *Strategic Direction of the Chinese Navy: Capability and Intent Assessment*" (2015). His three co- edited books are titled '*Maritime Power Building: New Mantra for China's Rise*' (2015); '*Security Challenges Along the Indian Ocean Littoral: Indian and US Perspectives*' (2013) and '*Technological Developments in the Maritime Domain and their Strategic Implications in the Indian Ocean Region' (2011)*. He is a Missile and Gunnery specialist and has also acquired an Advanced Diploma in Chinese language to complement his research work.

Captain Raghavendra Mishra

Raghavendra Mishra is a Research Fellow at National Maritime Foundation since Apr 2012. Prior to this appointment, he was with the Directorate of Naval Air Staff at IHQ-MoD (Navy) where he gained firsthand knowledge on planning, procurement and operational exploitation of naval aviation assets. He was commissioned into the Indian Navy in January 1989 and is a Seaking Observer with wide ranging experience on naval aviation operations afloat. He is also an Anti-Submarine Warfare specialist and has served extensively onboard frontline ships of the Indian Navy. He has commanded a minesweeper and INAS 330 (The Harpoons), the premier Seaking Squadron of Navy. His service also includes varied appointments in operational, training and staff appointments including an instructional tenure at the Defence Services Staff College (DSSC), Wellington.

Commander (Dr.) Kapil Narula

Kapil Narula holds an M.Tech. Degree in Electrical Engineering (IIT, Kharagpur) and a Ph.D. Degree in Economics (Indira Gandhi Institute of Development Research, a deemed university of the Reserve Bank of India). His naval appointments include sea time on INS Delhi and INS Khukri and he has served as an instructor at INS Valsura. His last appointment was (acting) Head of Faculty, Electronics and Communication Engineering at the Indian Naval Academy, Ezhimala. He is currently posted as a Research Fellow at the National Maritime Foundation, New Delhi where he is also the Executive Editor of the flagship journal 'Maritime Affairs'. Cdr Narula is a certified energy auditor from Bureau of Energy Efficiency (BEE) and he has been involved with various energy and environmental initiatives in the Indian Navy. His areas of competence are energy, sustainability, economic policy, climate change and he attempts to integrate multi-disciplinary aspects in his work.

Captain (Dr.) Gurpreet S Khurana

Gurpreet S Khurana is a serving missile specialist, who has been closely associated with the development of doctrines and strategy for the Indian Navy. His 27 years of service includes command of two warships. In 2002, he commissioned a Fast Attack Craft based in the Andaman & Nicobar Command as its first Commanding Officer. During his Research Fellowship at IDSA (2003-2008), he specialized in maritime security and strategic issues. His article of 2007 is accredited to be the first to use the term 'Indo-Pacific' in geo-political context. He authored a book titled 'Maritime Forces in Pursuit of National Security' (2008). While serving at the Navy's Maritime Doctrine and Concept Centre (2009-2013), he was awarded the Navy Chief's Commendation for co-authoring the Indian Maritime Doctrine, 2009. He also authored the Navy's first ever handbook on 'Law of Maritime Operations'. He holds a PhD in Defence Studies. He is presently serving as the Executive Director of NMF, New Delhi and represents India at the CSCAP Working Group on Search and Rescue.

Vice Admiral Anurag G Thapliyal (Retd.)

Vice Admiral Anurag Gopalam Thapliyal retired from the Indian Navy on 31 Jan 2015 after 38 years of service, the last two years of which were on deputation to the Indian Coast Guard as its Director General. He is a specialist in Navigation & Aircraft Direction and has held various operational and staff appointments both, afloat and ashore. In the rank of Rear Admiral, he served as the Chief of Staff, Headquarters, Eastern Naval Command, ACNS (Information Warfare & Operations) at IHQ, MoD (Navy) and Fleet Commander, Eastern Fleet. As Vice Admiral he held the appointment of the Commandant Indian Naval Academy and later as the Chief of Personnel at IHQ (MoD) before shifting on deputation to the Indian Coast Guard. He is an alumnus of the Naval War College, Newport, Rhode Island, USA and DSSC, Wellington and possesses two Masters Degrees in Physics and Defence Studies. He is also the recipient of the Ati Vishist Seva Medal (AVSM) and Bar to AVSM.

Dr. Shankari Sundararaman

Shankari Sundararaman is a Professor of Southeast Asian Studies and Chair of the Centre for Indo-Pacific Studies, at the School of International Studies of Jawaharlal Nehru University. She has been a visiting fellow at the Asia-Pacific College of Diplomacy at the Australian National University from May-July 2005. She is also the recipient of the ASIA Fellows Award in 2005 as part of which she was a Visiting Fellow at the Centre for Strategic and International Studies (CSIS), Jakarta, Indonesia in 2006-07. In 2009, she received a collaborative research grant from the Asian Scholarship Foundation (ASF) to study India-Indonesia bilateral relations, under the broad theme of 'Regional Powers and Global Politics'. She is the author of a book titled '*Cambodia: The Lost Decades*'. She had a monthly column on Southeast Asia titled "*Another Asia*" for the Asian Age from March 2009 till April 2013.

Antara Ghosal

Antara Ghosal Singh is presently working as a Research Associate at the National Maritime Foundation. She is an alumna from the Tsinghua University, People's Republic of China where her thesis was on "A comparison between higher/technical education between China and India.' She did her post-graduation from the Indian Institute of Mass Communication (IIMC) New Delhi in print journalism. Before starting her career in academics, she has worked as a professional journalist with several national dailies like the Times of India and the Deccan Chronicle Group. Her area of research at NMF is China's foreign policy, China-India relations, strategic-security developments in East Asia and the maritime diplomacy. She has a working knowledge of Mandarin Chinese and has pursued Chinese language courses at the Tsinghua University, Beijing Language and Culture University, China.

INDEX

A

'Act East' Policy xv, 54

Air Defence Identification Zone (ADIZ) viii, ix, 6, 45, 53

Air Sea Battle 17, 18, 39, 169

Andaman and Nicobar 52, 152

Areas Beyond National Jurisdiction 105

ASEAN viii, ix, xv, 10, 21, 22, 25, 26, 29, 31, 32, 33, 34, 36, 40, 42, 45, 46, 47, 52, 53, 54, 55, 57, 60, 62, 67, 68, 69, 75, 78, 92, 133, 137, 141, 142, 143, 144, 146, 147, 148, 150, 152, 153, 154, 155, 156, 157, 158, 159, 160, 161, 165, 166, 167

ASEAN Regional Forum (ARF) xv, 10, 33, 46, 55, 57, 60, 64, 65, 69, 137, 142, 144, 148, 155

Asian Development Bank (ADB) 28

Asian Infrastructure Investment Bank (AIIB) 8, 171

Asian Pacific Council (ASPAC) 141

Association of Southeast Asia 140, 141

B

Bab-el-Mandeb 71, 125

Balintang Channel 38

Bandung Conference 146

Bangladesh-China-India-Myanmar (BCIM) 125

Bashi Channel 38

Bay of Bengal vii, 8, 71, 84, 89, 93, 95, 122, 132, 152

Beidou satellites 18

Belt and Road Initiative (BRI) 168

BIMSTEC 10

Binh Minh 61, 70

Bintulu 50

Boko Haram 1

C

Cambodia People's Party (CPP) 29

Cam Ranh Bay 27

Carrier Battle Group (CVBGs) 12

Central Military Commission (CMC) 57

Chiang Kai Sheik 40

China-ASEAN Free Trade Agreement (CAFTA) 21

Chinese ballistic missile submarines 132

Chinese Foreign Affairs Office 60

Cold War 1, 29, 36, 37, 39, 44, 149, 165

Commission on the Limits of Continental Shelf (CLCS) 57, 60

Commonwealth Scientific and Industrial Research Organization (CSIRO) 98

Comprehensive Economic Cooperation Agreement (CECA) 32, 162

Comprehensive National Power (CNP) 121

Continental Shelf (CS) 42, 57, 69, 78, 79, 82, 84, 85, 87, 92, 179

Cuarteron Reef 85, 89

D

Department of Defence (DoD) 18

E

East Asian Summit xv

East Asia Summit (EAS) 143, 155, 157, 171

East China Sea viii, ix, 5, 37, 39, 40, 41, 138, 152, 170, 172

Eastern Naval Command v, vii, ix, xiii, 2, 174, 176

East Timor violence 154

Eldad Reef 89

Eurasia 2, 7, 164

European Economic Community (EEC) 140

Exclusive Economic Zones (EEZ) 21, 22, 23, 25, 38, 45, 47, 49, 55, 57, 60, 61, 64, 68, 70, 71, 78, 79, 82, 84, 87, 89, 101, 105, 108, 115

Expanded ASEAN Maritime Forum xv, 144, 161

F

Fiery Cross Reef ix, 45, 47, 49, 58, 85, 89

First Islands Chain 38, 39

Five Power Defence Arrangement (FPDA) 24, 154

Foreign Direct Investment (FDI) 28

Free trade agreements (FTAs) 32

G

Gaven Reef 58, 85, 89

Guangzhou 122

Gulf of Tonkin 38

Gwadar 8, 20, 121, 122, 160

H

Hainan 52, 57, 58, 72

Hambantota 121, 160

Hormuz Strait 125

Huangyan Island 55

Hughes Reef 59, 89

Humanitarian assistance and disaster relief (HADR) 24, 139

I

Indian Ocean Region (IOR) 53, 71, 120, 121, 122, 123, 124, 125, 126, 127, 128, 129, 130, 131, 132, 133, 138, 145, 168, 171, 172

Indian Ocean Rim Association (IORA) 127, 162

Indo-Asia-Pacific 3, 5, 8, 63, 151, 169

Indo-Pacific region v, vi, 1, 37, 51, 126, 172

INS Airavat 66, 72

International Commission for the Conservation of Atlantic Tunas (ICCAT) 108

International Court of Justice (ICJ) 81, 82, 84, 87, 90, 170

International Crisis Group (ICG) 44

International Fleet Review vii

International Hydrographic Organisation (IHO) 76

International Maritime Organization (IMO) 108

International Military Education and Training (IMET) 154

International Seabed Authority (ISA) 108, 126, 134

International Tribunal for the Law of the Sea 81, 95

Itu Aba island 56, 89

J

Japan India Maritime Exercise (JIMEX) 161

Johnson Reef 85

K

Kachin States 30

Karimata Strait 38

Kashgar 20

Kennan letter 14

Kurile Islands 36, 37

Kyaukpyu viii, 160

L

Line of Actual Control (LAC) 5, 53

Littoral v, xiv, 3, 20, 45, 49, 51, 53, 54, 71, 132, 152, 159

Littoral Combat Ship (LCS) 47, 51

Lombok Straits 38, 52

Long-range maritime reconnaissance (LRMR) 73

Look East policy xv, 147, 150, 171

Luzon Strait 39

M

Macclesfield Bank 76

Manmohan Singh 147

Mariana Islands 38

maritime manoeuver 6

Maritime Prepositioning Ships (MPS) 131

Maritime Silk Route (MSR) 16, 17, 18, 20, 45, 50, 53, 57, 121, 123, 124, 126, 127, 128, 130, 134, 163, 171

McKennan Reef 85

Military Operations Other than War 129

Military Sealift Command (MSC) 131

Mindoro Strait 38

Minimum Essential Force (MDF) 50

Mischief (Meiji Jiao) Reef 59

Mischief Reef 59, 85, 89

Modi, Narendra 66, 157

Monroe Doctrine 6

Myitsone Dam project 31

N

Narasimha Rao 147, 156

National Maritime Foundation iv

National Oceanic and Atmospheric Administration (NOAA) 98

Natuna Archipelago ix

Natuna Islands 22

North American Free trade Agreement (NAFTA) 16

O

Ocean Health Index 102, 103, 105, 106, 115, 116

Offshore waters defence 6, 43, 129

Okhotsk Sea 3

One Belt One Road 45

ONGC Videsh Limited 66, 67

Open sea protection 6

P

Paracel island 36, 38, 40, 45, 55, 58, 60, 61, 62, 75, 76, 153, 164

Peoples Liberation Army (PLA) 28

Permanent Court of Arbitration 81, 93

Philippine Sea 38, 63, 71

PLA Navy 6, 43, 53, 58, 59, 63, 129, 130, 131, 132, 135, 136

Q

Qing Dynasty 60

R

Reclamation in Spratlys

Fiery Cross (Yongshu) Reef 58

Gaven (Nanxun) Reef 58

Hughes (Dongmen) Reef 59

Johnson South (Zhigua) Reef 59

Mischief (Meiji Jiao) Reef 59

Subi (Zhubi) Reef 59

Republic of Korea 46, 137, 143

Ryukyu Islands 38, 48

S

SAARC 10, 137, 145

Samudra Manthan 1

Sand Cay 61, 89

Scarborough Shoal 23, 45, 60, 62, 76, 85

Sea Lines of Communication (SLOCs) 128, 169

Sea of Okhotsk 37

Search And Rescue (SAR) 161

Second Island Chain 38

Senkaku islands 5, 38, 39, 42, 45, 46, 48

Sittwe viii

Sonadia viii

South China Sea (SCS) viii, ix, xi, 1, 3, 5, 6, 7, 18, 21, 22, 24, 25, 26, 27, 29, 32, 33, 35, 36, 37, 38, 40, 41, 42, 43, 44, 45, 47, 49, 50, 51, 53, 54, 55, 56, 57, 60, 61, 62, 63, 64, 65, 66, 67, 68, 69, 70, 71, 72, 73, 74, 75, 76, 77, 78, 79, 80, 81, 82, 84, 85, 86, 87, 88, 89, 90, 91, 92, 93, 95, 96, 138, 149, 150, 152, 153, 154, 155, 159, 160, 161, 162, 164, 166, 170, 171

Southeast Asian Association for Regional Cooperation (SEAARC) 141

Southeast Asia Treaty Organization (SEATO) 154

Special Economic Zones (SEZs) 28, 31

Spratly Islands 36, 37, 38, 40, 42, 45, 47, 49, 50, 53, 55, 56, 58, 61, 62, 63, 73, 75, 76, 80, 81, 88, 153, 164

Straits of Malacca 8, 52, 71, 74, 152

Strategic deterrence 6

Subic Bay 23, 50

Subi Reef 45, 65, 85, 89

Sulu Sea 38

Sunda Straits 38, 52

Surigao Strait 38

Sustainable Development Goal (SDG) 112, 113, 114

Swallow Reef 56, 89

T

Taiwan Strait 5, 38, 51

Thitu Island 49, 56, 63

Trans-Pacific Partnership (TPP) 15, 16, 17, 25, 123, 134, 169, 171

Trans Pacific Strategic Economic Partnership 15

Trilateral Dialogue on Indian Ocean (TDIO) 162

U

Unified Command Plan 11, 12

United Nations Conference on Sustainable Development (UNCSD) 112

US-Japan Security Treaty 5

V

Verde Island 38

Viktor Chirkov 44

W

Weapons of Mass Destruction (WMD)
   14

Western Pacific Naval Symposium
   (WPNS) 26, 46, 53, 144, 145

X

Xi Jinping 5, 46, 121, 127, 133, 163

Y

Yunnan Province 30

Z

Zheng He 16